OUT OF THE SHADOWS OF NIGHT

THE STRUGGLE FOR INTERNATIONAL HUMAN RIGHTS

OUT OF THE SHADOWS OF NIGHT

THE STRUGGLE FOR INTERNATIONAL HUMAN RIGHTS

Marvin E. Frankel

with Ellen Saideman

Delacorte Press

Published by
Delacorte Press
Bantam Doubleday Dell Publishing Group, Inc.
666 Fifth Avenue
New York, New York 10103

Cover photo of the tiger cages of Con Son, South Vietnam, by Tom Harkin.

Library of Congress Cataloging in Publication Data

Frankel, Marvin E., 1920–
Out of the shadows of night: the struggle for international human rights / by
Marvin Frankel, with Ellen Saideman.
p.   cm.
Includes bibliographical references.
Summary: Examines the history of the modern international human
rights movement, violations of human rights in Latin America, the
Soviet Union, South Africa, the U.S. and elsewhere, and various efforts to
prevent or censure such abuses.
ISBN 0-385-29752-1 (hardcover edition)
0-385-29820-X (tr paperback edition)
1. Human rights—Juvenile literature.   [1. Human rights.]
I. Saideman, Ellen.   II. Title.
JC571.F643 1989
323.4—dc19   88-29419
CIP
AC

Manufactured in the United States of America
September 1989
10 9 8 7 6 5 4 3 2 1
BG

Out of the shadows of night
The world rolls into light;
It is daybreak everywhere.

—HENRY WADSWORTH LONGFELLOW
(from *The Bells of San Blas*)

To Rachel and Jeffrey
and the continued
blessings of freedom

Acknowledgments

As a belated newcomer to the study of international human rights, I am indebted to scores of people who have taught me by precept and example. A number of them are named in this book among the human rights heroes I've met or admired from afar. Others are mentioned in connection with the nongovernmental organizations they lead—including particularly my colleagues in the Lawyers Committee for Human Rights, Michael Posner, Arthur Helton, and Diane Orentlicher. To list others would be tedious for the reader and almost certain to lead to unintended slights. One above all, however, has to be recognized—my cherished friend Louis Henkin. Lou is undoubtedly our foremost teacher and advocate of human rights. He combines quiet passion with exquisite scholarship. I've been privileged to be his student for many years.

Several individuals connected with Amnesty International contributed their time and valuable information to this book. I would like to thank Linda Valerian, who was interviewed for Chapter 6, Pete Larson, Membership Communications Coordinator, Konstantine Dierks, volunteer leader of the New York City High School Cluster, and the Steering Committee of that group, who participated in the discussion in Chapter 6: Jennifer Appell, Nadya Engler, Simon Lee, Stacey Malacos, Donna Manion, Vivian Monterroso, Kimberly Noone, Natalia Olynec, Analía Penchaszadeh, and Diane Piltser. Nadya Engler and Donna Manion also read an early draft of the manuscript, and offered many helpful and insightful comments.

CONTENTS

INTRODUCTION

This book is about one of the wonders of our time: the struggle of people and governments to give every human being everywhere the right to live safely, with dignity and with freedom. It is about something almost, if not quite, new under the sun—an effort to build and enforce a world law of human rights. Like many births, this one begins with pain. But the pain that preceded the birth of international human rights was not a normal and expected kind of pain; it was the agony and the horror of the Holocaust engineered by Hitler and his fellow madmen who led Nazi Germany. World reaction against that wave of barbarity gave rise to a new idea: that every government in the world has some interest in seeing to it that no other government lawlessly silences or imprisons or kills people because they dissent or happen to be different.

While concern for human rights is and should be a governmental responsibility, both the leadership and the support depend on the work of devoted individuals. Incredibly brave people, like those who founded our country and its great rights, are risking their freedom and their lives to resist repressive governments. Individuals here and in other free countries devote themselves to seeking basic human rights for less fortunate fellow beings elsewhere in the world. Working with each other, caring for each other, these people—inside and outside of repressive countries—make up a still young, wholly inspiring, steadily growing movement for international human rights.

This movement became a personal commitment quite late in my own life. My first involvement was a three-week trip to the

1

Soviet Union, while I was still a district judge, paying wholly unofficial visits to human rights activists, to Jewish *refuseniks*, of whom you'll be reading below, and to government officials responsible for repressive measures. After leaving the bench in 1978 and returning to the practice of law, I became more regularly engaged—in missions to several countries, work for human rights within the United States, and, since 1980, as chairman of the Lawyers Committee for Human Rights. This work has been throughout a sometimes grim, always challenging, deeply rewarding experience.

From this personal experience has come a realization of how vitally important it is for my fellow Americans to enlist, along with people all over the world, in this greatest of causes. My purpose is to help spread the word about the inspiration and the opportunity embodied in the worldwide struggle for human rights. People everywhere, of all ages, should know and be involved in these efforts. It's never too late, and nothing is more important. At the same time, it's clear that young readers are a special and specially desired audience. The need for a peaceful and orderly world—for which human rights are indispensable—is a particular concern of the young. And it is the young, by the same token, who will carry the vital burdens of seeking such a world.

In that light I've tried to tell about human rights, a complex subject, in plain and direct terms. I've tried to convey some of the excitement and the sense of worthiness that come with working for human rights. I've limited the technicalities and details we lawyers cherish. But some important factual details cannot and must not be omitted. A great advance of our era has been the creation of international human rights *law*. So anyone who takes an interest in this subject, as everyone should, will want to become friendly with some of the international covenants, organizations, treaties, and legal practices.

For those who may be taking a first close look at this subject, this can be a start on one of the great pathways of your life. Not so long ago, awed by the selfless courage of people in many countries risking torture and death in the struggle for human rights, I decided that I could at least give some time and energy to support them. It turns out that I've received infinitely more than I've given. Their examples of heroism and devotion, some of which you'll encounter in the following chapters, have widened and brightened my horizons. Those who devote themselves to this cause are insisting on the sacred worth and dignity of every human being. Dedicating *their* lives to that belief, they bear witness to the value of *our* lives. They tell us that greatness is possible for all of us—together.

CHAPTER 1

Human Rights—Victims and Heroes

Taken from their homes in the dead of night or abducted in open daylight on the streets, these people are never seen again. Their relatives are left not just without their loved ones but without any certainty about whether they are alive or dead. The "missing" are deprived of more than their homes, their livelihoods, their children. They are also deprived of their graves.

ARIEL DORFMAN, *Widows* dedication, 1983

The story of human rights is constant and ever changing, for it is made up of the individual histories of the many people who have fought, and continue to fight, for freedom around the world. The best way to begin, then, is to focus on a few particular, ongoing stories, such as that of *los desaparecidos.*

In the 1970s the word "disappeared" became a noun in Spanish, meaning someone who had disappeared in a special way. A *desaparecido*—a "disappeared one"—was a man or woman or child picked up by a gang of armed men and spirited away in a car or van, perhaps never to be seen again, perhaps to reappear some time after being tortured, raped, and otherwise abused. The word itself—*desaparecido*—became a grim and horrible part of life in a number of South and Central American countries, particularly Argentina.

The military seized power in Argentina in 1976 and mounted a fierce campaign against leftist guerrilla groups, a campaign that came to be known as the "dirty war." It had two phases: conventional battles with guerrilla forces and secret operations by death squads under the control of the armed forces. The death squads abducted not only leftist guerrillas but people suspected of sympathizing with them, including trade unionists, liberals, and anyone who opposed the death squads. People who had only the barest connection with the political targets, or none at all, were caught up in the dragnet.

Thousands of people were abducted, many from their homes or offices, and then held at secret military detention centers for questioning. Many were tortured—with electric shocks, near-drownings, rapes, and beatings. Many were executed. In some cases the *desaparecidos'* young children were also seized and sometimes secretly placed for adoption with military families.

Families of the *desaparecidos* searched for their loved ones, going in vain from one government office to another, asking where their missing relatives were. Often the officials told parents that their sons or daughters had run off and didn't want their families to know where they were.

One day in April 1977, Azucena Villaflor de Vicenti went to the Argentinian Ministry of the Interior to ask about her son Nestor, who had disappeared in March 1976. The officials refused to give her any information. She turned to the other people waiting for news and cried, "It's not here that we ought to be—it's the Plaza de Mayo [a main square in Buenos Aires in front of the Casa Rosada, the presidential palace]. And when there's enough of us, we'll go to the Casa Rosada and see the President about our children who are missing."[1]

Thirteen other women joined de Vicenti for a silent walk around the Plaza de Mayo. One of them, Adela Antokaletz, was the mother of a lawyer who defended political prisoners; he had been taken into custody by six men at about 8:00 A.M. on November 16, 1976. Another of the women, Hebe Bonafini, who joined the group of women soon after the first march and later became its president, was the mother of two men who had been taken away—one with his wife—and kept, or murdered.[2]

In a land where disappearances were common and almost no one dared to speak up, that historic walk was astonishing. The police did not know what to do. Two officers approached and ordered

6

the women to leave, but they refused. One woman said, "Aren't you ashamed to attack defenseless mothers? You want us to leave; we want the same thing, so give us back our children, tell us what you have done to them."[3]

The women, who became known as Las Madres de la Plaza de Mayo (the Mothers of the Plaza de Mayo), were housewives, many from the working class, who had never been active in politics. But they began to march every Thursday afternoon, even though public protest was forbidden. They wore white handkerchiefs with the names of their *desaparecidos* or held photographs of them, and they cried: "Give us back our children!"

At first the government called Las Madres "*Las Locas* [the crazy women] *de la Plaza de Mayo*," but as their numbers and political activity grew, the government began to take them seriously. In October 1977 several hundred women appeared in front of the Congress building to present a petition with 24,000 signatures requesting the release of all political prisoners and the investigation of the *desaparecidos*. The police intervened and arrested two hundred people, including several American journalists.

In December 1977, death squads raided meetings of Las Madres and their supporters, abducting thirteen people, including de Vicenti and two French nuns, Alice Domon and Renée Duquet. These women were now among the *desaparecidos*. The story of their abduction, torture, and deaths was finally told in *Nunca Más* ("Never Again"), the factual, moving, and horrifying report of the Argentine National Commission on the Disappeared, which was published in 1984. They had been betrayed by Captain Alfredo Astiz, a navy lieutenant who had gained their confidence by posing as the brother of a *desaparecido*.[4] A witness who had been held at the same detention center testified before the commission that "the nuns had been beaten and were very weak, and when Sister Alice went to the bathroom she had to be carried by two guards. I asked her if she had been tortured, and she answered yes. She had been tied on a bed, completely naked, and the electric prod was applied to all parts of her body. . . . The nuns were in the Navy Mechanics School for about ten days, tortured

7

and interrogated. Then they were 'transferred' with eleven other people. The rumors in the prison, which were based on the speed with which they took these people away, suggested that they were killed."[5]

Nevertheless, on the Thursday following the raids, forty mothers turned up at the Plaza de Mayo. Further raids, arrests, and other forms of harassment did not stop them. Las Madres continued drawing national and international attention to their *desaparecidos* through the Thursday marches.

Early in 1979, however, the police became so violent that it was impossible to meet in the plaza. Las Madres then met illegally in churches, often in the dark and in silence, communicating through notes to spare the churches from the wrath of the government if they were discovered. Throughout their ordeal they were encouraged and strengthened by financial and moral support from sympathizers abroad. Late in 1979 they agreed to return to the plaza even if it meant dying there. Although the threats and beatings continued, Las Madres never again surrendered the plaza to the government. And on the fourth anniversary of the first march, more than two thousand people marched, including Adolfo Perez Esquivel, who had won the Nobel Peace Prize in 1980 for his human rights work in Argentina.

Economic problems and the disastrous war with Britain over the Falkland Islands in 1980 (the Argentines call these islands Las Malvinas) brought down the military government in 1983. Domestic and international concern for human rights seems to have played only a small part in the government's collapse. However, with the return of democracy and the election of human rights advocate Raúl Alfonsín to the presidency on October 30, 1983, it was clear that the Argentine government would seek to defend rather than to crush human rights. Still, the struggle to rescue surviving victims of the "dirty war" and to seek justice was not ended. The elections did not stop the marches of Las Madres. Hebe Bonafini, president of Las Madres, said, "We will not give up the battle until all the guilty are judged, until we reach the truth about where our disappeared ones are." That solemn vow—to punish the criminal violators of human rights—presents tough problems that we'll return to later on (in Chapter 7).

There are many counterparts of the *desaparecidos*—the victims—and Las Madres—the heroic crusaders—in too many other countries all over the world. For such people, whether victims, crusaders, or both, are what today's international quest for human rights is all about. It is vital as well as inspiring to have some sense of how and why these people struggle, risking their comfort and their lives against seemingly impossible odds.

Far away from Argentina, in the Soviet Union, the story of Andrei Sakharov and his wife, Dr. Elena Bonner, has become a great saga of the twentieth century. A scientific genius, highly decorated and privileged, with economic comforts and perquisites given to only a handful of the Soviet elite, he was an important contributor to the Soviet creation of the hydrogen bomb, after the United States had first achieved that "success." That achievement was to prove a moral breakthrough in Sakharov's life. He faced what he had done and was appalled. He became a persistent campaigner for peace and arms control, and that led him to a deep concern for human rights. His open and persistent campaigns for the rights of protesters and dissidents in the late sixties led to reprisals against him by the Soviet government. In 1968 he published an essay called "Thoughts on Progress, Peaceful Coexistence, and Intellectual Freedom," which became world famous. In his own country, however, Sakharov was rewarded with harsh pressure to make him shut up. He was barred from secret work and stripped of many privileges. When he won the Nobel Peace Prize in 1975, he was denied permission to travel to Stockholm to receive it; his wife went in his stead to deliver his acceptance speech. But he continued to speak out against increasing threats and reprisals and to be heard all over the world. He openly denounced the Soviet invasion of Afghanistan in 1980. For that he was banished to Gorki, 250 miles east of Moscow, and isolated from friends and scientific colleagues, until the last days of 1986.

The story of Sakharov is still unfolding. He and his wife have endured physical and moral struggles against brutal police, ruthless doctors force-feeding him during hunger strikes, spies, intruders, and other government agents seeking to silence him or punish him for speaking out. The Soviets have never been ready or able to silence him completely. If they did, a storm of world protest would follow. This international concern for Sakharov has probably limited the measures that his government took against him.

Throughout the Sakharovs' ordeal, some odd notes of inconsistency persisted. The lines of communication with the outside world were disputed and scrambled, but never completely broken. Even in the brutal times in Gorki, the Sakharovs occasionally managed to talk by telephone with Elena Bonner's son and daughter-in-law and some others in the United States. In 1977 Sakharov was taken to the U.S. embassy in an official car to receive a letter from President Carter. In 1985, after many refusals, Bonner was permitted to go to Italy for eye surgery and to America for heart surgery. That trip resulted in her moving book, *Alone Together*, in which she gave no quarter to her Soviet tormentors in telling the story of the years in Gorki. Through it all, the people in power never withdrew Sakharov's lofty status as an academician. And in the end, miraculously surviving, the Sakharovs were back in Moscow, still unyielding in their demands. By late 1988, under Gorbachev, they appeared to have regained their freedom, while continuing to speak their minds and champion human rights.

I was privileged to visit with them in October 1987, along with two colleagues from the Lawyers Committee for Human Rights. They sat together on a couch in a very comfortable Moscow apartment—the gentle, soft-spoken Sakharov and the more voluble, waspish Bonner, still utterly together, far less alone than during the Gorki exile. They were as strong as ever in their demands for human rights. Emigration should be free, they insisted, or restricted only under narrow, fair, and known rules of law. The Soviet army should get out of Afghanistan. Prisoners of conscience should be freed. And Soviet prisons—which they described as appallingly brutal—should be conformed to civilized standards. These demands should be pressed against their own government, they said, with all the persuasive means available to others to test the promise of Gorbachev's *glasnost*. Listening to them, I felt that nothing was impossible.[6]

In South Africa, a far different world, a contemporary of Sakharov's has conducted an even longer and more bitter struggle. Nelson Mandela, born in 1918 into a royal family of the Thembu tribe, has spent the whole of his adult life fighting and resisting the oppression of nonwhite South Africans by the white government. The white population, about a fifth of South Africans, is itself bitterly divided, but the majority party (the National Party), in power since 1948, has used military and police to enforce a system of repression, exploitation, and savage discipline against the black, "colored" (of mixed race), and Indian people. As this is written (in 1989), some of the harshest measures have been lifted. But the changes are relatively minor and woefully late.

The grim system of white rule of South African blacks is known as *apartheid*, an Afrikaans word meaning "aparthood," the condition of being apart. It was adopted in 1948 by the Afrikaaner government that took power in that year under Prime Minister D. F. Malan, to describe the policy of racial segregation enforced by the ruling white party. Under that policy, blacks were subjected to "pass laws": required to carry passes at all times and to show them to police on demand. Thousands of blacks were jailed over the years because they were found without passes in white areas. Apartheid confined most blacks to ghetto dwellings, to inferior education, to menial jobs, and to generally deprived and wretched lives. Places of amusement were segregated. There were "white" beaches and inferior "black" beaches. Marriage and sexual relations between whites and blacks were outlawed. In general, apartheid allowed a white minority to live in luxury at the expense of a powerless majority of exploited blacks.

In the years since 1980 some aspects of apartheid have been modified. The pass laws were repealed in 1986. Movie theaters and some other public places have been quietly desegregated. Mine workers and laborers in other large industries have formed labor unions, winning improvements in wages and working conditions. The sexual prohibitions have been removed, including the

11

ban against marriages between people of different races. Pressure from other countries, including trade sanctions, has led the South African government to make some gestures of improvement. But they are not much more than that. The basic evils of apartheid continue. The Nationalist government remains harsh and ruthless. Opposition leaders face execution in treason trials. Newspapers are censored and shut down for speaking out, even moderately, in opposition. There are scores of executions each year for the inevitable cases of violence—bombings, killings, and other crimes—by members of the black majority, a group that, on the whole, has been remarkably nonviolent. Individuals and organizations are "banned" for speaking out. "Banning" confines a person's travel and prevents him or her from being in gatherings of more than two people or making public statements, either in speech or in writing.

Nelson Mandela has been in prison since 1962. As a young man, while training to become a lawyer, he joined the African National Congress (ANC), which had been founded in 1912 to unite blacks against the system of subjugation by the white minority. Before long he rose to positions of ANC leadership in campaigns marked by strikes, boycotts, civil disobedience, and arrests. In 1952 he was president of the ANC for the Transvaal (the most populous of South African provinces, which includes Johannesburg and Pretoria), and he was soon made the subject of a government banning order.

Mandela never gave up. In 1955 he played a role in the adoption of the now famous Freedom Charter promulgated by the Congress Alliance of Africans, Indians, and trade unionists. The charter proclaims goals for democratic freedom and human rights in a nonracist society. In 1956 Mandela was arrested and charged with treason. There followed a five-year ordeal of trial by day and efforts to keep up his law practice by working late into the night. The trial ended finally with his acquittal in 1961.

Originally the ANC was a nonviolent organization. But after years of ineffective struggle against apartheid, its members despaired of this policy. In 1961 it created a group, Umkhonto we

12

Sizwe (Spear of the Nation), to employ tactics of force and violence, with Mandela as its leader. He had already gone underground, where he continued to direct acts of sabotage against apartheid. Betrayed by an informer in 1962, he was tried for inciting black workers and unlawfully traveling to Ethiopia. He was sentenced to five years in prison. While serving that term, he and other ANC leaders were charged with sabotage, convicted, and sentenced to life terms. He remains in custody today (early 1989). There are hints that soon he may finally be released.

One of the most remarkable facts about Mandela is that, through all his years of imprisonment, he continues to be a great leader as well as a symbol of black demands. His wife, Winnie Mandela, whom he married in 1958, is a leader in her own right. Like Nelson, she has marched, spoken, and protested fearlessly over the years, and suffered a series of cruel punishments, beginning with imprisonment when she was pregnant with their first child, and including banning and banishment from her home. Neither has yielded. In 1985, South African President Pieter Willem Botha offered to release Mandela from prison if he would unconditionally renounce violence as a political instrument. Mandela rejected the offer. In a statement addressed to his fellow blacks and read by his daughter Zindzi (because Winnie was banned), he said:

> It was only then when all other forms of resistance were no longer open to us, that we turned to armed struggle. . . . Let [Botha] renounce violence. Let him say that he will dismantle apartheid. . . . Let him free all who have been imprisoned, banished or exiled for their opposition to apartheid. . . . Let him guarantee free political activity so that the people may decide who will govern them. . . . I cannot and will not give any undertaking at any time when I and you, the people, are not free. Your freedom and mine cannot be separated.[7]

13

Those words, like Mandela's whole life, mark a selfless struggle that has struck responsive chords everywhere on earth. The government of the United States, like others, has called for his release. Botha offered to free him because even in a prison cell, Mandela has a tremendous impact on world opinion and continues to be a powerful force for human rights.

Elsewhere, similar lives of heroic leadership are beacons of hope for all of us. Like Sakharov and Mandela, many of them have become famous:

- Jacobo Timerman, the publisher and editor of the Buenos Aires newspaper *La Opinión*, which published lists of the *desaparecidos* and campaigned for the release of political prisoners, was abducted by the Argentine army in April 1977. His newspaper was seized. He was tortured in prison and released (and exiled to Israel) only after he had become the subject of pressure from all over the world, including protests from President Carter and the pope.
- Kim Dae Jung, South Korea's best-known advocate for human rights, spent years in prison, under house arrest, and in exile for his beliefs. Returning from America in 1985, he took up his role as an opposition leader. In that role he was criticized by some for failing to unite with a rival opposition leader against the ruling party, which won a relatively free election in 1988. He remains nonetheless a stalwart leader in the international human rights movement.
- Benigno Aquino, who fought President Ferdinand Marcos for political and economic rights in the Philippines, spent nearly eight years in jail and three years in exile in the United States before he returned to the Philippines. At the end of his flight home he was shot to death as he left the airplane in the Manila airport. His death led to a revolt against Marcos, and in 1986 his wife, Corazon ("Cory"), became president of the Philippines, and an immensely popular leader in her own right.

14

- Jorge Valls, a poet, teacher, and student activist, survived twenty years in Fidel Castro's Cuban prisons. He had been charged with "activities against the powers of the state and leading anti-government organizations."[8] He was freed after an international campaign led by his wife, Cristina.
- Adam Michnik, the Polish historian and literary critic who helped to found KOR (the Workers' Defense Committee), which inspired the people's movement known as Solidarity, has been imprisoned repeatedly for his beliefs and his active opposition to the communist regime in Poland.
- Dr. Joel Filartiga, a physician in Paraguay, long opposed President Alfredo Stroessner, who ruled Paraguay with an iron hand until he was overthrown in a coup in January 1989. Because of Filartiga's political activity, his seventeen-year-old son, Joelito, was tortured and killed by the Paraguayan police in 1976.
- For many years Anatoly Sharansky (now known as Natan Sharansky) was one of the Soviet Union's most prominent *refuseniks*—the word created to describe Jews denied permission to emigrate. Sentenced to a term of thirteen years for "treason" in 1978, he was released on February 11, 1986. He has continued to devote himself to the battle for human rights, in the Soviet Union and elsewhere.[9]

In addition to heroes with worldwide recognition, there are many who are not famous, or who are wholly unknown, who have fought and continue to fight for human rights. Since they are not well known outside their own countries, such people are liable to be more harshly treated. They are more vulnerable. What happens to Las Madres, a Sakharov, or a Mandela is front-page news around the world, and a matter for international diplomacy. This is not to belittle their evident courage, but to acknowledge that the spotlight shone on them may make the difference between life and death. Winnie Mandela believes that international concern prevented South Africa from sentencing Nelson Mandela and the other ANC leaders to death, and Andrei Sakharov has said that international pressure brought about his release from exile in

Gorki. International support does not mean that their lives are safe or easy. Still, knowing that others care gives them hope, and they in turn give hope to the rest of us.

All of the famous and anonymous people who have put their lives on the line for basic human rights have one important thing in common: they're all volunteers. They aren't accidental "victims." All of them made a choice to enlist in the human rights cause. They could easily have chosen to avoid the confrontations, the dangers, the physical horrors they suffered and the threat of violent death. It is this deliberate risk and self-sacrifice for noble goals that leads us to call such people heroes.

What makes people heroes? As Shakespeare said, "Some are born great, some achieve greatness, and some have greatness thrust upon them" (*Twelfth Night*, II, v, 159). Some, like Nelson Mandela and Benigno Aquino, are brought up to be leaders. Others, like Las Madres de la Plaza de Mayo, are stirred to action out of love for their families.

Some scientists, like Andrei Sakharov, feel a sense of responsibility for the weapons they have created or other aspects of their special knowledge and power. Some are motivated by their religious beliefs. Some, like Corazon Aquino, accept a role they might never have sought but for challenges "thrust upon them." Others are struck by injustice they experience or witness as youths and determine then to fight for change. For many heroes there is a mixture of reasons ranging from pure altruism to selfishness.

Most of us do not desire to be famous. Most of us are not heroes. But we wonder what we would have done under the same circumstances. Would we have marched in the Plaza de Mayo or demonstrated against apartheid in South Africa? Would we have returned to Manila if we were Benigno Aquino? Living in freedom in the United States in the late twentieth century, it is hard to imagine how we would act in those totally different situations. These great people are models and reminders of our best aspirations for ourselves.

If we accept that we might not be heroes, we tend to believe we would not be villains. But the government leaders who approve torture and the torturers are human beings too. They, too, love their families. They don't see themselves as villains, but as patriots who inflict pain on their government's enemies. They believe torture can break a prisoner's spirit and serve some "higher" cause, and they usually refuse to recognize that their victims are human.

Doctors who work with torturers in violation of their Hippocratic oath "to do no harm" are perhaps the worst of moral monsters. In the Soviet Union, psychiatrists have committed dissidents to mental hospitals by diagnosing political dissent as schizophrenia, a severe mental illness. One influential doctor, Andrei V. Shezhnevsky, developed the diagnosis of "sluggish schizophrenia" for individuals who exhibited "obsessive desires 'to seek social justice,' camouflaged by seemingly normal behavior."[10] In Chile, government doctors have assessed detainees' ability to bear pain by examining them before and during torture sessions; minimized the evidence of torture on victims' bodies; and issued false medical statements certifying that torture victims left the detention center in good health.

It is vital to think about these villains because they too are human, like you and me. Their evil impulses are not those of aliens from another planet. All of us feel anger and aggression now and then; all of us are capable of cruelty. Most of the time we try to control our emotions. Torturers do not. Torturers often have a warped sense of righteousness—the idea that dissenters are "subversives," the evil ones who must be broken and defeated in the service of the nation. This kind of thinking is perverted and extreme, certainly, but not wholly unlike the way most of us tend to join in the popular view without questioning it, and to distrust or look askance at people who are too noticeably different or unpopular. For most of us the easy, most common way to get along is to go along, especially with directives that come from official quarters. This inclination goes far to explain how, during World War II, so many "good Germans" were able to operate Nazi death camps during the week and still go to church on

Sunday. Identical impulses enabled many white Americans in the segregationist South to join in lynch mobs.

Like gas chambers and lynch mobs, many of humankind's worst horrors have sprung from perverted notions of patriotism, or religion, or justice. Devotion to the nation and "our way of life"—to protecting "us" and our virtues against "them" and their viciousness—has a great, and often deceptive, appeal. Demands in the name of government and law tend to evoke ready acquiescence. If the law is warped to achieve cruelty and oppression, the government itself becomes an instrument of terror. The law, which is meant for security and good order, becomes a nightmare.

This kind of perversion is a central aspect of modern concern for international human rights. Leaders who distort the law in order to use imprisonment, torture, and murder to stifle anyone who opposes, or merely questions, their regimes violate our most basic rights: the right not to be imprisoned, except after a fair trial for violation of some known and acceptable law; the right never to be tortured; and certainly, the right not to be murdered by thugs holding government office or wearing government uniforms. (As we'll see, many people, including me, wish to see capital punishment outlawed as a violation of international human rights, but this remains debatable, notably in the United States, where a large majority still supports the death penalty.)

In the next chapters we'll examine how these rights have come to be recognized, and how they've grown in very recent times. Above all, we'll be taking an overview of the ways in which governments protect—or violate—these basic rights. We will look at political goals and diplomatic strategies. And at every point we will focus on the humans involved in the struggle for *human* rights; for in the end, of course, at every point we are talking about people and the way they deal with each other.

CHAPTER 2

Lawless Governments

In most of the world today, most people live in communities that are held together by the rule of law. The system of law is so basic and familiar that the majority of us take it for granted or are unaware of it. We routinely expect that drivers will stop for that red light while we cross the street. We not only hope but reasonably expect that stronger people or gangs of thugs won't beat us or kill us or invade our houses to take our property. The daily newspaper and television news reports focus, of course, on the cases in which these expectations prove wrong—when people rob or murder or cause accidents by running through red lights. Because that's what news is, we sometimes think life is a series of crime "waves" and that laws exist only to be broken. But consider it for a minute and you'll recognize how marvelously the great majority of us respect the law and each other, and in that way make civilized life possible. Watch cars stay in line, pedestrians sort themselves out in decent order, public and private property generally respected and left intact.

The whole thing works because we all grow up being "socialized," being conditioned to play a willing part in the complex

19

tasks of living together in a crowded world. It would not work if a majority, or even a large minority, chose to break the rules and run amok, assaulting and robbing their neighbors. This rarely happens because we feel the strong arm of the government near at hand to deter or punish lawbreakers. Even if police officers are not always close by, and most disputes don't wind up in the courthouse, we know that government muscle behind the law stands ready to carry out the official threat that violators will be punished. Of course, we also expect that the government will obey the rule of law and arrest only those it has good reason to believe have committed criminal acts, and punish them only after they have been found guilty.

All that, which is so obvious when you think about it, is a fundamental beginning of the subject of human rights. The grim problems of the Mothers of the Plaza de Mayo and other victims are a result of the uses and misuses of force and violence by those who control the apparatus of government at any given time. This is something to keep in mind when we consider human rights and the endless struggle to preserve them.

Because it seems necessary for a civilized society to create structures of power to enforce the domestic rule of law, most of us accept the existence of police forces as essential parts of government. We also accept the need for armed forces to protect us from outside threats. It is only a very distant hope that large nations will find a way to do without them. (One or two small countries— Costa Rica is a current example—have no army or navy, but these are rare though glowing exceptions.) So one way or another the monopoly of physical force is a critical part of the institutions that we have called governments throughout recorded history. How those governments have come to exist is, of course, a long, complicated, and varied story. In many cases, both in the past and in the present, the use of military and police power has been the means by which rulers, including both dictators and kings, installed and maintained themselves and their heirs. Still others acquire political power by less violent and more civilized means, such as election in democratic countries, and in that way take charge of police and military forces. However governments originate, and however rulers come to lead them, the sundry ways of continuing them—by force, by rules of succession, by consent, by some of each—are a large part of the human story. Without pretending to pursue that story, we know that the subject of human rights is tied tightly to the organized force of governments.

Law-abiding people who want to live in peace rely on that organized force as a benefit of civilization. As a last resort against violence, we count on being able to call the police. If we can't settle disputes over property rights or family relations among ourselves, we can turn to the courts. None of that works perfectly by any means. But it works well enough so that we are usually satisfied that the rule of law is in place.

But what if that machinery of law—especially the human "machinery" made up of police and soldiers—should itself become an instrument of lawlessness and violence? What if you call the police for help and they arrive and proceed to beat you up and destroy your house? Worse yet, what if they come uninvited to assault and murder? This kind of nightmare is not imaginary. It happens to law-abiding people all over the world. Imagine the case of a small urban family—father, mother, and two daughters—learning that those who run the government have decided to round them up and send them away to concentration camps, where they may be starved, put to forced labor, tortured, and probably killed. Suppose the father's coworkers offer to risk their own lives by hiding the family in a secret annex to the warehouse where he worked. The father and his associates smuggle the family's belongings and food supplies to the hiding place, bit by bit, to avoid suspicion. And then one day the government calls the oldest daughter to be taken away, and the father tells the family that it is time to go into hiding. Imagine the father inviting another family (father, mother, teenage son) and another man to share the small hiding place, and imagine them hiding there for more than two years, being fed and protected by his coworkers, but shrinking into silence at every unexpected noise or sudden visit to the warehouse below. Even coughing is forbidden; anyone

21

with a cold is drugged with codeine to suppress coughs. Of course, when someone is ill, he or she can't go to a doctor. Picture the younger daughter living her early adolescence that way—keeping a diary that manages to record bright moments, her first kiss, quarrels in the tight living quarters, hopes for the future as well as fears in those ghastly circumstances.

This is the story preserved for us by *The Diary of a Young Girl* (better known by the name of the play, *The Diary of Anne Frank*), a book that everyone should read, a diary that ended when a betrayer led Nazi police to the secret annex in Amsterdam. The diary was dropped on the floor by the Nazis, who were only interested in taking the family's last valuables, their silverware and their Hanukkah menorah, and was hidden by one of the father's coworkers. Then, as the world should not forget, Anne Frank, age fifteen, was taken off to a concentration camp and murdered, as were all the other occupants of the secret annex except her father. He survived Auschwitz, the infamous concentration camp. This family's "crime" was being Jewish, a crime for which some six million other people died at the hands of the Germans during World War II.

Anne Frank's short life history belongs in the story of human rights for more than one reason. She had been born in Germany, but her family fled to Holland in 1933 when the Nazis came to power, only to fall under Nazi rule after they invaded Holland. The Germans' official bestiality was practiced within Germany and in all the occupied nations—against Jews, Gypsies, homosexuals, mental patients, "subversives," and others that Nazi doctrine had declared unfit to live. As we shall see, martyrs like Anne Frank are an immortal part of the world's strivings for human rights.

The horror of a government like that, run by gangsters with official titles and uniforms, comes to life for us in her diary:

> Countless friends and aquaintances have gone to a
> terrible fate. Evening after evening the green and gray
> army lorries trundle past. The Germans ring at every

front door to inquire if there are any Jews living in the house. If there are, then the whole family has to go at once. . . . In the evenings when it's dark, I often see rows of good, innocent people accompanied by crying children, walking on and on, in charge of a couple of these chaps, bullied and knocked about until they almost drop. No one is spared—old people and babies, expectant mothers, the sick—each and all join in the march of death. . . . I get frightened when I think of close friends who have now been delivered into the hands of the cruelest brutes that walk the earth. And all because they are Jews![1]

Farther to the east, the Soviet Union experienced an even longer reign of terror than Germany under the Nazis. This period began in the late 1920s and lasted until 1953, when Stalin died. Among the first victims were the peasants. Soviet theory called for collectivized farms, with the land and machinery owned by the state rather than individuals. Large numbers of peasants resisted giving up their land and equipment, especially the more prosperous ones called *kulaks*. In 1929, Stalin declared his intention to "liquidate the kulaks as a class,"[2] and a period of violent conflict began in which thousands were killed. The struggle led to a drastic decline in Soviet farm production. In the resulting famine, deaths from starvation are estimated to have numbered between 5 and 10 million. (Ironically, under Mikhail Gorbachev, the Soviets seem to be returning from collective to individual farms.)

Stalin imprisoned and executed anyone who dissented, or who was suspected of dissenting, from the "party line." Sweeping "purges" in the 1930s featured fake, forced confessions and large-scale executions of Communist Party and military leaders. In a nightmare regime millions of innocent people were sentenced to wretched prisons, to exile in Siberia, or simply to death. The unspeakable conditions of the Siberian camps, where many died of disease brought on by hunger and brutal mistreatment, have been recorded in detail in Aleksandr Solzhenitsyn's *Gulag Archi-*

pelago. After the end of World War II, Stalin appeared to be starting a new round of purges, prevented only by his death in 1953.

The account of imprisonments and killings does not describe the full horror of regimes like Hitler's and Stalin's. The whole nation in the grip of such totalitarian control lives in a state of fear and dread. People are afraid to speak openly or to trust one another. It is always possible that a neighbor or a supposed friend will betray or fabricate "disloyal" actions. The arbitrary powers of secret and other police as well as the military are an overhanging threat. There is steady pressure to cheer and salute the tyrants and their lieutenants. For those of us who cherish personal freedom, it is hard to believe that millions of Germans and Russians truly seemed to believe in those governments and to support them. The explanations for this belief are complex and still far from satisfactory. But one thing is perfectly clear: totalitarians are the prime and implacable enemies of human rights.

Here in the Western Hemisphere, though not on the scale of the Nazi or Soviet atrocities, thousands of similar individual stories have been documented—in Argentina, Brazil, Chile, and other places. After the ouster of the Argentine junta in 1983, the democratically elected government of Raúl Alfonsín created a commission to collect evidence on the *desaparecidos*. The commission's report, published in 1984 under the title *Nunca Más* ("Never Again"), summarized more than fifty thousand pages of documents and several thousand statements and testimonies telling, in harrowing detail, what it means when the government itself becomes a criminal organization. In the prologue, Ernesto Sabato, the Argentine novelist who chaired the commission, described the effect of the "dirty war" on his fellow citizens:

> A feeling of complete vulnerability spread throughout Argentine society, coupled with the fear that anyone, however innocent, might become a victim of the never-ending witch-hunt. Some people reacted with alarm. Others tended, consciously or unconsciously, to justify

24

the horror. "There must be some reason for it," they would whisper, as though trying to propitiate awesome and inscrutable gods, regarding the children or parents of the disappeared as plague-bearers. Yet such feelings could never be whole-hearted, as so many cases were known of people who had been sucked into that bottomless pit who were obviously not guilty of anything. It was simply that the "anti-subversive" struggle, like all hunts against witches or those possessed, had become a demented generalized repression and the word "subversive" itself came to be used with a vast and vague range of meaning. In the semantic delirium where labels such as Marxist-Leninist, traitors to the fatherland, materialists and atheists, enemies of Western, Christian values, abounded, anyone was at risk—from those who were proposing social revolution, to aware adolescents who merely went out to the shanty towns to help the people living there.[3]

Argentine President Alfonsín, a staunch advocate of human rights and a steady opponent of the junta he succeeded, has described the human and institutional wreckage caused when the government itself embarks on a terrorist reign:

This loss generated fear, uncertainty, self-criticism and, above all, insecurity stemming from the impossibility of predicting the arbitrary exercise of public authority. One result was a general and self-defensive withdrawal; people sought shelter in the private realm, abandoning all interest in public affairs. In some sectors of society, this attitude was related to a certain indifference towards, and even tolerance of, the aberrant acts committed first by pseudorevolutionary terrorists and then by those who from positions of power promoted their own terrorism, which demonstrated the same contempt for the dignity of the human person.[4]

25

In South Africa today, children have been special targets of the government's violence. In 1985 more than two hundred children were killed by the police. This violence is random; the police often fire on crowds for no reason at all. In one case a four-year-old child was killed when police fired into a crowd celebrating a wedding; on another occasion two babies were killed by fumes when police fired tear gas into a crowd. Any child who tries to flee the security police is shot, and often children are caught in crossfire as they play or run errands. Entire schools full of children have been arrested. Children as young as seven have been arrested and detained without anyone telling their parents. While under arrest, children are routinely beaten and often tortured with electric shocks and other devices.

Abuses of human rights are not restricted to lawlessness and random violence. In many instances the laws themselves violate individual human rights. Until the Civil War, American law allowed black people to be bought and sold as slaves. Slaves who escaped had to be returned to their owners. Until 1954 the laws of most southern states required that blacks and whites attend separate schools. The anti-Semitic laws of Nazi Germany that required Jews to wear yellow stars and barred them from professions and school violated human rights. Today in South Africa the problem is not only that the government flouts the law in its use of torture and force against unarmed civilians, but also that the elaborate legal system of apartheid, which limits where people may live, work, and eat because of the color of their skin, itself violates human rights.

Criminal governments, unlike the more candid breeds of private criminals, package their atrocities in ideological wrappings. In Hitler's view, aggressions and mass murders were necessary to destroy "subversives" and "inferior breeds" like Jews and Gypsies, who "threatened the racial purity of the German people," and to overpower assorted conspiracies of communists, international bankers, and other "enemies of the state." The prisons of the Soviet Union, Cuba, and other communist states have been filled with political enemies who "slander" the state and are denounced as "criminals" trying to obstruct the forward march of the masses. In Cambodia over a million died when the Khmer Rouge took power, summarily executed soldiers and "educated" people, and sent urban residents on forced marches into the countryside to create a rural society through forced labor. South Africa imprisons thousands of black people, including many hundreds of children, and kills hundreds because they too are "subversive" and "traitorous," which means they resist apartheid. Similar ideological "explanations" account for the misery and murder of uncounted people during the recent history of Chile, Poland, Indonesia, China, Turkey, Zaire, Paraguay, and many other nations.

In Iran, the peaceable adherents of the Baha'i faith, who seek universal equality and tolerance, are considered "misguided infidels" and are the target of a genocide campaign by the Moslem fundamentalist theocracy. Baha'is, a minority of 300,000, believe they must obey the laws of the governments where they live, and do not participate in partisan politics. Yet two hundred have been executed since 1979, when the Ayatollah Khomeini came to power. Several hundred are in prison, without charges, often tortured. Their property is confiscated, they are prevented from earning a decent living, and their children cannot attend Iranian schools. Since they are forbidden to emigrate, they are trapped in a nightmarish system where they are considered "nonpersons" under the Iranian constitution, and have no protection in the courts.[5]

What can be done about these atrocities? For the most part, the struggle must be carried on from within each particular country. The great burdens are borne by heroes like those we spoke of in Chapter 1, who lead the fight of oppressed people against their oppressors. It is a fearsome undertaking. If a country does not have a tradition of keen vigilance against dictatorial threats, a repressive regime may come into power before people are aware of its real nature.

For instance, the debate continues about how far the German people understood, and supported or resisted, Adolf Hitler's seizure and use of the national power. His book *Mein Kampf*, his speeches, and his officers made no secret of his racist theories and

27

his goals of conquest. While others fought him at the polls and even in the streets, the rapid growth of his mass following leaves no doubt that hundreds of thousands of Germans shared his outlook. And when he had taken the reins of power, the possibility of overthrowing him was nearly hopeless. A few people tried, but it is clear that the great majority of Germans ignored or opposed these attempts.

It took an awful world war with many millions of deaths to end the Nazi regime. And it was not Hitler's atrocities against human rights that led to the war. In fact, there has never been an invasion or a war by one nation against another for the purpose of ending the other country's violations of its own people's human rights. For the most part that remains the brutally difficult task of the suffering people within each country's borders.

But in our time we have seen the beginnings of significant change in this situation. Human rights have become an international concern, and Hitler gets "credit" for this in the sense that his depraved regime had a lot to do with bringing it about. We'll discuss that development in Chapter 3.

Today it is generally understood that it is proper for one country to care whether basic human rights are being respected in another country. It is still true, and it probably should and must remain true, that nations won't go to war to enforce human rights elsewhere. But it is also clear that people and governments everywhere now take a new and encouraging interest in human rights within any particular country and have mobilized in a variety of ways to make that interest meaningful. The development is still young, intertwined with political goals other than human rights. This means, for example, that selected countries are specially prominent targets of human rights criticism while violations in other countries go largely or wholly unnoticed. Nevertheless, ideas and actions supporting *international* human rights have taken strong and deepening root since World War II.

South Africa is a prime illustration of the continuing development. For many years that country has been condemned by just about every nation in the world for its serious offenses against human rights through its apartheid system. South Africa was deprived of its seat in the General Assembly of the United Nations by a lopsided vote in 1981. A number of countries, including the United States, have imposed trade sanctions on South Africa— refusing to sell South Africans things they need or to buy things they export. A number of American and other companies have withdrawn investments from South Africa to demonstrate their opposition to apartheid. South African athletes have been excluded from a great many international events, including the Olympics. Many cultural exchange programs with South Africa have ended, and many artists boycott South Africa. South Africa, in a word, is being isolated from the international community.

Measures that aim at a whole country in this fashion raise serious questions. Many people, within South Africa and elsewhere, are against sanctions of various kinds, though they oppose apartheid. Economic boycotts, they say, hurt blacks more than they hurt whites, and cutting off cultural exchanges isolates the champions of human rights within the country from friends and allies around the world. These arguments make sense. But the vocal black leadership in South Africa favors sanctions, and their international supporters elsewhere tend to accept that judgment.

The pressures from outside make the South African government vividly aware that its human rights abuses generate anger and hostility all over the world. And the outrage of other nations has made many South Africans question and even oppose their government's policies. There are others, of course, who want their government to thumb its nose at the rest of the world. It appears, however, that a large number from within the white ruling class are weakening their support of apartheid. Of course, there have always been a few brave whites—like the late Alan Paton, author of *Cry, the Beloved Country*; Donald Woods, author of *Biko–Cry Freedom*; and Helen Suzman, a white liberal member of the South African Parliament—who have opposed apartheid, but they have been a distinct minority.

What is still more important, outside pressures have given South African blacks moral and material support in their struggle.

They know they are not alone. Individuals and governments contribute money to help in many ways, ranging from legal battles in the South African courts to the guerrilla warfare waged by the African National Congress.

In gauging the impact of outside pressures, we have to keep in mind that "government" is not a monolithic or superhuman apparatus. There are human beings within every government who are capable of being affected by human influences, both from within the country and from elsewhere. At some point soldiers and police officers may become unwilling to brutalize their fellow citizens. This is what happened in the Philippines, when nonviolent masses assembled to support Corazon Aquino and to oppose dictator Ferdinand Marcos. The very top leadership may change under the pressure of foreign demands and sanctions. We've seen this over and over again, as in the peaceful Filipino revolution of 1986 and in the transformation of governments like that of Argentina. In every case, the evidence is clear that the happy change might have been delayed longer, or might not have happened at all, without the support of the international community.

CHAPTER 3

Out of the Ashes

International human rights as we know them today are a recent phenomenon. A whole complex of new elements—international law, treaties, debates, the way nations see themselves and others—began during World War II and its aftermath. But the source for these new ideas lies deeper in our cultural history. Nothing in human history is wholly unconnected with what has gone before.

Beginning with the waves of liberating thought and ideals that characterized the eighteenth century in Europe as the Age of Enlightenment, and extending to around the period of World War I (1914–18), the western world enjoyed a strongly optimistic sense that the human race and its environment were growing steadily better and better. Knowledge expanded rapidly. Science and technology produced one marvel after another. Medical advances brought longer lives and greater well-being. Enlightened governments widened the benefits of education and participation. Slavery was ended. To be sure, there were plenty of negatives. The blights of colonialism, racism, and human exploitation continued to spread misery in large areas of the world. But the idea of progress and human perfectibility rode high into the second decade of the twentieth century.

The carnage of World War I—a war fought for reasons that seemed more and more questionable as people thought about them—was a sobering experience. The brief and troubled span before the outbreak of World War II in 1939 brought the horrors of communist and fascist dictatorships. In 1917, after the despotic czar had been overthrown in the Russian Revolution, the Bolsheviks seized power from the new liberal government under Prime Minister Aleksandr Kerensky and installed V.I. Lenin as leader. In 1922, Benito Mussolini formed a fascist government in Italy. After the German economy collapsed in 1927, heralding the onset of a worldwide depression that reached the United States in 1929, Hitler's Nazi movement gained strength. In January 1933, Hitler was appointed chancellor of Germany, and by April, boycotts against Jews had begun and the first concentration camp had been established at Dachau.

In *Mein Kampf* (My Struggle), a book that should have given ample warning to the world, Hitler pronounced his theories of a master race (which for him was the Aryan race) entitled to rule the world. This mythical master race was a supposed stock of blond Nordic types. That racist doctrine would have been monstrous even if it had had a basis in fact. Ironically, however, it was also a scientific absurdity. Hitler himself, with his black hair and mustache, did not answer to the Aryan description. Over the course of modern times there has been so much intermarriage between people of different races, religions, and nationalities that the idea of "pure races" is idiocy in any case. But not for Hitler and his followers.

According to Hitler, the Aryan race was the only culture-creating race, the one that had built civilization by conquering and enslaving inferior people. But Hitler contended that the Aryan race had lost its full power through mixing with the inferior races: "As soon as the subjected peoples themselves began to rise . . . , the sharp separating wall between master and slave fell. The Aryan gave up the purity of his blood and therefore he also lost his place in the Paradise which he had created for himself."[1]

32

All the white Germanic folk blessed with his approval were by that token entitled to deem themselves lords and masters over other, "lesser" people—Jews, blacks, Gypsies, Slavs, and others. Hitler opposed what he called the "Jewish" view of the equality of man: "It is a criminal absurdity to train a half-ape until one believes a lawyer has been made of him, while millions of members of the highest culture race have to remain in entirely unworthy positions; that it is a sin against the will of the eternal Creator to let hundreds and hundreds of thousands of His most talented beings degenerate in the proletarian swamps of today while Hottentots and Zulu Kafirs are trained for intellectual vocations."[2]

Hitler blamed Germany's loss in World War I on Jewish participation in German life. He made it his goal to rebuild and rearm Germany.

Launching World War II with his attack on Poland in September 1939 (earlier invasions of the Rhineland and Czechoslovakia having been allowed with scarcely a whimper by the other European nations), Hitler proceeded to put into practice his diabolical master-race theory. Millions were enslaved to produce munitions and other goods for the German war machine that aimed to dominate the world. Large numbers of slave laborers were starved and worked to death.

Hitler was obsessed with the Jews. He made a top priority a "final solution" to the "Jewish question"—the murder of all Jews in Europe. After German forces invaded the Soviet Union, the Nazis established *Einsatzgruppen* (special action groups) to liquidate Jews and others. The *Einsatzgruppen* rounded up people in tens of thousands, forced them to dig their own mass graves, made them strip, and shot them dead on the spot. Millions more were herded into concentration camps, transported in tightly packed boxcars without food or water so that large numbers died en route. Gas chambers were built for large-scale extermination. Other killing methods were created for "efficiency" in a methodical course of insanity that most of us would find impossible to imagine if it had not really happened. The infamous names of the death camps—Auschwitz, Majdanek, Treblinka, and Belzec were the largest—evoke one of the most miserable chapters of human history.

It is recorded that 6 million Jews were killed by the Nazis, nearly 2 million at Auschwitz alone. A million Jewish children were murdered, as well as hundreds of thousands of Gypsies, Poles, Russians, and others of all religions and nationalities, including many who bravely opposed the Nazis. The Nazis ruled the nations they occupied by terror and often murdered innocent civilians in reprisal for resistance activity. When the Nazi chief of security in occupied Czechoslovakia, Reinhard Heydrich, was assassinated by the Czech underground, the Nazis destroyed the village of Lidice and murdered all its male inhabitants.

The Germans' wartime allies, the Japanese, behaved similarly in places they occupied. In the six weeks after seizing control of Nanking, China, the Japanese gang-raped more than twenty thousand women, ranging in age from eleven to seventy, and murdered at least ten thousand civilians.

By 1940 the Nazis controlled almost the entire continent of Europe. Sweden, Spain, Switzerland, Ireland, Portugal, and Turkey were neutral. And the Germans and Soviets had made a pact, agreeing on a division of the continent. England was the only western country still at war and was pounded daily by the German air force, the Luftwaffe. A Nazi victory appeared to be inevitable. But the would-be world conquerors overreached. By the end of 1941, the Nazis, together with the other Axis powers (Italy and Japan), were at war with the Allies (England, the Soviet Union, and the United States) throughout most of the world—Europe, Africa, and Asia. For the next four years, military victory against the Axis powers was the primary concern of the Allies.

In those desperate times, for a variety of reasons (often not good reasons), the Allied leadership paid less attention than it should have to the atrocities of Germany and Japan against civilian populations. The extent of those atrocities was not fully known or believed until the last days of the war, as the countries under Axis occupation were liberated.

However, as knowledge of Nazi and Japanese crimes against

humanity grew, waves of revulsion spread through the world. Earlier, in 1941, the Allies had declared the standards of right and the freedoms for which they fought. The American president, Franklin Delano Roosevelt, had announced a basic commitment to Four Freedoms—freedom of speech, freedom of religion, freedom from want, and freedom from fear. These became cornerstones of the Atlantic Charter (August 14, 1941) under which England and the United States declared their allied goals. In that charter they disavowed any interest in increasing their territories and stated that they would respect "the right of all peoples to choose the form of government under which they will live." They would collaborate with all other nations in trade and economic advancement. They stated that "after the final destruction of Nazi tyranny, they hope to see established a peace which will afford to all nations the means of dwelling in safety within their own boundaries and which will afford assurance that all men in all the lands may live out their lives in freedom from fear and want." Finally, they pledged to work for peace and to disarm nations that threatened or might threaten force outside their frontiers.

The Allies also warned that war crimes would be punished. In 1943 they laid the foundations for the United Nations War Crimes Commission. For their part, the Germans and Japanese persisted both in waging war and in committing atrocities until the bitter end. Even when defeat was certain, the Nazis went on with their "final solution." Transporting Jews to the gas chambers remained a top priority at a time when the German army needed trains to transport troops and equipment. When the Allies approached the concentration camps, the Nazis often sent their victims on forced marches into Germany. Many prisoners died in the very last days of the war.

After World War II the victorious nations undertook to carry out some of their wartime pledges. Nazi and Japanese leaders were brought to trial for war crimes and crimes against humanity. The largest and most significant proceedings were the Nuremberg Trials, in which twenty-one top German leaders sat in the dock as defendants while one, Martin Bormann, was tried in absentia.

35

Hitler had committed suicide in the final days of the war. Hermann Goering, the brilliant and evil deputy who had presided over the formation of the Gestapo (the Nazi secret police), commanded the Luftwaffe (the air force) during the war, and had signed the only existing written orders giving responsibility for preparing a "final solution" of the "Jewish question," escaped execution by managing to obtain and swallow a fatal dose of poison two hours before his death sentence was to be carried out.

Of the others, ten were sentenced to death and were hanged on October 15, 1946, three were sentenced to life imprisonment, and four were sentenced to prison terms of between ten and twenty years. Martin Bormann was also sentenced to death by hanging, but he was never found. Three were acquitted, but were found guilty of lesser offenses in later trials. A few served their terms and lived to be released. One weird figure, Rudolf Hess, remained imprisoned in Berlin until his death at age ninety-three in August 1987. Hess had flown to Scotland in 1941, allegedly to talk peace, shortly before Hitler invaded the Soviet Union. Hitler had denounced him as a madman, but the Soviets suspected that his mission had been to arrange a deal with England so that Hitler could focus the full powers of the Nazis on the Soviet Union. The Soviets would never thereafter consent to releasing Hess from his life sentence.

The Nuremberg Trials and others like them raised a deep issue that is still debated. Were they proper "trials," or only a means for the victors to exact revenge from the vanquished? The defendants had not committed "crimes" at all, this argument ran, because their wartime acts as leaders of their countries, however monstrous, had never been proscribed as "criminal" in any orthodox legal sense. Accordingly, under this view, the Nazi leaders and others were punished under ex post facto laws—that is, were tried and sentenced for conduct that was only declared "criminal" after their actions had occurred. If this view was sound, it laid a serious charge against conducting the war crimes trials. It is a nearly universal principle of modern law that a person may be tried and punished only for conduct that was criminal under the law at the time when he or she engaged in it. Departure from this principle—punishment under ex post facto laws—is generally considered unacceptable.

A majority of scholars and political leaders rejected the ex post facto label for the Nuremberg Trials. They felt that the bestialities of the Nazi and Japanese leaders had long been condemned as criminal by known standards of international law. This was most clearly true of "war crimes"—violations that were well defined for many years in international treaties and conventions. Both the Nazis and the Japanese had unquestionably violated international law in their treatment of prisoners of war by putting them to forced labor and, on at least some occasions, murdering them. In one infamous incident, which came to be known as the Bataan Death March, the Japanese forced 72,000 American and Filipino prisoners of war to march for seven days with no food and under brutal treatment; more than ten thousand died.

While the treaties specifically condemned the murder of prisoners of war, they did not address the murder of civilians. But the Allies justified the charges and sentences for "crimes against humanity" by arguing that law, especially international law, is not made only by treaties and statutes; it is also generated by the customary usage and beliefs of the civilized people of the world. They took the position that mass murder of civilians had become an international crime before World War II and that, in any event, the Axis powers had been repeatedly warned that such actions were criminal and would be punished.

The subject of that debate has filled many volumes and will undoubtedly fill many more. Without pretending to give a full account of it, this one writer records a vote in favor of the Nuremberg Trials.

Most important, these trials led to judgments of right and wrong that are now international law. The idea of a master race lording it over inferior races generated worldwide abhorrence that we hope will continue down the centuries. If any single thing could account for complex developments like the international human rights movement, it is Hitler's repulsive theory and the

37

barbarities committed under the Axis aegis. The key premise in the concept of human rights is that every human being, by virtue of being a human being, is to be assured the basic rights and freedoms that Hitler denied. Today no civilized country dares openly to question that premise.

The international human rights movement began before the end of World War II with the Allied statements of the principles for which they were fighting and the organization and definition of the United Nations. On June 25, 1946, delegates in San Francisco signed the Charter of the United Nations. The preamble stated in part that "We the Peoples of the United Nations [are] determined . . . to reaffirm faith in fundamental human rights, in the dignity of and worth of the human person, in the equal rights of men and women and of nations large and small."

Key provisions of the United Nations Charter were Articles 1, 55, and 56. Article 1 states that one of the central purposes of the United Nations is "to achieve international cooperation in solving international problems of an economic, social, cultural, or humanitarian character, and in promoting and encouraging respect for human rights and for fundamental freedoms for all without distinction as to race, sex, language, or religion." Article 55 prescribes that the United Nations shall promote "universal respect for, and observance of, human rights and fundamental freedoms for all without distinction as to race, sex, language, or religion." Article 56 provides that "all Members pledge themselves to take joint and separate action in cooperation with the Organization for the achievement of the purposes set forth in Article 55."

Americans had hoped to annex an international bill of rights to the charter, much like the American model. But there had not been time to draft such a document.[3] Before the end of 1948, however, the Universal Declaration of Human Rights was completed. This is one of the great documents of modern times. Chapter 10 discusses it in detail.

We Americans are entitled to take pride in the major role played by our leaders in creating the Universal Declaration and in the extent to which fundamental American conceptions are echoed in that document. We have not always stayed in the forefront of the human rights movement, but our leadership, along with bedrock ideas in our Declaration of Independence and Constitution, are solidly recorded in the Universal Declaration.

Of course, Americans speak with more than one voice on all subjects. From the very beginning of the United Nations, a minority opposed declarations or treaties on international human rights. Some southern whites feared that American blacks might enlist the United Nations in their struggles against racial discrimination. Their fears were not unfounded. In 1947 the National Association for the Advancement of Colored People submitted a petition to the United Nations Human Rights Commission seeking condemnation of the segregation and discrimination practiced in the United States against black Americans.

Overriding the opposition, the American government supported the creation and adoption of the Universal Declaration. Tasks like these are always the work of teams of people. Frequently the most significant and creative work is performed by professionals whose names are not widely known. But one prominent person who played an outstanding role in fashioning the Universal Declaration was Eleanor Roosevelt, the widow of President Franklin Roosevelt. President Harry S Truman asked her to sit as a member of the U.S. delegation to the General Assembly of the United Nations, undoubtedly because he was impressed by the fine work she had done as First Lady during the Great Depression and World War II. She was asked to serve on "Committee Three," which dealt with humanitarian, educational, and cultural questions. In her autobiography she said that she "could just see the gentlemen of our delegation puzzling over the list [of committees] saying: 'Oh, no! We can't put Mrs. Roosevelt on the political committee. What would she do on the budget committee? Does she know anything about legal questions? Ah, here's the safe spot for her—Committee Three. She can't do much harm there!' "[4]

Mrs. Roosevelt's work on Committee Three and the U.N. Human Rights Commission earned her the affectionate title "First

Lady of the World." When the Human Rights Commission was formed in January 1947, she was unanimously elected to chair it. Under her direction, the commission set as its first goal the drafting of a Universal Declaration of Human Rights. A "declaration" required for its adoption only a majority vote of the General Assembly and would not be binding on the member nations. A binding treaty would require ratification nation by nation, and Mrs. Roosevelt recognized that such a process would be very difficult and time-consuming. She thought that to start with drafting the technical language of a treaty and then to await ratification by the nations of the world would block progress in human rights. She also foresaw the likelihood of Senate opposition to a treaty binding the United States to honor human rights. She undoubtedly remembered the League of Nations, the first world organization founded after World War I. Although President Woodrow Wilson was its most ardent supporter, the Senate failed to ratify membership in that organization. That probably accounted in substantial part for the essential failure of the league as an agency for peace and may well have been a factor leading to World War II.

Eleanor Roosevelt proposed that after the Universal Declaration was adopted, the commission should focus on drafting specific covenants creating binding obligations and on methods for implementing the declared rights. Her instincts proved correct; the declaration was ratified in 1948, but the vital covenants were not approved by the General Assembly until eighteen years later (in 1966), and as of this date (1989), the United States has still not ratified them.

Mrs. Roosevelt's commission faced the formidable job of composing a declaration that would be acceptable to a wide array of religions, cultures, and ideologies. The Chinese delegate, P. C. Chang, wanted to incorporate the teachings of Confucius. Charles Malik, a Lebanese Catholic, wanted to reflect the philosophy of Thomas Aquinas. The Soviet bloc wanted the declaration to emphasize social and economic rights, and viewed the inclusion of rights listed in the French Declaration of Human Rights and the

American Bill of Rights as "remnants of archaic bourgeois thought." Mrs. Roosevelt and the British delegate, who was a trade unionist, compromised by agreeing to include articles guaranteeing full employment, adequate housing, decent health care, and cradle-to-grave social security.[5]

At 3:00 A.M. on December 10, 1948, the United Nations General Assembly adopted the Universal Declaration of Human Rights. The final vote was 48 nations in favor, 2 absent, and 8 abstentions. The Soviet bloc abstained because the declaration did not give sufficient weight to economic, social, and cultural rights. Saudi Arabia abstained because, its delegate explained, it believed that freedom of religion was contrary to the Koran.[6] South Africa also abstained; its white government could not subscribe to Article 6, which states in part: "All are equal before the law and are entitled without any discrimination to equal protection of the law." No nation voted against the declaration. After the vote the delegates gave Eleanor Roosevelt a standing ovation in honor of her leadership.

As mentioned earlier, the Universal Declaration is in major part a reflection of civil rights and freedoms familiar to Americans from our Constitution, and to the French from their Declaration of the Rights of Man. It also resembles similar ideas or documents in other democracies. Less familiar are the portions of the Universal Declaration (and later treaties and covenants) that provide *economic and social rights*. Under this heading are the provisions in Article 23 that declare "the right to work, to free choice of employment, to just and favorable conditions of work and to protection against unemployment." Rights like these—and others in the Declaration like the "right to rest and leisure" (Article 24)—are absent from the American Constitution and seemed strange and questionable to some Americans. Despite the fact that the United States is in the forefront of nations in meeting such needs, many Americans thought rights like these sounded "socialistic." They raised questions about what governments could fairly be expected to do about them, and whether economic and social rights were compatible with civil and political rights of the kind

41

familiar to us under our Constitution. We'll glance at this complex subject again later on. For the moment, let's just note that there is no incompatibility when welfare rights and traditional American freedoms are fairly understood.

CHAPTER 4

Governments as Human Rights Guardians

Governments are the main violators and the main protectors of human liberty. At any given moment, any government, including our own, is likely to be safeguarding and violating people's basic human rights. While the United States does protect the fundamental freedoms and guard against government abuse, our treatment of the hungry and the homeless, the conditions of our prisons, and our continued use of the death penalty are reminders that there is much work to be done right here.

There are violations all over the world—and millions of tragic victims. But just as we overlook the fact that thousands of cars pass through the same intersection on any day without colliding, while a fatal accident makes the headlines, so too the widespread compliance and desire to comply with international human rights principles is often ignored.

Most nations, most of the time, like most people, would prefer to abide by the law, including the law of international human rights, rather than to be violators. If that were not so, the whole subject would be hopeless—or, really, nonexistent. As we noted earlier, the same thought applies to *domestic* law. If most of us

43

were not law-abiding individuals, no police force of any realistically imaginable size could enforce the law and keep the peace among us. And so it is with nations, which have no police force to regulate them. They have all come to agree that each is better off under a system of effective international law. And no such system can exist without substantial voluntary compliance.

Voluntary compliance has been the normal habit of nation-states over the centuries. The rules of international law, apart from human rights, are observed in countless undramatic ways. Governments respect the rights of foreign diplomats. They don't cross borders or fly aircraft over the territories of others without permission. By and large, they keep the promises they make in treaties.

The same is true with respect to the evolving law of international human rights. Again, no nation wishes to be seen as a violator. There is a strong disposition to honor the safeguards for human rights that have come to be internationally accepted. This good tendency has a positive momentum of its own. As the habit of compliance spreads and increases in the community of nations, it becomes less acceptable to offend against human rights. Nations may deny or try to conceal violations. They may debate whether particular actions are violations—as when the Soviet government or the Castro government in Cuba maintains that people claiming to be political prisoners are just ordinary criminals. But it is no longer acceptable for any government to ignore the rights of its people not to be wantonly imprisoned, abused, tortured, or killed by government officers.

Still, as we've said, compliance is far from perfect, and some nations are persistent violators. The violations are often offenses against international law, which means that other nations have a right to complain and to demand that the abuses cease. What can governments do to bring other governments into compliance?

Force is not the answer. No one believes that one country should invade, or threaten to invade, another as a means of ending human rights abuses. Nobody imagines that the United States and the U.S.S.R. would so much as hint at forcible measures against each other to foster human rights. And the same holds essentially true even for powerful governments confronting weaker ones. The rules against military aggression in international relations are too solidly established to permit exceptions.

It does not follow that governments must stand by in silent helplessness when gross abuses of human rights are being committed by oppressive regimes. There is a variety of possible measures, and we'll be noting specific cases as we go along in this book. For the moment, speaking generally, governments can act singly or in groups against human rights violations. Public protests are an obvious form of reaction. A dramatic example was President Reagan's visit to Moscow for a summit meeting in the spring of 1988, when he used the occasion to speak publicly against the Soviet Union's denials of the right to emigrate, restriction of religious freedom, continued holding of political prisoners, and other abuses. The Soviets were not happy with that, which suggested that the criticisms hit home.

Probably the most desirable form of action is collective measures taken by regional or world bodies of nations. The main agency of this kind is of course the United Nations, which has a wide array of techniques at its disposal. The two most powerful organs of the United Nations are the Security Council and the General Assembly. The Security Council is the prime means for establishing and maintaining international peace. The five superpowers (the United States, the Soviet Union, the United Kingdom, France, and China) are permanent members, and ten other members are elected by the General Assembly for two-year terms. The Security Council is the only U.N. body with the power to compel member nations to act—for instance, by imposing economic sanctions—but each of the superpowers has the right to veto any such decision.

Normally, however, the General Assembly is the more active body with respect to human rights. It is composed of the 159 U.N. member nations, representing approximately 98 percent of the world's population. Each nation, whether it's as small as Luxembourg or as big as China, has one vote in the General Assembly, which serves as the principal forum for debate on international human rights. Although the General Assembly has no power to compel action, it may initiate studies and make recommendations on human rights to the member nations, the Security Council, and other U.N. bodies. The General Assembly's Third Committee (Social, Humanitarian, and Cultural) prepares recommendations for approval in sessions of the full assembly.

The Economic and Social Council (ECOSOC) is composed of fifty-four members of the General Assembly who are elected by that body to three-year terms. Acting under the authority of the General Assembly, ECOSOC coordinates the economic and social work, including human rights work, of the United Nations. ECOSOC created the Human Rights Commission, which receives direction from the Security Council and the General Assembly as well as ECOSOC.

The commission has forty-three members serving in official capacities selected on the basis of geographical distribution. At first the commission's main task was drafting international human rights treaties and declarations. After the two main covenants had been approved by the General Assembly, the U.N. began to focus on the implementation of human rights. From the outset the commission has focused attention on South Africa. After the 1967 war between Israel and Egypt, the commission focused on Israel's conduct in the territories of the West Bank and Gaza. In 1969 the commission appointed a special working group to investigate alleged human rights violations in the Israeli occupied territories. (As we'll see later, the singling out of some countries and not others is in some degree the result of international politics and bloc voting. In order to make fair judgments, each country, and its differing circumstances, should be studied as a separate case.)

After General Augusto Pinochet Ugarte seized control of Chile in a 1973 coup, the commission added that country to its list of human rights abusers, and established an ad hoc working group with five members to study the Chilean situation. Unlike South Africa and Israel, which have refused to participate in U.N.

studies, the Pinochet government actively joined in the debate, providing lists of people arrested and permitting the group to make an on-site visit in 1978. In 1979, the group was disbanded and a special rapporteur was appointed with the same mandate.

The commission has continued to appoint special rapporteurs to make reports on specific nations. Felix Ermacora, the special rapporteur for Afghanistan since 1984, found, after meeting with Afghan refugees in Pakistan, that conditions under the Soviet occupation in Afghanistan were "far removed from respect for human rights" and that there had been mass killings and attempts to destroy irrigation facilities and food production. Ermacora said that the Afghan authorities' plan to resettle 300,000 people from a number of provinces in the southwestern region would result in people being displaced against their will, creating an internal exile. He recommended the withdrawal of "foreign troops." Afghanistan responded that this report "frame[d] the Government and its sincere and trustworthy friend, the Soviet Union" through "dishonesty, fabrication, and gross distortion of facts."[1]

Beginning in 1980, the commission changed its emphasis from specific nations to particular human rights abuses. A five-member Working Group on Enforced or Involuntary Disappearance was created in 1980. The working group's mandate included seeking information from governments, international organizations, human rights organizations, and other reliable sources, and making a report to the commission at its next session. The commission continues to renew the working group's initial one-year mandate and to require annual reports, but it did not expand the mandate to include the making of recommendations to eliminate the practice of disappearances until 1984. The pace is slow—many would say maddeningly slow—and the work proceeds quietly, usually in private rather than with public fanfare. But these are, after all, pioneering efforts on an international scale.

The commission has also appointed special rapporteurs to make reports on other specific human rights abuses. In 1982, Amos Wako of Kenya was appointed the special rapporteur on summary or arbitrary executions. Wako has appealed, with some success,

47

for an end to summary executions. After his interventions, some sentences have been commuted. He also entreated the United States to block executions of convicts who were under eighteen at the time of the offense, since such executions violate the Covenant on Political and Civil Rights. (The United States has signed but not yet ratified the covenant. At the time of this writing, the U.S. Supreme Court has begun to grapple with the question of whether the Constitution bars execution of a person who was under fifteen, or some other minimum age, when the crime was committed, and is expected to rule sometime in 1989.) In December 1985 the General Assembly requested that Wako consider standards for measures to be taken by authorities when death occurs in custody, because such deaths are particularly suspicious. When a prisoner dies in confinement, as the black student leader Steve Biko did in 1977 while in prison in South Africa, many people believe that the authorities are responsible for the death.

In 1985 the commission appointed a special rapporteur on torture, Professor P. H. Kooijmans of the Netherlands. He received allegations of torture in thirty-three nations during the first year, and made urgent appeals to prevent torture in Chile, the Comoros, Ecuador, Honduras, Indonesia, South Africa, the U.S.S.R., and Uganda. It is not realistic to hope that the ghastly practice of torture, still so widespread, will soon disappear. But we *can* hope that the work of the rapporteur, along with many other efforts by groups like Amnesty International, will save lives and decrease the suffering.

Other U.N. organs consider specific kinds of human rights problems. The Office of the United States High Commissioner for Refugees, two-time winner of the Nobel Peace Prize, has worked heroically in many parts of the world to protect refugees and help them to seek asylum. The United Nations Fund for Children (UNICEF) concerns itself with the health and welfare of children around the world. The International Labor Organization, a U.N. agency since 1946, focuses on the freedom and security of working people. The World Health Organization and other specialized agencies deal with other aspects of human rights and well-being.

The interplay among U.N. organs concerned with human rights can be seen in the case of South Africa. In 1946, at the very first session of the General Assembly, India asked for an investigation of the treatment of South Africans of Indian origin. The General Assembly expressed the view that South Africa should abide by its agreements with India and by the U.N. Charter and later called upon South Africa to enter into negotiations with India and Pakistan. The wider question of apartheid was first debated in the U.N. in 1952. The South African government has consistently taken the position that this matter is purely "domestic" (internal, not international) and that, therefore, the U.N. cannot consider it under its charter.

The United Nations has continued, however, to keep South Africa under intense scrutiny. The Security Council has called on South Africa to abandon apartheid, and the General Assembly established a Special Committee Against Apartheid in 1962. During Nelson Mandela's trial in 1963, the General Assembly, by a vote of 106 to 1, demanded his release and the release of all South Africa's political prisoners. That same year, the General Assembly passed the Declaration on the Elimination of All Forms of Racial Discrimination, and called for a voluntary embargo on the sale of arms to South Africa and what was then Rhodesia (now Zimbabwe).

In 1965 the General Assembly approved the Convention on the Elimination of All Forms of Racial Discrimination, which came into force on January 4, 1969. Pursuant to that convention, a Committee on the Elimination of Racial Discrimination, with eighteen independent experts, was formed. In 1973 the General Assembly approved the International Covenant on the Suppression and Punishment of the Crime of Apartheid, and in 1977 it enacted an International Declaration Against Apartheid in Sports. On November 4, 1977, fourteen years after the General Assembly had recommended an embargo, the Security Council finally approved a mandatory embargo on the sale of arms to South Africa.

These are just a few of the actions taken by U.N. bodies against South Africa's policy of apartheid.

Certainly, the United Nations has done a first-rate job of setting standards for international human rights. In addition to the Universal Declaration and the two major covenants the commission has drafted, the General Assembly has approved and many nations have ratified a number of other documents setting forth universal standards for protecting human rights, including conventions on genocide, torture, slavery, and racial discrimination. Almost every nation on earth has at least agreed that these are rights worthy of protection.

There are all kinds of things "wrong" about U.N. action. Clearly, the United Nations can go no further than its members permit. Since many members are violators of human rights, this is a substantial limitation. Among other limitations is the fact that a state which is itself a violator is unlikely to denounce others for similar violations. During the "dirty war" in Argentina, discussed in Chapter 1, Argentina's delegate to the Commission on Human Rights was Dr. Mario Pena, a judge who had permitted approximately 650 bodies to be buried as "NNs" (*non nombres*—"no names"). Many bore bullet wounds.[2] Clearly, Dr. Pena was unlikely to be vocal on behalf of *desaparecidos* and their families.

Further, the U.N. is large and unwieldy. Its proceedings are slow and cumbersome. On May 27, 1970, ECOSOC Resolution No. 1503 authorized the Human Rights Commission to examine private communications received by the U.N. charging a consistent pattern of human rights violations. Such communications go through a labyrinthine review process. First, the working group of the Subcommission on the Prevention of Discrimination and Protection of Minorities reviews the communication. If the working group finds that a consistent pattern of abuses has been shown by reliable evidence, it refers the communication to the subcommission, which in turn refers it to the commission. Since these bodies meet only briefly once or twice a year, the process can take many years. Meanwhile, innocent lives are disrupted, prisoners are taken, and people die while the committees ponder.

There are other grave defects. The U.N. makes errors of judgment and decisions that are more the result of international politics than of strict principle. But for all the gap between the ideal and the reality, U.N. measures can be meaningful and often deserving of support. The imperfections are challenges rather than reasons to give up.

Often, U.N. member nations give only lip service to the human rights standards they agree to. One of the clearest examples of such a discrepancy is Czechoslovakia, which in December 1975 became the thirty-fifth nation to ratify the Covenant on Civil and Political Rights. With that ratification, the covenant came into effect, in March 1976. In January 1977 over 240 Czechs signed a document called Charter 77, which asked their nation to honor the U.N. covenants both as international treaties and as domestic law, and also to honor the Helsinki Final Act (to be discussed later in this chapter) and the Czech constitution. The Czech government interrogated and arrested many of the signatories of Charter 77 and dismissed many others from their jobs in contravention of the covenant that it had so recently signed. The Charter 77 signatories did not ask for help from the U.N. However, they did appeal to world opinion by sending documents abroad and directly contacting foreign institutions and individuals. Their struggle continues though their number has been severely reduced by imprisonment, exhaustion, and death.

Possibly the most common criticism of the U.N.'s human rights activities is that they are not fair and even-handed. The principles are applied not to all violators alike but only to countries unpopular with the Third World nations (the developing nations of Africa, Asia, and Latin America), who are now a majority in the U.N. Thus, the argument goes, the U.N. has paid a great deal of attention to violations by South Africa and Israel but has practically ignored substantial violations in Cambodia, Malaysia, Uganda, Zaire, Zimbabwe, and other Third World countries.

Because international relations must be handled cautiously, there are often delicate questions about the choice of tone and tactics for U.N. efforts to improve compliance with human rights standards. For example, when the special representative's 1985 report on Iran was criticized for not being sufficiently negative, it was suggested that the U.N. had decided not to affront Iran because that might set back the secretary general's effort to mediate the war between Iran and Iraq. After the mediation effort failed, the 1987 report was far more critical of the Iranian government. It estimated that seven thousand people had been executed after the fall of the shah in 1979 and found that torture and summary executions were still common.

There are degrees of severity of U.N. measures against human rights violations. The least harsh is a resolution merely censuring or denouncing a violator. But even this relatively mild action can be useful. It exposes the violator to shame in the eyes of the world community. This is real and painful. "Governments" are not abstractions, after all. They are made up of people exercising authority over millions of other people. And people, as we all know, suffer from being shamed in the eyes of others. Both leader and citizen are likely to feel, perhaps in different ways, the sting of international disapproval. There may be adverse practical effects on trade, international loans, and tourism, hurting the always sensitive national pocketbook.

Victims of violations welcome international censure of their governments—as an expression of support for their plight, as a form of pressure to change, as a possible means of weakening those in power. After the General Assembly passed a resolution against an address delivered by the South African minister of foreign affairs in 1962, Nelson Mandela said, "The increasing world pressure on South Africa has greatly weakened her international position and given a tremendous impetus to the freedom struggle inside the country."[3] After the election of a democratic government in Uruguay, Senator Albert Zumran told the Human Rights Commission:

> We cannot forget nor fail to express our heartfelt appreciation to members of this United Nations Human Rights Commission for all they have done to defend human rights in Uruguay.[4]

Citizens who are not victims may come to withdraw support from their government and ally themselves with its victims. Gary Player, the white South African golfer, began to speak in favor of candidates who had broken with the National Party because of its failure to yield its doctrine of white supremacy. Early in 1987 he said:

> South Africa is now the skunk among nations. With six million miles behind me, I've traveled more than any other athlete in history, and I've always held that this is the greatest country in the world. But where there was once friendliness, there now is growing hatred.[5]

Another reaction, of course, may be simple rejection and defiance of a U.N. resolution. Here again South Africa and Israel are notable examples, though their situations are otherwise quite dissimilar. Both nations have completely disregarded numerous U.N. resolutions, contending that they have been singled out for political reasons, not principled ones. When the U.N. imposed sanctions, South Africa termed this a "supreme example of hypocrisy," and said that in over half of the Security Council member nations, the concept of freedom of expression hardly exists.[6]

Statements and resolutions only protest against human rights violations; sanctions are more stringent. Sanctions vary, but essentially they consist of cutoffs of cultural, social, scientific, and educational exchanges, arms, trade, transportation, and travel. Because such measures are relatively severe, because they can hurt those who impose them, and because the U.N. continues to walk softly through the minefields of international law and politics, sanctions are rare. The Security Council approved sanctions against a member nation for the first time on November 4, 1977, when it enacted a mandatory embargo on arms to South Africa.

Although the General Assembly called for economic sanctions against South Africa and Rhodesia beginning in 1962, sanctions against Rhodesia were first imposed in 1966 and then expanded in 1968. The United Nations had failed to vote economic sanctions against South Africa. Still, the General Assembly has voted with some effect for voluntary sanctions: in 1968 it suspended cultural, educational, and sporting exchanges with the South African government and South African organizations that practice apartheid; in 1970 it ended preferential trade treatment for South African exports; and in 1975 it called for a voluntary embargo on petroleum and petroleum products.

While there are sometimes other reasons, human rights abuses have been the principal grounds for U.N. sanctions. For example, when sanctions were voted against Rhodesia (now Zimbabwe) in 1968, the U.N. condemned "the recent inhuman executions carried out by the illegal regime in Rhodesia which have flagrantly affronted the conscience of mankind and have been universally condemned" and recognized "the legitimacy of the struggle of the people of Southern Rhodesia to secure the enjoyment of their rights as set forth in the Charter of the United Nations."

Why were sanctions voted against Rhodesia and not South Africa? The answer rests on a political distinction. Whereas South Africa is an independent country, Rhodesia was under British authority until 1965. Rhodesia was to be granted independence only if it provided for majority rule, i.e., rule by the black Rhodesians. But in November 1965 the white Rhodesian government under Ian Smith made a unilateral declaration of independence, purporting to create an independent country with minority rule. Rhodesia was in rebellion against the United Kingdom, and the United Kingdom and its allies—the United States and France—supported economic sanctions against Rhodesia.

Are sanctions effective? As we've noted earlier, there are many drawbacks. First of all, the sanctions may not be fully honored even by the nations voting for them. Other nations can sabotage sanctions. For example, South Africa and Portugal (which had African colonies) dealt with Rhodesia in open defiance of the U.N. sanctions. Another concern is that the people hurt most by the sanctions are those at the bottom of the economic system—for instance, in the case of South Africa and Rhodesia, the blacks in whose name the sanctions were adopted. And sanctions may stiffen the oppressor's resistance. After the arms boycott was imposed, South Africa's foreign minister, Roelof Botha, said, "I think the superpowers, if they want to overcome us, will have to do it with a force of a very vast nature. It will be a very expensive effort. And I'm not bragging."[7]

There is no absolute certainty about where and when and to what extent sanctions are a good idea. But they bolster the morale of human rights victims, squeeze the people in power, and may lead to reconsideration of harsh policies. There is evidence that economic sanctions were a factor in Rhodesia's eventual agreement to majority rule in 1979, although Rhodesia had also suffered a bloody civil war that lasted seven years and cost over 27,000 lives.

But trade is a two-way street. The trading partners of a sanctioned nation will suffer losses and inconveniences—lost profits, lost access to vital minerals, etc. Sometimes one partner is the United States. In 1971 the U.S. Congress enacted its own resolution directing that America disregard the U.N. sanctions and continue importation of Rhodesian chrome and other strategic metals unless imports from communist nations were also banned. Rather than proposing a ban on such imports, President Richard M. Nixon acquiesced in a blatant violation of the sanctions.

Currently, in a far more poignant situation, the "front-line" nations of Black Africa—Mozambique, Zimbabwe, Angola, Botswana, Lesotho, Swaziland, and Zambia—are genuinely and profoundly opposed to the South African system of apartheid. At the same time, they are heavily dependent on economic relationships with their Afrikaaner neighbor. The landlocked nations need South Africa's modern ports and railroads to transport their imports and exports; several of the front-line states rely on South Africa to employ their excess workers, who in turn provide their nations with foreign currency; and several also rely on South Africa as a trading partner. As a result, they engage in a variety of evasions and compromises. It is another of the trade-offs between human rights ideals and the practicalities of life.

There is no single, final formula for resolving problems of this nature. But there are guiding principles—among them the principle that human rights must surely be at the top of any list of values when we come to the task of balancing various interests against each other.

Up to this point we've talked about actions against human rights abuses to be taken by the world community of nations as a whole. There is also the possibility of action by a group of governments that may have special concerns about a particular country. One such example, mentioned above, is the group of Black African countries versus the white government of South Africa. Zimbabwe and Zambia had set sanctions against South Africa, but both let the deadline pass without action or comment. President Kenneth Kaunda of Zambia, an impoverished country, had bravely said, "If in striving to ease their [black South African] suffering we have to suffer too, then we shall suffer." But when food prices in Zambia doubled in December 1986, bloody riots erupted. Members of Parliament pressed President Kaunda to focus on the plight of his own people, and to pay less attention to foreign liberation struggles. Only one African nation, Malawi, has candidly maintained diplomatic relations with South Africa. Its President, Hastings Kamuza Banda, scornfully says, "Those African countries who talk about boycotting South Africa, they just talk. They can't do it."[8]

South Africa has not been timid about exercising its own economic power. When Zimbabwe's prime minister, Robert G. Mugabe, called on the British Commonwealth to impose economic sanctions on South Africa and threatened his own, South Africa slowed rail traffic to Zimbabwe for two weeks. Since then South Africa has threatened to send sixty thousand Mozambican miners home, and then relented to the extent of reducing the number by half. South Africa has also launched military assaults into seven countries on what it claimed were strikes against African National Congress targets. Complicating matters still further, many South African corporations have large investments in the front-line countries, which puts them in conflict with their own government.

The front-line states have struggled to overcome their economic dependence on South Africa. In 1980 nine nations founded the Southern African Development Coordination Conference "to liberate our economies from their dependence on South Africa." The goal remains distant.

Still another means by which nations can work together is by international agreements. The Helsinki Final Act, signed on August 1, 1975, by the nations of Europe, the Soviet Union, Canada, and the United States, has surprised its western signatories by becoming an important vehicle for improving human rights in the Soviet bloc. The act was designed to acknowledge territorial changes resulting from the war and to promote mutual confidence and security. The Soviet Union got what it wanted—western recognition of its post–World War II borders, including its absorption of the Ukrainian and Byelorussian parts of eastern Poland as well as the division of Germany into two nations. But the act also provided that the signatories respect human rights and fundamental freedoms, including freedom of thought, conscience, religion, and belief.

The Soviets placed a high value on the Final Act, and this became the key to the development of the Helsinki process. Because of their pride in what they saw as a victory, the act was printed in *Izvestia*, the official national publication of the Soviet government. Spontaneously, in May, 1976, voluntary "Helsinki Watch Committees" sprang up in Moscow, Leningrad, Kiev, Vilnius, Tbilisi, and Yerevan to monitor Soviet compliance with the act. Other monitor groups sprouted in Eastern Europe, including Charter 77 in Czechoslovakia and the Workers' Defense Committee (KOR) in Poland. An unanticipated consequence of the act was the birth of hope in Eastern Europe.

However, by the next review meeting in Madrid, which began on November 11, 1980, human rights in the Soviet bloc had suffered serious setbacks. Afghanistan had been invaded, Andrei Sakharov was in exile in Gorki, emigration had been reduced to a trickle, and the Soviet Helsinki Watch members had been subjected to brutal treatment. Anatoly (now Natan) Sharansky was in prison, serving a long term under conditions he described after his release in his book *Fear No Evil*. Of the 71 original members, 19 had been sentenced to a total of 159 years of forced labor and exile, 11 were under arrest, 9 were in prison for prior offenses, 7 had been forced to emigrate, and 2 had been stripped of their citizenship while traveling abroad.

Given the bad relations between East and West, caused in large part by the Soviet invasion of Afghanistan and the corresponding western sanctions, the Soviet Union came to the 1980 meeting with the aim of agreeing only to a conference on military détente and disarmament. The United States gave human rights a high priority and denounced the Soviets for a detailed list of human rights abuses. All the western and neutral nations branded the invasion of Afghanistan a violation.

Although Soviet repression continued during the Madrid meeting, which lasted three years, there is some reason to believe that the Helsinki process helped to blunt it. After Sakharov's first hunger strike was discussed at the Madrid proceedings, his stepson's fiancée was allowed to emigrate. When Soviet prisoner Iosef Mendelevich went on a hunger strike in November 1980, the camp administration tried to dissuade him. Mendelevich responded that his life was not important to the Soviet Union. But the administrator answered, "You are wrong because you are not alone. There is a Madrid conference at the present time, and many things have happened in the world which the Soviets have to take into account."[9] Mendelevich was released a year before the end of his twelve-year sentence and allowed to emigrate to Israel.

The Helsinki process became a valuable part of American human rights policy, serving as a forum for reminding the Soviets of their failure to live up to their side of the bargain. At the very least, it has been a setting for a dialogue between East and West even during the coldest spells of the Cold War.

CHAPTER 5

The United States and Human Rights Abroad

The ringing words and the inspired ideas of our Declaration of Independence and the Bill of Rights in our Constitution are still at the heart of the liberties sought by people everywhere. Although the American record is far from perfect, especially with respect to race, America has moved much closer to living up to its ideals in the period since World War II. Our leadership in creating the United Nations and its Universal Declaration of Human Rights is another great chapter in world history. But what have we done for international human rights lately?

There is no doubt that we have the *power*—economic, cultural, and military—to influence other governments. "Military power" means our ability to give or withhold military assistance, not, in general, an attack or invasion. Economic power involves the various ways we can encourage or discourage trade, as well as giving or withholding aid. Tariffs can be raised or lowered as types of pressure or reward for approved behavior. Scientific, artistic, and intellectual emissaries can be encouraged, discouraged, or cut off altogether. We have used these techniques in dealing with the Soviet Union, Poland, Cuba, and others that we view as "adversaries" because they have ideologies and national interests different from ours. With countries like these, there are no guarantees that our foreign policy objectives will be furthered no matter what we do. But even without guarantees there is good evidence that economic and other pressures made a difference with unfriendly as well as friendly governments.

For example, when General Wojciech Jaruzelski declared martial law in Poland on December 13, 1981, and moved to suppress Solidarity, the independent trade union that had become a political movement, the United States responded by imposing sanctions against both Poland and the Soviet Union. The United States believed that the crackdown was due to Soviet pressure to destroy Solidarity, which had called for a national referendum on the future of Poland's communist government and reconsideration of Poland's military alliance with the Soviet Union. Solidarity's support among Polish workers was strong; at its height, 10 million Poles belonged, about 25 percent of the population. Probably because of this widespread support, the crackdown was harsh and brutal; thousands were arrested, including Solidarity's leader, Lech Walesa (winner of the 1983 Nobel Peace Prize).

The United States was the only western nation to impose sanctions. When France refused to break off trade, President François Mitterand said: "After all, those who are hungry aren't the ones who run the government." But for many Poles who were both hungry and opposed to their government, U.S. sanctions were a welcome support.

Poland's martial law ended in 1983. In turn, some of the American sanctions were lifted in 1984. In September 1986, General Jaruzelski released all detained political prisoners except suspected spies and traitors. Soon afterward, Lech Walesa and Josef Cardinal Glemp called for the United States to lift its remaining sanctions, particularly the loss of most-favored-nation status for trading to help Poland toward economic recovery. (A "most favored nation" is one that is granted the lowest tariffs on imports and therefore has an advantage in selling goods to Americans.) The Polish government had blamed the American sanctions for the nation's problems, claiming they had cost Poland $15 billion. That was probably exaggerated. The fact remained that sanctions had hurt and the lifting of sanctions was welcomed by the Polish government.

In September 1986 Jaruzelski declared an amnesty and many prisoners were released. The United States responded positively but warily. The last of the sanctions were lifted in February 1987. In a statement announcing that step, President Ronald Reagan noted that conditions in Poland had improved dramatically since sanctions had been imposed and said, "We will be watching to see that further steps are taken toward national reconciliation in Poland, and that the progress made is not reversed."[1]

On another front, the U.S. Congress moved against South Africa when it passed the comprehensive Anti-Apartheid Act of 1986 over President Reagan's veto. The act, among other provisions, barred the importing of Krugerrands and other gold coins, uranium, coal, iron, steel, textiles, and agricultural items produced or manufactured in South Africa. The act also deprived South African Airlines of landing privileges in the United States and prohibited most loans to the South African government and American exports of computers or other technology to the South African military, police, prison system, and any agency charged with enforcing apartheid. The act further provided that American policy would call for further sanctions if there was no progress toward ending apartheid and establishing a nonracial democracy within a year.

The act required the president to issue a report within six months naming the nations that violate the U.N. embargo on the sale of arms to South Africa "with a view to terminating United States military assistance to those countries" (Section 508). As a result, on March 18, 1987, Israel, one of the prime beneficiaries of American military aid, decided not to sign any new military sales agreements with South Africa. In a report to Congress on April 2, 1987, the State Department found that prior to March 18, the Israeli government had been "fully aware of most or all of the trade" in arms to South Africa carried on in violation of the embargo.

Of course, sanctions are no panacea. In 1979, when the Soviet Union invaded Afghanistan, the United States and several western nations responded with sanctions. Most notably, the United States boycotted the 1980 Moscow Olympics and curbed sales of wheat to the Soviet Union. Many Americans argued that the boycott harmed American farmers, and athletes who had spent years preparing for the Olympics, more than they hurt the Soviets. In fact, as things turned out, the Soviets won the lion's share of Olympic medals and bought wheat from Argentina, Australia, and Canada. Moreover, the sanctions had little effect on Soviet policy. When the Soviets finally decided (in 1988) to pull out of Afghanistan, their reasons had little to do with the sanctions. But the United States had had few peaceful alternatives and was unwilling to risk nuclear war. In the long run, moreover, the sanctions may well have bolstered the pressures (including the morale of rebel resisters) that led ultimately to the Soviet withdrawal.

The sanctions became an issue in the 1980 presidential election. Fulfilling a campaign promise, President Reagan lifted the grain curb on April 24, 1981. He said, "As a Presidential candidate, I indicated my opposition to the curb on sales because American farmers had been unfairly singled out to bear the burden of this ineffective national policy."[2] However, he did not lift the restrictions on Soviet fishing privileges in American waters or on trade in high technology products. You can see varieties of pressures and "politics" in these policies. The Reagan pattern of hostile measures against the Sandinista government in Nicaragua was far less selective and fine-tuned.

A different form of economic power to promote American foreign policy is our program of assistance to comparatively poor countries. Since World War II the United States has spent hundreds of billions of dollars in foreign aid, first for the war-torn countries of Europe under the Marshall Plan, later for the underdeveloped countries of Africa, Asia, and Latin America, many of which had recently been parts of colonial empires. United States motives in giving aid range from magnificent generosity to calculated self-interest. Expenditures of this kind have since declined considerably. Other nations—Japan, France, Canada, and Norway, among others—have taken up part of the burden of foreign aid. Even so, American grants remain substantial; in 1987 the United States spent over $7 billion in foreign aid.

Granting or withholding economic and military aid can be powerfully persuasive influences. In the late 1970s the American government showed its displeasure with the vicious junta running Argentina by severely cutting its aid programs. In 1978, Vice President Walter Mondale threatened a lower credit rating for Argentina on its export-import loans. Our government relented only when Argentina's President Jorge Videla agreed to permit the Organization of American States to send a fact-finding mission to Buenos Aires to investigate the cases of the *desaparecidos* and other human rights problems. These and other actions helped to weaken the junta's power and accelerate its downfall. In early 1984, I was one of a group of lawyers visiting with Raúl Alfonsín, then recently installed as Argentina's first democratically elected president since the junta. He assured us that American policies toward Argentina in those critical years had probably saved thousands of Argentine lives.

A couple of other cases in recent history illustrate the powerful effect of American economic pressure:

- In early 1985 the United States abstained on votes in international lending agencies on loans to Chile in response to President Pinochet's declaration of a "state of siege" in November 1984. The abstentions probably influenced Pinochet's decision, on the eve of further votes on international loans, to lift the state of siege in June 1985. Regrettably, the United States then resumed support for further loans despite clear evidence of torture by Chilean officials and continued repression by the Pinochet government.

63

- In 1986, Rumania responded to congressional hostility to renewing its most-favored-nation trading status by releasing several prominent political prisoners and allowing over a thousand people to emigrate.

Sometimes the United States fails to make use of economic and political influence, with tragic results. There is solid reason to believe that the repressive martial-law regime of Ferdinand Marcos in the Philippines would have ended much sooner than it did (in February 1986) or that Marcos would not have declared martial law in the first place, if he had not received signals that the U.S. government would accept that outrage (and the tyranny that followed it) without protest or interference.

It is apparent that in a world of widespread human rights violations, the American government acts against some, not against others. We sometimes pretend that the violations do not exist. With governments we don't like, we see violations all the time. What determines the courses we take? Once more, there is no single, simple answer, but a number of factors that play a role. Let's look at some.

Competing Interests

International human rights is not and cannot be the sole concern of foreign policy. American diplomats, like others, often believe that other goals must take a back seat to national security considerations, and that there are times when we must overlook rights violations by countries whose friendship is vital to our national self-interest. At such times, "enemies" can become "friends." This attitude recalls the observation of Winston Churchill, a fierce anticommunist, about Britain's alliance with the Soviets against Hitler in World War II; he said, "If Hitler invaded Hell, I would make at least a favorable reference to the Devil in the House of Commons."[3]

The American State Department regularly considers military

and security interests more important than human rights. Government officials defend their policies by arguing that the Soviet Union is the prime violator of human rights, and that it is necessary to tolerate some human rights abuses by friendly governments to contain the spread of communism, because communism brings worse abuses. Recent history affords numerous examples of the United States winking at outrages against human rights because it was felt that the perpetrators, like Ferdinand Marcos or Augusto Pinochet, were important allies against communist powers or regimes sympathetic to the Soviet position. At times this has led the United States government to take positions that are both shameful and ridiculous.

The Filipino experience, again, is one example. By 1981 the whole world could see Marcos for the brutal dictator that he was. He had been ruling the country by military force for over eight years. Violent and undisciplined troops and an even more savage constabulary roamed through the islands terrorizing and murdering critics or suspected opponents of the regime. Instead of crushing opposition, the repression was producing an increasingly powerful armed communist resistance. Because Marcos was anticommunist and because of his continued approval for United States air and naval bases in the Philippines, the American government continued to support him while he brutalized and pillaged his own country.

Vice President George Bush went on a state visit to Manila on June 30, 1981, following the inauguration of Marcos after a sham election. At a luncheon, the American vice president raised his glass in a toast to Marcos and said, "We love your adherence to democratic principles—and to the democratic process."[4] The episode remained a bitter joke among Filipinos for years.

Pakistan is another recent example. After the Soviet invasion of Afghanistan, military and strategic interests led to intensified American support of General Mohammad Zia ul Haq, who had seized power in Pakistan, Afghanistan's neighbor, in a military coup d'état in July 1977. Pakistan was providing refuge for millions of Afghans despite severe strains on its economic resources and its already difficult ethnic division. Pakistan was also subjected to Soviet attacks on the refugee camps, since the Soviets believed that Afghan guerrillas were trained and supplied there. American support for Pakistan included a six-year military and economic assistance program mounting to a cost of $3.2 billion by 1987.

But General Zia's government was a persistent human rights violator; it imprisoned and otherwise abused anyone who opposed him. Zia ended martial law as of January 1, 1986, but abuses persisted. Our government remained a staunch supporter of Zia. The failure to press harder for human rights reforms, though debatable, was a regrettable lapse. We should not fail to demand respect for human rights from our strongest allies. (Zia was killed in an airplane explosion in August 1988 that had earmarks of sabotage. At this writing—early 1989—the explosion is being investigated and the world waits to see how Pakistan will develop after Zia and under the first woman leader of an Islamic nation, Benazir Bhutto.)

In addition to military and strategic interests, the protection of American economic interests often has more effect on foreign policy than does the protection of human rights. American industry and American workers have strong interests in the profits and jobs that depend on arms deals and trade. When foreign nations nationalize industries owned by American companies, the companies complain to the U.S. government. Thus, when Chile's socialist President Salvador Allende Gossens nationalized the copper mines, the State Department placed heavy emphasis on payments by the Chilean government to the American copper companies, regardless of the cost to the impoverished Chileans or to the stability of President Allende's government. When General Pinochet overthrew Allende, who was murdered or committed suicide in the process, the Nixon administration welcomed Pinochet. Because of his hospitable view of private economic enterprise, American leaders were willing to overlook his human rights abuses.

After fifteen years of his dictatorship Pinochet's regime was voted down in a plebiscite on October 5, 1988. Some Chileans fear a return to the economic instability and disorder of the Allende years, but most people look forward to a new era of democracy. "I think we Chileans have learned a lot in the past fifteen years," said Roberto Semprevivo, a restaurateur, on the day after the vote. "We have to move cautiously to build a stable democracy."[5]

Favoring Our "Friends"

The United States has tended to ignore the forces of change in country after country such as the Philippines, Iran, Zaire, Kenya, and South Korea, and to be taken by surprise when those forces overwhelmed the regimes that our government has supported. We have ambled into traps of our own making, awakening too late to the fact that in a new era the freed—or at least freer—people of these countries will tend to view us as the supporters of their former oppressors.

In this recurrent scenario, our insufficient regard for human rights makes for foolish policy in the most unsentimental terms. Needing friends and allies everywhere, we have frequently overlooked the reality of "people power," as demonstrated in the peaceful Filipino revolution of 1986. In cases like these, forsaking our basic ideals has resulted in unsound calculations of national self-interest.

Iran may be one such example. The survival of the shah of Iran, who came to power in a coup backed by the CIA in 1953, rested heavily on American support. Not only did Iran have a strategic geopolitical location, bordering the Soviet Union, but it had vast oil deposits as well. The shah maintained power through fierce repression; his internal security police, SAVAK, was feared for its brutality. In 1979 the rabid anti-Americanism of the Iranians who deposed him led to Iranian students holding sixty-two Americans hostage for over a year. Many people, in the United States and elsewhere, attribute this hostility to resentment over our long support for the shah. What can we learn from this? People who say we were right to support the shah point out that he was less repressive of human rights than the Ayatollah Khomeini, who replaced him. On the other side, more democratic elements present in Iran might have emerged and taken control if we had supported them rather than the shah. It is not easy to resolve this complex question. But anyone who values human rights can say that only the most extreme and overwhelming necessity can justify our alliance with a repressive regime. There was no such justification in the case of the shah.

Though we are often timid when it comes to embarrassing our friends, we are outspoken in denouncing adversaries such as the Soviet Union for their human rights abuses. But even then there are times when American policymakers are willing to overlook violations. At Secretary of State Henry Kissinger's urging, President Gerald Ford refused to meet with the noted Soviet dissident writer Aleksandr Solzhenitsyn, in order to avoid angering the Soviets. The stakes are often high: a new arms control treaty or a nuclear test ban may seem to be in the balance. Which is more important, diminishing the worldwide threat of nuclear annihilation, or helping a few hundred dissidents? If that is really the issue, the small group of dissidents may have to be neglected. Too often, however, diplomats are prepared to sacrifice human rights when that is not realistically necessary for the sake of other interests.

Generally, in dealing with the Soviet Union and the other communist regimes, we have tried to reach past the governments and beam our messages directly to the people. At the same time, we have used a variety of forums and techniques to maintain a steady barrage of attacks against violations, and we have pressed demands for human rights reforms as conditions for trading and other advantageous relationships.

When a dissident is freed, we deserve some credit. The new era of *glasnost* sounds as if some of our basic ideas of freedom may be taking root in the U.S.S.R., though we can't forecast the long-run effects of such things.

Although international human rights had been an American concern from time to time—our government issued protests to

68

Russia about pogroms in the early nineteenth century, and in the early 1960s we pressured South Korea's President Park Chung Hee to hold elections—it did not become an integral part of American foreign policy until the 1970s. The development was somewhat unusual in that the main impetus came from the pressure of an activist Congress.

Basic doctrine has it that foreign affairs is the special province of the executive—of presidents and prime ministers and, once upon a time, of kings—rather than legislatures, or still more clearly, of judges. Our Constitution makes the president the commander in chief of the army and navy and gives him the power, "by and with the advice and consent of the Senate," to make treaties and nominate ambassadors. Negotiations, diplomacy, consuls—the paraphernalia of international relations—are by definition executive business. This has been the agreed wisdom of both the legal profession (including the courts) and political scientists in the United States. Logically applied, this would make the president and the people he appoints (primarily, of course, the secretary of state) the key figures in defining and pursuing American interests in international human rights. This is likely to be the case in fact over the long haul.

But in the 1970s a possibly unique combination of events tended to shift this normal balance toward congressional control. The shift was a result of the "power of the purse," the Constitution's grant of power to Congress to collect taxes and appropriate money for federal expenditures. The president cannot spend money for aid, among other things, without congressional approval. Congress used this power to strike blows for human rights.

During the scandal-ridden terms of Richard Nixon, the issue of human rights was far from a top priority in the White House. It was a period of sometimes brilliant, and sometimes disastrous, *realpolitik*—of shrewd international dealings and hard-nosed practicality as those in power defined it. The Vietnam disaster was brought to its whimpering conclusion. *Détente* (French for the relaxation of tensions) became the byword for U.S.-Soviet relations. A carefully designed course opened a door to China and produced a better approach toward the communist powers. A cynical investment of American power helped destroy an elected leftist regime in Chile and to replace it with the brutal military dictatorship of General Pinochet. Elsewhere—in the Middle East, in Africa, in Central America—the primary focus of American foreign policy was on the manipulation of power relationships, not the quality of the lives of people living under the regimes with which we dealt. When our ambassador to Chile became concerned about human rights outrages there, Secretary of State Henry Kissinger is said to have told him to "cut out the political science lectures" and get back to business.[6]

At that time the Congress effected a rather remarkable departure. Largely due to the disastrous Vietnamese War, in which nearly sixty thousand young American men died fighting for unclear reasons, and in part due to President Nixon's downfall because of the Watergate scandal, in the mid-1970s the Congress took some of the foreign affairs leadership into its own hands, particularly with respect to human rights.

One constant theme in the bitter discussions of the Vietnamese War was that Americans were giving their lives to help a South Vietnamese government that was antidemocratic and undeserving of our support. Many Americans felt that we were fighting to maintain a corrupt dictator. In 1970 Tom Harkin, then a congressional aide, now (1988) Senator Harkin, discovered the "tiger cages," the cramped cages used to imprison opponents of the South Vietnamese government.

Various legislators attempted to reduce funding for the South Vietnamese government, but met little success while American troops were still in combat there. By 1973, however, the United States had withdrawn its troops and Congress was eager to restrict presidential action. The War Powers Act, limiting the ability of the president to involve the United States in hostilities abroad, was adopted in 1973 over President Nixon's veto. Soon congressional action spread to other foreign policy concerns.

On August 1, 1973, Representative Donald Fraser, chairman of the House Foreign Affairs Subcommittee on International Organizations and Movements, opened hearings on the international protection of human rights. The subcommittee's report concluded:

> The human rights factor is not accorded the high priority it deserves in our country's foreign policy. Too often it becomes invisible on the vast foreign policy horizon of political, economic, and military affairs. . . . Unfortunately, the prevailing attitude has led the United States into embracing governments which practice torture and unabashedly violate almost every human rights guarantee pronounced by the world community. Through foreign aid and occasional intervention—both covert and overt—the United States supports those governments. Our relations with the present governments of South Vietnam, Spain, Portugal, the Soviet Union, Brazil, Indonesia, Greece, and the Philippines exemplify how we have disregarded human rights for the sake of other assumed interests. . . .
>
> A higher priority for human rights is urgently needed if future American leadership in the world is to mean what it has traditionally meant—encouragement to men and women everywhere who cherish individual freedom.[7]

The subcommittee concern was fueled in part by the circumstances that led to and followed the fall of the democratically elected government of Salvador Allende Gossens in Chile. President Nixon had opposed Allende's leftist regime, and there was evidence that the United States had been involved in the military coup that brought General Pinochet to power. The administration staunchly denied any such connection, but there was widespread disbelief.

Congress took another tack in 1974 when it passed the Jackson-Vanik Act, conditioning most-favored-nation status of nonmarket economies such as the Soviet Union on relaxed immigration policies. The act had been two years in the making. It began as a response to the 1972 Soviet decision to tax emigrants for their education, from $5,000 to $25,000. Almost all the emigrants were Jews, who suffered from Soviet anti-Semitism and restrictions on religion in general. The Soviets hoped that the tax would either deter people from emigrating or fill Soviet coffers with foreign currency. President Nixon and Henry Kissinger, eager for détente, persuaded the Soviets to agree to end the tax, but congressional leaders then upped the ante by demanding that the Soviets permit more to leave. The U.S.S.R. refused to make any public concessions, and Congress finally passed the act in 1974 together with the Stevenson Act, which required congressional approval for the Export-Import Bank to extend to the Soviets more than $300 million in credits over a four-year period.

That same year Congress banned U.S. training support for foreign police officers. The program had been instituted to fight terrorists, but Congress was horrified to discover that American-trained officers had been responsible for many cases of torture and assassination.

Determined to put sharper teeth into American human rights policy, in 1975 Representative Harkin (as he was then) proposed tying economic assistance to respect for human rights. His amendment passed, prohibiting developmental assistance to any country that had "a consistent pattern of gross violations . . . unless such assistance will directly benefit the needy people in such country." Gross violations were defined as "torture or cruel, inhuman or degrading treatment or punishment, prolonged detention without charges or other flagrant denials of life, or security of person."

In order to enforce the new laws, Congress needed information about human rights in the countries that receive American security and developmental assistance. Congress therefore passed a law requiring the State Department to prepare annual reports on the state of human rights in every country that receives such assistance. These country reports, as they are called, are significant, and often controversial, documents dealing with the state of human rights all over the world, whether or not the countries receive assistance.

72

The country reports state the administration's view on human rights in every country that receives American aid. They are usually accurate when discussing our adversaries, but often evade difficult issues when discussing friendly nations. For example, the 1983 report on Uruguay admitted that there were allegations of torture by the military regime then in power, but downplayed the charges by saying that they had not been independently verified. The American embassy in Uruguay had not made any attempt to verify the allegations, and was roundly (and rightly) criticized for what amounted to condoning gross violations. Because the reports, as in that instance, are public, they are open to criticism and correction by human rights activists. On many occasions, such criticism has led to better reports the following year.

As noted earlier, complex problems of foreign policy make it impossible to have consistent and uniform positions supporting human rights everywhere. The conflicting pressures are reflected in inconsistencies within any single administration. President Carter, an earnest advocate of human rights, called upon Congress to reduce military aid to Argentina, Uruguay, and Ethiopia because of human rights abuses, but made no mention of any comparable reduction for the Philippines or South Korea, despite well-known and widespread violations in those countries.

Accidents of history also play their part. International human rights abuses, as might be expected, draw special American attention when Americans are involved. One such case is that of the four churchwomen—Jean Donovan, Dorothy Kazel, Sister Ita Ford, and Sister Maura Clark—who were murdered in El Salvador on December 2, 1980, after being sexually abused. When it appeared that the Salvadoran government would simply ignore these atrocious crimes, heavy pressure was brought on our State Department by the victims' families, church people, and many others demanding action to find and punish the murderers. Representatives of the Lawyers Committee for Human Rights, assisting the bereaved families of the four women, worked unceasingly in this case. Through investigations led by American embassy personnel, six members of El Salvador's National Guard were identified as suspects. Long after the murders, arrests were made, a trial was held, and five defendants were convicted of aggravated homicide. The United State Congress withheld $19 million in U.S. military aid (about one third of the annual total) until a verdict was reached.

Interested Americans were far from satisfied with the verdict. The men convicted were low-level soldiers, and there was powerful evidence that they had acted on orders from higher up. No amount of American pressure was adequate to reach those upper levels. But the trial and convictions were still a breakthrough. This was the very first time military killers had been tried, let alone convicted, in El Salvador's long and bloody history.

Another case in which American interest was heightened because a victim was connected to this country was the savage episode of the *quemados* (burnt ones) of Chile. On July 1, 1986, Rodrigo Rojas de Negri, a nineteen-year-old Chilean-born resident of Washington, D.C., was on a visit to his native land. There had been a public demonstration called to support a national strike. It is not clear whether he had participated in that. In any event, he and Carmen Gloria Quintana Aranciba, an eighteen-year-old student, were seized by Chilean soldiers about a block away from the scene of the demonstration. Both were interrogated. Then the soldiers poured gasoline on them and threw an incendiary device between them. After the flames subsided, the two were left in a ditch. The young woman was horribly burned, requiring a long course of plastic surgery. Rojas died. The American ambassador attended his funeral, undoubtedly because Rojas had been a United States resident. Even so, the ambassador's action was condemned by U.S. Senator Jesse Helms, who said the funeral had been a "pro-Communist event."[8] I disagree; the ambassador's action was a decent and useful gesture against the barbaric regime of General Pinochet.

At the same time, Senator Helms's position reminds us that domestic politics inevitably impinges on American actions touching international human rights. For Helms and others like him, fighting communists is the overriding international preoccupation, and human rights have a very low priority except as a weapon against communist states. Many individuals who truly value human rights have found ways to go beyond the constraints of international politics by creating "nongovernmental organizations." The next chapter tells part of their remarkable story.

Worldwide Volunteers

THE APPEAL FOR AMNESTY

Open your newspapers any day of the week and you will find a report from somewhere in the world of someone being imprisoned, tortured or executed because his opinions or religion are unacceptable to his government. There are several million such people in prison—by no means all of them behind the Iron and Bamboo Curtains—and their numbers are growing. The newspaper reader feels a sickening sense of impotence. Yet if these feelings of disgust all over the world could be united into common action, something effective could be done.
PETER BENENSON, *The London Observer*, Sunday, May 28, 1961

This quotation is the basic premise that led to creation of a remarkable organization, Amnesty International. It is the best known of a few dozen nongovernmental organizations (NGOs) around the world that work for the protection of human rights. These NGOs play powerful roles in exposing violations, pressuring and pleading with government violators, arousing world opinion, prodding governments and international agencies to move against abusive states, promoting improved standards of human rights, and acting in a host of other ways to promote the cause of human rights. Unlike governments, NGOs can devote themselves wholeheartedly to the cause of human rights. The story of these organizations and the people who run them is an inspiration for our time.

It can also serve as an inspiration and a challenge to anyone who would like to become involved in this vital crusade. There is endless work to be done. Volunteers are needed! Amnesty itself has local chapters throughout the United States and elsewhere in the world. Other human rights groups mentioned later in this chapter also need all the help they can get. It is the most urgent and rewarding kind of enterprise. People of all ages and skills have roles to play.

Amnesty International, founded in 1961, "was the product of the imagination of one man, Peter Benenson, a Catholic lawyer of Jewish descent, born of English and Russian parents, described by some people who knew him as a 'visionary,' even a saint."[1] Long active as a lawyer in human rights causes, Benenson hit upon the idea that widespread publicity and barrages of letters might lead dictatorial and abusive governments to release political prisoners.

Benenson and two colleagues published the "Appeal for Amnesty, 1961," on Trinity Sunday, May 28, 1961, when Britain's *Sunday Observer* published an article by Benenson, appealing for "forgotten prisoners" in eight countries ranging from Portuguese Angola (now the People's Republic of Angola) to Rumania, and including the Reverend Ashton Jones, a sixty-five-year-old minister who had suffered repeated beatings and jailings in Louisiana and Texas for his work in support of equal rights for blacks in the American South. Similar articles followed within days in newspapers all over the world. Those initial pleas for offers of "help and information" were the beginning; by 1987, Amnesty International had more than 500,000 members and subscribers in over 150 countries. In 1977, Amnesty was awarded the Nobel Peace Prize, which was presented on December 10, Human Rights Day.

Since its founding, Amnesty has evolved into a worldwide structure of branches, procedures, and organizational principles. The centerpiece of its activities remains the "adoption" of "prisoners of conscience." Amnesty's central office in London researches the abuses and meticulously documents each case to be sure that the individual in question is in fact a "prisoner of conscience." Under Amnesty's definition, prisoners of conscience are persons who are "imprisoned, detained or otherwise physically restricted by reason of their political, religious or other conscientiously held beliefs or by reason of their ethnic origin, sex, colour or language, provided that they have not used or advocated violence." Controversy erupted around this definition in 1964, as it affected one of the human rights heroes profiled in Chapter 1, Nelson Mandela.

Mandela had been adopted as a prisoner of conscience after his arrest in 1962 on charges of organizing a strike of black workers and unlawfully traveling to Ethiopia, "crimes" that fall within Amnesty's mandate. But in 1964, Mandela was convicted of sabotage and sentenced to life in prison. He admitted that he supported resorting to violence after decades of nonviolent protest had failed to end apartheid. His British adoption group decided that this approval of violence meant they could no longer consider him a prisoner of conscience. A vigorous debate ensued, leading to a poll of all of Amnesty's members. The vast majority supported Amnesty's strict definition, but a compromise was struck: although Mandela would no longer be called a prisoner of conscience, Amnesty would complain to the South African government if it thought that his trial was unfair or the prison conditions severe or that he was being tortured. This basic compromise has been used many times since; Amnesty will adopt only those who meet its strict definition of prisoner of conscience, but will oppose all human rights abuses no matter what the victim may have done.

Amnesty's "adoption groups" are small numbers of people who organize themselves to "adopt" two or more prisoners of conscience as their special and intense concern. Each group is assigned prisoners from different countries and political systems. Thus, if three prisoners are assigned to a group, one will be from the West, one from a communist nation, and one from the Third World. The group will use a variety of measures on the prisoner's behalf—writing to the prisoner and his or her family as a means of moral support; writing to or telephoning the jailers and government authorities to seek release or less harsh prison conditions, or at least a fair, orderly, and open trial; doing whatever imaginative people can do to end or ease the prisoner's confinement. The spotlight of publicity is sought and employed in knowledgeable and effective ways. Public meetings and vigils are organized.

As a matter of Amnesty policy—evidently to reflect the impartial, independent, and international character of its concerns—Amnesty people do not act on behalf of prisoners in their own country. They may, however, work in their own country on such tasks as promoting human rights legislation, protecting refugees, and opposing export of equipment that may be used in torture or other violent forms of human rights violations. In the United States, Amnesty members have urged ratification of the international human rights treaties and abolition of the death penalty.

Amnesty members come from all walks of life—homemakers, high school students, professors, doctors, lawyers, and retired people, among others. Adoption groups may be formed through a church, a neighborhood, or other community organizations. Through this kind of simple arrangement, Amnesty has marshaled enormous strength for its cause while spreading the message of human rights in the most effective way, through personal care and involvement. Many a fruitful engagement with human rights has begun from such grassroots efforts.

Amnesty groups can also be formed through schools, and are organized at the high school and college level. At present there are 860 high school groups around the country and more than 500 college groups, a number that is steadily increasing, due in part to Amnesty's 1988 Human Rights Now! worldwide concert tour to celebrate the fortieth anniversary of the Universal Declaration of Human Rights on December 10, 1988. The tour featured Bruce Springsteen, Sting, Peter Gabriel, Tracy Chapman, and Youssou N'Dour.

Student members are important to Amnesty. "The fact that half the world is under twenty-five means that young people must and do play a major role in the movement to protect universal human rights," says Jack Healey, executive director of Amnesty International USA. "They may not use the sophisticated language of government diplomacy but their message is hard and forceful—they want action."

Although school groups cannot "adopt" prisoners, they support Amnesty's work in many other ways. They can write articles, work with student newspapers, and organize events to publicize human rights abuses, join activities sponsored by other Amnesty groups, and write "Urgent Action" letters, a form of campaign designed to stop torture even before Amnesty's research confirms that the individual imprisoned is a prisoner of conscience. Many school chapters often get together in a larger group with members from other schools in the area to share ideas and work on programs. Ellen Saideman and a Delacorte editor spoke to members of the New York City High School Cluster of Amnesty International, all students who have been working for human rights causes for some time. The participants in the discussion were: Nadya Engler of the Brearley School in Manhattan, Donna Manion and Jennifer Appell from Townsend Harris High School in Queens, Natalia Olynec and Stacey Malacos from St. Francis Prep, Analía Penchaszadeh and Simon Lee from the United Nations International School, Vivian Monterroso and Diane Piltser of Forest Hills High School, and Kimberly Noone, from the High School of Telecommunication Arts and Technology in Brooklyn. They talked about why they had joined Amnesty, how working for human rights had affected them, and what they felt they had done to help victims around the world.

Some of the students joined because their own families or friends had suffered under repressive governments. Analía Penchaszadeh's family left Argentina for political reasons. "I've always been involved in human rights, one way or the other," she said. "I think the biggest problem in human rights violations is ignorance. So we've been preventing human rights abuses by spreading awareness."

Most joined out of general interest in and concern for human rights. "Writing the Urgent Action letters is such an easy thing to do, and you're helping to free people all around the world," said Jennifer Appell. "Here we are in America, and we have so many rights. And meanwhile there's somebody who's out there rotting in a prison cell. Personally, I just can't sit back and let that go on.

Working with Amnesty has made me appreciate life here more, but I also see more problems. This is not a perfect society. Far from it. But I think we're very lucky in a sense that we are here."

Amnesty does not take a position on human rights violations before 1961, when it was founded, but some of the students felt their human rights work had given their history and political science courses more immediacy. "Getting involved with Amnesty coincided with learning about Nazi Germany, and it was so powerful I had to do something," said Kim Noone.

"Amnesty has made me more aware of abuses here, even though members don't work on cases in their own countries," Donna Manion said. "I take a class where we're discussing the Native American experience and it really struck me to learn that Americans have caused the genocide of a people, of a culture, and that most Americans aren't even aware of this. Indians weren't even given rights in the Constitution. They were left out."

"When you look at history," said Nadya Engler, "—and right now we're studying the French Revolution—you realize we are still talking about the same thing. The rights of man. Joining Amnesty has made me more politically aware. I know that I read the papers in an entirely different way now."

Simon Lee agreed. "You get caught up in schoolwork this, schoolwork that, and when you don't have work you go out with your friends. But being in Amnesty gives me a sense of awareness that I'm actually in the world."

"You begin to realize that if it happens over there it could happen here," said Analía.

"But wherever I go in the world," Simon added, "I would like to have the same rights I have here."

"I can be sitting at home and I don't have to worry that someone is going to barge in and arbitrarily arrest me," Jennifer said.

"Which sounds extreme," said Simon, "but it's the extreme that we all have to worry about. Even if it's not happening to you it's happening to someone else. Looking at it as if you were them makes a big difference."

"Yes," said Vivian Monterroso, "but my parents don't understand why I'm so involved. They're from Guatemala and they feel, 'See, I've grown up there, I've lived with this, you don't understand.' It's really hard to try and help them understand a bit, to tell them, 'Okay. Because you've lived with this doesn't mean we still have to. We still have to try, we can't just sit back and watch it happen.' "

Another dedicated, longtime Amnesty member is Linda Valerian of Minnesota's Twin Cities. In the past ten years Linda has seen most of her group's adopted prisoners released—including people in Argentina, the Philippines, and South Korea. Two adopted prisoners from Argentina who were released and came to live in the United States stopped first in Minneapolis to thank the group for its efforts on their behalf. As this is written, Linda is working on behalf of an Ethiopian prisoner, Tsehai Tolessa, who has been held for seven years without charges, apparently because of her membership in the Oromo ethnic group. Tolessa's husband, who headed the Lutheran church there, disappeared in 1979 and is believed dead. The work on Tolessa's case has been particularly frustrating; there is usually no response from the Ethiopian government. However, the group has been able to make contact with Tolessa; it knows two people in Addis Ababa who visit Tolessa regularly as well as a Lutheran missionary who goes to Ethiopia from time to time. The group has also met with Tolessa's daughter, who lives in the United States. Linda finds some satisfaction in knowing that she and her colleagues have been able to provide some relief to Tolessa, usually money, but once they sent her long underwear, desperately needed in her poorly heated prison cell.

Linda joined Amnesty eleven years ago after receiving a fundraising appeal in the mail. She had been appalled by the widespread existence of torture and jumped at the opportunity to help. She began by writing Urgent Action letters. Soon afterward an adoption group was formed in the Twin Cities, and Linda joined. She has since become very active in human rights. Today she serves as administrative assistant for the Center for Victims of

Torture, which runs a treatment program. After work she volunteers as a "trainer," leading workshops with Amnesty adoption group members to develop new strategies for dealing with difficult cases and countries and new legislation. She also serves as an expert witness on Ethiopian human rights abuses in American hearings on applications for political asylum and deportation proceedings.

It is not uncommon for Amnesty's work on behalf of a prisoner to continue after the prisoner has been released. After years of writing letters and conducting campaigns, the adoption group knows the prisoner and often his family. On occasion, groups assist prisoners who are forced into exile by helping them find refuge. In Kansas City, one group helped Ernesto Dominguez Amaral, a former political prisoner in Uruguay who, like many political prisoners there, remained jobless for years after his release from prison.

When Amnesty mounts a campaign for a particular prisoner of conscience, it is not usually possible to say with absolute certainty that its efforts account for the prisoner's release. But the evidence is overwhelming that the campaigns make a huge, often decisive, difference—as in the case of Julio de Pena Valdez, a trade union leader in the Dominican Republic. After he was freed, he acknowledged his debt to Amnesty:

> When the first two hundred letters came, the guards gave me back my clothes. Then the next two hundred letters came and the prison director came to see me. When the next pile of letters arrived, the director got in touch with his superior. The letters kept coming and coming: three thousand of them. The president was informed. The letters still kept arriving and the president called the prison and told them to let me go.
>
> After I was released, the president called me to his office for a man-to-man talk. He said: "How is it that a trade union leader like you has so many friends all over

the world?" He showed me an enormous box full of letters he had received and, when we parted, he gave them to me. I still have them.[2]

The letters from Amnesty also boost prisoners' morale. While incarcerated in a Soviet psychiatric institution for political prisoners, Viktor Davydov was given two letters from Amnesty members in West Germany. He later explained what they meant to him:

> When you are in confinement, you have no contact with friends, or anyone. You feel completely cut off, deprived of the outside world. Suddenly I got the letters. It is difficult to explain what that meant. These two letters I got gave me hope. I understood how important this human rights support, and defense from the West, was for me, because only thanks to it did I keep my mind and my brain alive.[3]

Davydov credits his release to the work of human rights activists. He said, "The only reason why I am not in a psychiatric hospital, why I was not arrested again, is the activity in the West in defense of Soviet human rights."[4]

There are thousands of stories like these two. But Amnesty's work does not stop with its interventions in individual cases. It also sends missions of inquiry—over five hundred since 1961—to countries believed to be human rights violators, and publishes influential reports of its findings. Since at least 1973, it has conducted a global campaign for the abolition of the death penalty—not only for "political" crimes but for any crime whatsoever—holding that execution by the state "must now be seen as a violation of the human right not to be subjected to torture or cruel, inhuman, or degrading treatment."[5] (In continuing to countenance capital punishment, the United States departs from all of the western industrial democracies—with the exception of South Africa, which styles itself western and a democracy though, in fact, it is neither.)

Since 1972 Amnesty has concentrated on investigating the practice of torture, using publicity to bring some improvements in countries that consider themselves civilized but continue systematically to torture political prisoners. Their instruments range from primitive sticks to the more modern electric shock. Amnesty has documented cases of torture in more than eighty countries. The list includes countries as varied as Italy, Spain, Syria, Kenya, and Malaysia. Amnesty is opposed to all torture—of any kind and for any reason. Today Amnesty is urging ratification of the U.N. Convention on Torture. It has also campaigned against the sale of military and police equipment to nations where the authorities routinely violate human rights.

In a 1978 campaign, Amnesty focused international attention on the brutal mistreatment of children. Far too often, governments punish parents for their acts of conscience by detaining and even harming their children. In one instance documented by Amnesty, the seventeen-year-old son of Dr. Joel Filartiga, an opponent of the brutal Stroessner dictatorship in Paraguay, was abducted from his home and tortured to death. (See the discussion of the legal sequel to this crime in Chapter 8.)

As an offshoot of Amnesty's work, two Toronto doctors, Frederico Allodi and Philip Berger, founded the Canadian Center for the Investigation and Prevention of Torture in 1982. The center provides psychiatric care, legal aid, and other support services for torture victims who have immigrated to Canada. Although release means the end of the physical torture, for many victims the agony continues. They suffer from insomnia, nightmares, fear of authority, paranoia, and dependency on alcohol and drugs. At the Canadian center, over thirty doctors, twenty lawyers, and many other volunteers donate their services to alleviate that suffering.

While Amnesty remains unquestionably the most prominent and important NGO, an array of other organizations work for human rights. They vary in their membership, tactics, and support. While they often pursue the same goals as Amnesty, they also focus on aspects that are outside Amnesty's program. The

NGOs often work together—for example, in jointly sponsored missions and appeals. If the number of NGOs were multiplied a hundredfold, there would still be urgent work for all of them.

Probably the oldest, and among the most distinguished, of the NGOs is the International League for Human Rights. The league traces its origins to La Fédération des droits de l'homme (Federation of the Rights of Man), which was founded in 1902, sparked by the French orgy of anti-Semitism remembered as "the Dreyfus Affair."[6] Roger Baldwin, founder of the American Civil Liberties Union, had first come into contact with the federation in 1926. Later, when members of the French group sought refuge in New York during World War II, they enlisted Baldwin and joined with him in founding the International League in 1942. The league, of which Baldwin soon became director, was one of the first NGOs to gain consultative status with the United Nations. It participated in the drafting of the Universal Declaration and other human rights documents and treaties. The league investigates human rights abuses and sends observers to political trials. Its Family Reunification Project concerns itself with the cases of more than a thousand families whose members are forced to live apart because governments deny them the right to emigrate. Its Human Rights Defenders Project works for the protection of human rights monitors, those generally unknown as well as the famous ones. The league has forty worldwide affiliates.

The league's chairman, Jerome J. Shestack, is among the most distinguished and best known of American human rights advocates. Among his many contributions to the cause of human rights was his service in 1979–80 as United States representative to the U.N. Commission on Human Rights. Like other activists he has devoted a good part of his career to constructive criticism of our government as well as serving it in the role of human rights ambassador.

Today, the Human Rights Watches are probably the best known of the American human rights groups. Helsinki Watch, which is a member of the International Helsinki Federation, was founded in 1979 to monitor and promote human rights in the thirty-five nations of Europe and North America that had signed the 1975 Helsinki Accords. Americas Watch was founded in 1981 to promote human rights in the Western Hemisphere, and Asia Watch, of course, focuses on Asia.

Robert Bernstein and Aryeh Neier are two of the top leaders who have worked long and hard to make the Human Rights Watches successful. Bernstein first became interested in human rights because of the Vietnamese War; he says, "Vietnam is what made me realize I couldn't sit around and just talk." As president of Random House and chairman of the Association of American Publishers, Bernstein had a strong interest in the freedom to publish. He chaired the association's International Freedom to Publish Committee, which investigated human rights abuses against writers. But he was not satisfied with the limited work he could do as a publisher, so in 1975 he founded the Fund for Free Expression, which is the parent of the Human Rights Watches. He says the Watches' mission is to "influence American foreign policy toward protecting human rights wherever they are violated."[7] Today he is the chairman of Helsinki Watch and a member of the other Watch committees.

Aryeh Neier, like many others, came to human rights from involvement in American civil rights. He had been executive director of the New York Civil Liberties Union from 1965 to 1970 and of the American Civil Liberties Union from 1970 to 1978. Today he serves as vice chairman of all three of the Human Rights Watches. Like Bernstein, Neier has led human rights missions to all parts of the globe. Both have often testified before Congress and written many articles on human rights. The Watches publish detailed reports of human rights violations.

The International Commission of Jurists (ICJ), which is headquartered in Geneva, Switzerland, focuses on the supremacy of the rule of law and particularly on safeguarding the independence of the judiciary and the legal profession. The ICJ's many activities include holding international conferences of lawyers to formulate detailed legal standards for human rights, sending international observers to political trials, and publishing reports of its human rights missions. In more than fifty countries, national sections of the ICJ have been established. There is an American section, the American Association for the International Commission of Jurists.

There are other NGOs in which particular professional groups undertake to defend their colleagues from human rights abuses— most prominently, PEN (Poets, Playwrights, Essayists, Editors, and Novelists), and the Committee of Concerned Scientists, which aids people like Andrei Sakharov. Psychiatrists have formed the Campaign Against Psychiatric Abuse and the Working Group on the Internment of Dissenters in Mental Hospitals. The Committee of Forensic Scientists and Physicians, headed by Dr. Jorgen L. Thomsen, a forensic pathologist in Copenhagen, sends delegations all over the world to examine victims. The committee was inspired by the work of the Argentine Forensic Anthropology Team, which, with initial assistance from forensic scientists from the American Association for the Advancement of Science, has done an incredible job of documenting the deaths of many of the *desaparecidos*. Forensic specialists can determine many crucial details of death, such as whether a person was shot in the back or in the front, and whether a woman had given birth before her death. Such evidence has been, and continues to be, crucial in the trials of human rights abusers in Argentina, a topic to be discussed in the next chapter. The evidence is also necessary to identify the *desaparecidos*, and to learn what happened to them.

Among the numerous NGOs in Europe that join the international organizations in the struggle for human rights are Médecins sans frontières (Doctors Without Borders) and Médecins du monde (Doctors of the World), which were both formed by French physicians to deal with international health problems. Médecins sans frontières began working in Biafra and Bangladesh with refugees who had dire medical problems. More recently, both of these medical groups have worked with refugees in Ethiopia and Afghanistan. The physicians who have treated torture victims have also provided evidence of human rights abuses.

89

Other, more general European human rights groups include the Kairos Working Group in the Netherlands, the Association for Human Rights in Paris, the Swiss Committee Against Torture, the Danish Center for Human Rights, and Interights in London.

Another prominent NGO is the New York–based Lawyers Committee for Human Rights. Its first chairman and one of the people mainly responsible for creating the Lawyers Committee in 1978 was Jerome Shestack. But beyond his significant efforts at the creation, the major credit for the committee's splendid contributions belongs largely to its devoted full-time staff and the many hundreds of volunteers who give evenings and weekends to its projects.

Michael H. Posner, the executive director, led in the founding of the Lawyers Committee in 1978, continuing a career commitment to the cause of human rights. His introduction to international human rights had come while he studied law at the University of California at Berkeley and spent a semester working with the ICJ researching human rights violations in Uganda. Although he was denied permission to enter Uganda, he was able to interview almost a hundred Ugandan refugees throughout Europe. He describes the interviews as "cloak-and-dagger experiences. . . . They would meet me under the clock in the railroad station or . . . clandestinely in little cafés. I really traveled everywhere I could to find Ugandans."[8]

Diane F. Orentlicher, as director of the committee's Human Rights Program, was responsible for setting many of the program's priorities and has personally led many missions. She led the first human rights delegation to Cambodia, which met with members of the Khmer Rouge (the notorious Pol Pot regime responsible for the "killing fields").

Arthur C. Helton, as director of the Lawyers Committee's Political Asylum Project, aids refugees seeking asylum in the United States and has trained hundreds of volunteer American lawyers in handling asylum applications. These volunteers constitute a growing corps of lawyers who are sensitized and alert to international human rights concerns in a particular sector where

90

the United States must often be pressured and prodded toward the performance of a role fitting its traditional values.

We can get an idea of the range of NGO activities by comparing the relatively modest Lawyers Committee (annual budget just over $1 million) with the far-flung Amnesty International operation (annual budget roughly $9 million). Dollars alone don't tell the full story, since NGOs rely heavily on the free labor of volunteers—from the few thousand Lawyers Committee volunteers to the more than 500,000 Amnesty members worldwide.

The Lawyers Committee has sent groups to over thirty-five countries, including Argentina, Cambodia, El Salvador, Israel, Nicaragua, Pakistan, the Philippines, Poland, South Africa, and Uganda. Staff member Helena Cook's 1986 study *The War Against Children* has become a widely known, much-cited document on the savagery of white South Africa's repression of its black majority. On occasion, Michael Posner and Diane Orentlicher have joined forces with Amnesty International and other NGOs as members of their missions to other countries—for example, to Chile, Cuba, and Uganda.

Like Amnesty, the Lawyers Committee tries to establish contact with individual prisoners such as Maina wa Kinyatti, who had been imprisoned in Kenya for being in possession of seditious literature, and was released after six years, four months, and seventeen days. Kinyatta spent the last year of his sentence in solitary confinement. A medical examination after his release revealed that he had suffered damage to his heart, stomach, teeth, and ears, and that his vision was impaired and he would have to undergo eye surgery.

While in prison, Kinyatta received messages from the Lawyers Committee that sustained him. After his release, he wrote to Michael Posner in January 1988:

"I walked out of the prison gate . . . with my shoulders unbent, my head unbowed. The main reason why the prison, brutality, and inhumanity did not break me was the fact that I drew my strength, courage, and determination from you, from many friends all over the world who fiercely, consistently fought for my release.

Without their support, and understanding, without their commitment to the truth and justice, to a just world, I don't think I would have survived. . . . The 'messages' you sent . . . connected me with the rest of humanity; they gave me strength and courage . . . love and faith which I badly needed."

To know that a prisoner has been released, and to receive such a letter, is one of the greatest rewards for the committee and its supporters.

In addition to international campaigns and individual cases like Kinyatta's, the Lawyers Committee pays particular attention to the performance of the United States on international human rights issues. It works to encourage the president and the Congress to take effective measures against violations by other governments. To this end, reports go regularly to every congressional office and to appropriate State Department and other executive offices. Other ways it exerts pressure and shares information include formal testimony before congressional committees, informal correspondence and conversations with government leaders, lectures, and op-ed articles in many of the nation's leading newspapers.

The Lawyers Committee also insists that the United States should respect the human rights of its own citizens and others who either seek to come here or may otherwise be affected by actions of our government. There are numerous American groups that work at home against human rights abuses. The NAACP Legal Defense Fund and the American Civil Liberties Union promote and expand our Bill of Rights. The Lawyers Committee has focused intensely on our treatment of aliens, as refugees or otherwise. From time to time the committee has sued federal agencies for mistreatment of detained people seeking asylum, for excessively narrow interpretations of rights of asylum under international laws and treaties, or other arguable departures from human rights standards. Win or lose, the cases remind those in power that in our system the government is under the law rather than the other way around.

I should also add that I've been chairman of the Lawyers Committee since 1980, and have been moved by professional ties to pay somewhat particular and loving attention here to its brilliant staff leaders. The fact remains, quite apart from personal associations, that they and the committee are recognized widely, here and abroad, as models of what NGOs can do in support of human rights.

But how can private people and groups hope to exercise meaningful power over governments? This is a steadily challenging question *within* any country that tries to be democratic. It is even more difficult when private people try to reach into other countries and affect what their governments do. While there are many obstacles and failures, there are actually ways and means for NGOs to make a difference.

Consider, for instance, how NGO missions learn the facts about human rights violations. Country X is accused of imprisoning, torturing, and killing "enemies" of the regime. The NGO sends a group of two or three people to look into the charges. Can Country X simply pull in the welcome mat and tell them to go away? It can, and that happens from time to time. But the result is not necessarily happy for Country X. When charges of torture and killings have been made, walling off the evidence usually leads people and governments on the outside to ask, what does Country X have to hide?

The walling-off technique is sometimes used, nevertheless. And the results usually boomerang. To cite one personal example, in April 1984, I was one of a group of four lawyers on a bar association visit to Paraguay, where charges of gross violations, including torture, had been widely made and credited for all thirty years of the harsh Stroessner regime.[9] We were arrested at the Asunción airport, held in custody all day, and sent on our way without being allowed to interview the human rights activists, victims, and officials we'd come to see. The experience was unpleasant, of course, and not the usual treatment of people on such missions. On the other hand, given the savage character of the Stroessner government, it was not altogether astonishing. But NGOs are not helpless in such cases; they can enlist governmental as well as other forces. Our strong protests to the American

93

ambassador there and to our State Department led to diplomatic objections, a Paraguayan apology, and an entreaty that we come back for a more agreeable visit. Two members of the group accepted that invitation. In due course, they confirmed that Paraguay had not much improved its police-state character. The important point here is that the effort to seal the borders had proved to be dumb and worse than useless.

An even worse case, an arrest in Kenya in January 1988, is described in the op-ed article reprinted at the end of this chapter. There again, the episode will probably cause an increase, rather than a decline, in pressure against human rights abuses.

The NGOs don't give up on reporting human rights abuses just because they're not allowed into a violator country. News of abuse usually gets out; the NGOs hear the stories of refugees, exiles, other visitors, and foreign government officials. The NGOs also review documents and are often able to talk with victims and activists on the phone. The violators become known and are publicized. For example, in 1972, Amnesty International released a significant and detailed Report of Allegations of Torture in Brazil despite the fact that the Brazilian government had denied entry to the Amnesty observers.

Many countries guilty of human rights abuses take the opposite tack of receiving human rights missions and even appearing to welcome them. And in such places all kinds of interesting, often appallingly significant, information proves to be readily available. Much of it comes from victims and their families; it is usually impossible to silence such brave people. Often, victims and their relatives form groups like Las Madres de la Plaza de Mayo, discussed in Chapter 1, that give evidence of the violations.

Oddly, many abuses may be admitted by government officials. In Argentina, for example, the bloody junta that seized power in 1976 never really denied the thousands of lawless arrests, "disappearances," and killings that were later documented in *Nunca Más* (see Chapter 1). Instead, the military "explained" that they were engaged in a "dirty war" with subversives and that the savage tactics were necessary for the good of the country. For those who could swallow such an explanation, the price was acceptable. For the great majority believing otherwise, the facts of wholesale human rights violations were revealed without question in 1979 when the Organization of American States Commission on Human Rights visited and heard testimony from thousands of victims.

There are many variations from country to country. Concealment of the most brutal atrocities is undoubtedly attempted and undoubtedly works in many times and places. Incessant, sometimes risky probing often succeeds, however, in piercing the cover. This is how the tiger cages of Con Son, South Vietnam, were discovered in July 1970. Tom Harkin, who is now a United States senator, was a staff aide to a committee of visiting U.S. congresspeople. He had heard about the horrible prison conditions from Don Luce, an executive secretary for the World Council of Churches, who had spent eleven years in Vietnam. Luce introduced him to a former prisoner, who said the tiger cages were hidden. The prisoner drew a map and said, "Look for a vegetable garden. A door leading from the garden is the only way to the cages."[10]

A routine visit to Con Son prison was on the committee's itinerary. Luce, who spoke fluent Vietnamese, joined Harkin, Congressman William Anderson and Congressman Augustus Hawkins. Of course the planned tour did not include the tiger cages. When Luce and Harkin thought they were close to the cages, they went off on their own. As Harkin later described it:

> I was in a vegetable garden when I saw a wall, and a door that didn't seem to go anywhere, and I was sure that was it. I whispered to Congressman Hawkins that I'd found the entrance in a vegetable garden. All of a sudden he started asking the prison's commandant about vegetables, and pretty soon we were all in the garden, very near that door. I asked the commandant, a Vietnamese colonel named Ve, what was behind the door. He said it led to another compound but that we couldn't use the door. I insisted that he open it, and he insisted

he couldn't. Then there was a clanking sound, and the
door swung open. Apparently the guard inside had heard
the colonel's voice and thought he wanted to come in.
He looked mortified. But before the colonel could say
anything, Congressman Hawkins and I barged through
the door, and inside, there were the tiger cages.[11]

With South Vietnam heavily dependent on American military
and economic support, it was unlikely that the prison officials
would have harmed the two congressmen or Harkin or Luce.
Representatives of international NGOs are usually safe because
they are protected by their own governments and the international media; any harm done to them might create an international incident.

The risk is much higher for the domestic monitors who live
under life-threatening regimes. The international NGOs therefore
devote considerable time and energy to providing support and
assistance to the domestic monitors. In 1985, after three of its
attorneys had been murdered and five more had been arrested,
the Free Legal Assistance Group (FLAG), a Philippine human
rights organization, asked for help. In response, an international
delegation, with representatives from the United States, Australia, New Zealand, Thailand, and Japan, visited the Philippines. The delegation found that "lawyers have been murdered,
detained and otherwise threatened or intimidated because of their
activities as human rights advocates."[12] Soon afterward there was
a letup in the persecution. Some of the credit for that is probably
due to the delegation's discussions with government officials and
subsequent reports.

In a similar case, in response to a request from the Chilean Bar
Association, Diane Orentlicher and two colleagues from the Association of the Bar of the City of New York visited Chile in
October 1986 to study the administration of justice there, including violent harassment of human rights lawyers and activists.
They heard "credible accounts of outright attempts at assassination; death threats; summary detention and prolonged incarcera-

tion of attorneys, frequently without charges being filed against them; prosecution, or threats of prosecution, for making statements to the press concerning specific cases or for protecting the confidences of clients; raids on offices; the burning of files; surveillance, by electronic means and otherwise—the list goes on."[13] They were given specific, terrifying accounts of individual targets of the violence.

One tale they heard was that of Luis Toro, a full-time attorney with the Vicaría de la Solidaridad, a human rights group operating under the aegis of the Roman Catholic Church. On September 12, 1986, his sister, whose telephone number was unlisted, received an anonymous telephone call informing her that all the lawyers at the Vicaría would be killed and that Luis Toro would be the first. At approximately 2:00 A.M. on September 13, several armed men dressed in civilian clothes arrived at his home and proceeded to throw themselves against the doors. Toro called his neighbors and the police. The group left, but a different vehicle soon arrived. Six men rang the doorbell and claimed that they were investigating the earlier disturbance. Toro turned on all his lights and made a lot of noise. By a prearranged signal, his neighbors did too. Toro refused to leave his home, and the men departed. At about the same time, four others were abducted and murdered.

The bar association's report on Chile was widely publicized. It was published in the Chilean newspapers. It is still too soon to tell whether the report will lead to any lasting changes in the Chilean government's conduct toward human rights lawyers and other activists. Past experience gives reason to hope—and, of course, to continue the struggle.

There is no pat conclusion to the ongoing story of NGOs and their work in the world. There are some triumphs. Soon after the publication of the Lawyers Committee's report *The War Against Children*, 269 of the 280 detainees under age sixteen in South Africa were released. However, the majority of the young people detained were from sixteen to eighteen years of age, and they were not released. Any progress—any life saved, torture ended, prisoner released—is significant. For the most part, the struggle tends to lack clear, dramatic, "victorious" outcomes. Many of the violator governments remain almost impenetrable and impervious to outside influences. Where lives are saved, a prisoner released here and there, a particularly horrible practice or regime changed or ended, there is no positive way of saying whether this or that NGO was responsible. But by now the evidence is overwhelming that the NGOs helped bring about the change. NGOs are an extraordinary opportunity to do volunteer work that truly makes a difference in the world.

Another illustration of a government's hostile reception to human rights inquirers from abroad, the following op-ed account is quoted from the *Boston Globe* of February 4 and *Newsday* for February 5, 1988:

KENYA'S RIGHTS ABUSES—INSIDE LOOKING OUT

BY MARVIN E. FRANKEL

"Why bother Kenya?" President Daniel arap Moi asked Dec. 12, in a speech that angrily denounced human rights organizations for speaking out about his government's severe crackdown on dissent.

In the last two years, Kenya has seen an increase in politically motivated arrests, illegal detentions, disappearances, torture and deaths in custody. Moi's remarks came on the day he ordered the release of Gibson Kamau Kuria, a prominent lawyer who had been held for nine months without charge. Kamau Kuria, who defends politically unpopular clients, was arrested after he initiated legal action on behalf of three political prisoners who charged the government with torture. His detention led to sustained pressure on the Moi government for his release, including efforts by Amnesty International, the American Bar Association and the Lawyers Committee for Human Rights.

"Why bother Kenya?" Because of cases like Kamau Kuria's. Because of government harassment or detention of independent journalists. Because of political trials that lack basic procedural safeguards. Because Kenya is an authoritarian state that brooks no opposition. Because of several deaths in police custody, including that of Peter Karanja in February, 1987.

Kenyan police officials have claimed that the 43-year-old Karanja, a businessman not known to have been involved in politics, was arrested for alleged membership in a banned opposition group. The official postmortem described "the body . . . of a male who is emaciated, dehydrated with sunken eyes. He appears older than the stated age." There were allegations of torture. Three inquest hearings were postponed. The Lawyers Committee cleared with the Kenyan government its plan to attend the reopened inquest into Karanja's death on Jan. 11.

En route to Nairobi, it seemed fitting to re-read the story of the inquest of Steve Biko, who died in detention at the hands of the South African police just over 10 years ago. Recalling that, one was aware that Kenyan political leaders have understandably condemned South Africa's persistent violations of the human rights of the black majority.

Like that of Biko, the death of Karanja, while he was being held without charge in secret custody, looked suspicious. Evidence of violent trauma was found in and on his body. The causes of death were the issue of disputes between the government's pathologist and one retained by the family.

The inquest began shortly after 10 a.m. in a small courtroom. I was there with Dr. Robert Kirschner, a forensic pathologist who attended on behalf of the American Association for the Advancement of Science and Physicians for Human Rights.

Less than 30 minutes into the proceedings, we were

99

summoned out of the courtroom by the Kenyan security police and placed under arrest, without formal charges. The dour plainclothesman in charge of the operation asked us incredulously whether we were not aware that it was a contempt of court to "cover" a judicial proceeding without due accreditation.

We were taken to separate jails, "booked," stripped of valuables, ties, shoes, newspapers. I joined three other residents in a filthy concrete cell. I heard cries and sounds like blows, and was told by a cellmate that prisoners were being beaten.

Removed from the cell after 4½ hours, I was taken to the headquarters of the security police and interrogated. For more than three hours, six men questioned me relay fashion, one, two and three at a time. The questioning was angry, accusatory, a little threatening, mostly pointless. "Who appointed you overseer of Kenya?" "Admit you're a spy." "If you can't say the exact year of Kenya's independence"—as I could not—"how can you come and govern Kenya?" There was no physical violence.

The U.S. embassy learned indirectly of our situation and responded effectively. I am sure we would have been held longer but for that spirited intervention. Our papers, including passports, were taken and not returned until after I'd left the country, despite diplomatic protests.

What about the Karanja inquest? Dubious to begin with, the case is only made more suspicious by the exclusion, arrest and harassment of international observers.

What about human rights in Kenya? The Moi government is right to join the chorus of protests against South Africa. This does not, however, erase the deep concerns closer to home. Neither human rights organizations nor the American government nor American citizens—given our deepest commitments—are anything but friends of the Kenyan people when we press to share those concerns and demand that Nairobi move closer to what it preaches for Pretoria.

CHAPTER 7

Punishing Human Rights Violators

We will not give up the battle until all the guilty are judged, until we reach the truth about where our disappeared ones are.[1]
HEBE BONAFINI, president, Las Madres de la Plaza de Mayo

"Never again," the cry of the Holocaust survivors, is echoed in the Spanish of Argentina—*"Nunca Más"*—and in the Portuguese of Brazil—*"Nunca Mais."* In country after country, when a dictatorship falls, its victims cry for justice. Their demand to punish offenders may persist for decades. World War II ended in 1945, but in 1987 Klaus Barbie, "the Butcher of Lyons," was convicted and sentenced to life imprisonment for his work as the Nazi Gestapo chief in Lyons, in Occupied France. In 1988 an Israeli court sentenced Ivan Demjanjuk, "Ivan the Terrible," to hang for his cruelty as a guard in the infamous Treblinka death camp. These two cases are grim examples of the campaign for retribution.

The call to punish human rights criminals can present complex and agonizing problems that have no single or simple solution. While the debate over the Nuremberg trials still goes on, that episode—trials of war criminals of a defeated nation—was simplicity itself as compared to the subtle and dangerous issues that can divide a country when it undertakes to punish its own violators.

A nation divided during a repressive regime does not emerge suddenly united when the time of repression has passed. The human rights criminals are fellow citizens, living alongside everyone else, and they may be very powerful and dangerous. If the army and the police have been the agencies of terror, the soldiers and the cops aren't going to turn overnight into paragons of respect for human rights. Their numbers and their expert management of deadly weapons remain significant facts of life. As Aryeh Neier, cochair of Americas Watch, an American NGO focused on Latin America, has said, "There are a lot of governments . . . where democracy is paper thin, and the military elite exercises most of the power and can act with impunity, where democratic governments are more of a show."[2] The soldiers and police may be biding their time, waiting and conspiring to return to power. They may be seeking to keep or win sympathizers in the population at large. If they are treated too harshly—or if the net of punishment is cast too widely—there may be a backlash that plays into their hands. But their victims cannot simply forgive and forget.

These problems are not abstract generalities. They describe tough realities in more than a dozen countries. If, as we hope, more nations are freed from regimes of terror, similar problems will continue to arise.

Since the situations vary, the nature of the problems varies from place to place. The simplest situation, but also the rarest (at least nowadays, when superpower conflicts raise the specter of nuclear annihilation), occurs when the former regime is utterly overthrown and destroyed from the outside—as were those of Hitler, Mussolini, and Tojo in World War II. The Allied forces demanded unconditional surrender, disarmed the Axis nations, established new governments, and punished war criminals. Even so, many of the people responsible for the Axis atrocities—like the notorious Josef Mengele, whose crimes included cruel medical experiments on humans at Auschwitz—succeeded in escaping and thereby evading trial.

It is more difficult to punish violations by the armed forces. Recent events in Argentina are a dramatic example of the problems. There the disgrace of defeat in the Falkland Islands discredited the military junta and led in 1983 to its peacefully giving up power to a democratically elected government without quite being thrown out. Although the military was essentially defeated, it remains a largely intact, potentially threatening force. Military coups in Argentina have overthrown democratically elected governments in 1930, 1943, 1955, 1962, 1966, and 1975.

Before the Argentine election was held, the military sought "understandings" from the major political parties, including the "understanding" that the military would not be investigated or prosecuted for any crimes during the "dirty war." But no political party was willing to make such a promise in the face of widespread public opposition. The military tried then to insulate itself from any future punishment. Two weeks before the election, the military government issued a general amnesty for all criminal offenses during the "war against subversion." But the presidential candidates denounced this, and promised to investigate the cases of the *desaparecidos*. On October 30, 1983, Raúl Alfonsín, who had promised to try to annul the self-amnesty, won with 52 percent of the votes.

Raúl Alfonsín was inaugurated as president on December 10, 1983, Human Rights Day. With the support of the democratically elected Congress, he began immediately to take action against human rights violators. The military's self-amnesty was declared null and void. President Alfonsín ordered the prosecution of all the members of the three juntas that had ruled the nation during the "dirty war" and created an investigative commission (CONADEP) on the *desaparecidos*. He also signed international human rights treaties, which were in turn quickly ratified by the Congress.

President Alfonsín later sparked controversy among human rights advocates when he introduced new legislation to regulate the trials of violators. The debate centered on two key provisions: first, the requirement that all cases of human rights violations be tried before the Supreme Council of the Armed Forces, and second, a provision that defendants would be presumed to have acted "in error about the legitimacy of their actions" if they were obeying orders, unless they exceeded their orders. The military was thus given an opportunity to clean its own house. Argentine human rights activists doubted that the Supreme Council would punish military officers for human rights abuses. The law would allow human rights violators to escape punishment because they were following orders. Opponents pointed to the Nuremberg trials, which had established the principle that obedience to orders is no excuse for crimes against humanity.

As a result of these protests, the law was altered somewhat before it was finally approved by the Congress. The civilian Federal Court of Appeals were given the power to continue as trial courts if the Supreme Council had not completed both the investigation and the trial in 180 days. The civilian courts were also given jurisdiction to hear appeals from the decisions of the Supreme Council. Further, "atrocious and aberrant acts" were exempted from the "due obedience" provision.

As predicted, the Supreme Council proceeded at a glacial pace in prosecuting military officers for their activities while in uniform. By July 1984 the Supreme Council had not even acted on the cases of the junta members. Human rights advocates petitioned the civilian court to assume jurisdiction, as more than 180 days had passed since the cases were initiated. The court instead granted the Supreme Council more time to complete the process.

In marked contrast to the military's lackadaisical approach, CONADEP enthusiastically met the challenge of investigating human rights abuses. On September 20, 1984, the commission delivered its report, with fifty thousand pages of documentation, to President Alfonsín. The summary, published under the title *Nunca Más*, immediately became a best-seller. The book set forth the details of the "dirty war," including 340 secret detention centers, the disappearances of at least 8,961 individuals, torture, murder, and the dumping of bodies into the ocean. The report came to the conclusion (p. 9) that the "system of repression was deliberately planned to produce the events and situations which are detailed in this report. The typical sequence was: *abduction— disappearance—torture.*"

Soon after the release of the CONADEP report, the Supreme

Council submitted an amazing memorandum, stating that it could find "nothing objectionable" in the orders given by the junta in the "struggle against subversive and terrorist delinquency," while at the same time asking for still more time from the civilian court. As a result, the Federal Court of Appeals finally lost patience and decided to proceed as the trial court. The first trial began in April 1985 and lasted five months. The prosecutor offered evidence on 711 cases of illegal abduction, torture, and murder, including testimony from survivors. Pablo Alejandro Diaz, who had disappeared at the age of seventeen along with several classmates, testified about the brutal torture they had undergone for the "crime" of organizing petitions to seek a reduction in bus fares for students. He was the only survivor. His story has since been made into a movie, *The Night of the Pencils.*

On December 9, 1985, the court issued its ruling, holding that a number of the defendants had devised a secret plan to combat supposed terrorist subversion by means that included torture and murder. The court found that the high command had supervised the plan and had given specific orders to carry it out. General Jorge Videla, president during the junta, was sentenced to life imprisonment and loss of military rank. Four other military leaders were also convicted and sentenced to terms ranging from four and a half years to life imprisonment. The defendants appealed the verdict, and Argentina's Supreme Court affirmed the decision in all respects.[3]

With the top junta members convicted, public attention turned to the other abusers. After convicting the junta members, the Federal Court of Appeals had sent evidence to the Supreme Council so that prosecutions could be started against the officers who had been in command positions or had operational responsibilities. But the military trials continued to move at a snail's pace, and the civilian courts assumed jurisdiction in many cases. On December 2, 1986, General Ramon Camps, the former chief of police for the province of Buenos Aires, was convicted of human rights crimes by a civilian court and sentenced to twenty-five years in prison. At the same time, four of his aides were convicted of torture and sentenced to terms ranging from four to twenty-three years. These included Dr. Jorge A. Berges, who had used his medical skills to determine the limit of victims' endurance. The court specifically refused to apply the "due obedience" law, holding that military discipline does not create the duty (or a right) to obey illegal orders.[4]

Soon after General Camps's conviction, President Alfonsín submitted to the legislature a bill calling for a *punto final* (full stop, or period) to human rights prosecutions. The proposed law provided that no new criminal charges could be brought later than sixty days after the passage of the legislation. Alfonsín explained that the law was necessary to break with the bitter past. He said, "No one should forget what happened to us. It is necessary not to forget so that it does not happen again. But I want all of us to understand, all of us to accept, that we can no longer live chained to our decadence."[5] Human rights groups protested vigorously. They argued that as long as evidence was still being found, people should be able to bring charges against those responsible for human rights abuses. Over 55,000 marched in a demonstration against the proposed law. But the bill passed. Judge Guillermo Ledesma, the presiding judge of the Federal Appeals Court, resigned in protest. He explained that he thought Argentina should show that it would not be more generous to military officers than to street criminals.

The *punto final* law backfired. It was designed to end the trials of military officers, but it prompted hundreds of victims and their families to file suits against those responsible for their sufferings. Courts suspended their usual summer recesses to give claimants the opportunity to file suits. At least thirty more active-duty officers were named in the new suits. Further, the Federal Court of Appeals took over important cases from the Supreme Council of the Armed Forces. By the end of the sixty-day period, perhaps three or four hundred officers continued to face charges.

The result was that the military was provoked, not pacified. Many in the military believed that no wrong had been done. Vice Admiral Ramon Antonio Arosa, the navy chief of staff, said that the navy leadership would "neither abandon nor scorn those who complied with their duty in the difficult situations created by the antisubversive war." Previously, he had said that Argentine democracy was "possible because of the defeat of those who wanted to create chaos in order to bring oppression." Admiral Arosa did direct the nineteen men charged with torture at the Naval Mechanics School to appear for trial before the Federal Appeals Court, which had taken over the case itself because the Supreme Council of the Armed Forces was "negligent" in prosecuting it. However, he also said that the navy would defend those accused of torture.

The problem with the military came to a head in April 1987, when army rebels seized the Campo de Mayo military base, about twenty miles from downtown Buenos Aires. The army rebels acted after Major Ernesto Guillermo Barreiro refused to answer charges of human rights abuses. Barreiro had been the chief of interrogation at the notorious La Perla detention center. The rebel leader, Lieutenant Colonel Aldo Rico, demanded an amnesty, stating that the group was protesting "injustices and humiliations" suffered by the army and wanted "political solutions" to the problems stemming from the "dirty war."[6]

President Alfonsín declared that democracy meant "submitting absolutely and without exception to the juridical system."[7] He called for public support for the democratic government, and the people responded. In the days of the junta, Las Madres de la Plaza de Mayo had marched in fear; now hundreds of thousands gathered in spontaneous demonstrations, keeping a vigil outside the presidential palace. Union leaders warned of nationwide strikes if democracy was threatened. The army, however, did not fully support the civilian government. General Antonino Fichera reported that officers under his command refused to arrest Major Barreiro, who had been dismissed from the army, because they "resist using arms against a comrade."[8] Since President Alfonsín could not rely on the army to suppress the rebellion, he acted himself. On Easter Sunday he went by helicopter to meet with the rebels. Before leaving, he said that he would not negotiate with them, because the Argentines "do not want to return to being the pariahs of the world."[9]

President Alfonsín persuaded the rebels to end their rebellion. Although he denied making them any promises, subsequent events suggest otherwise. The next month Alfonsín proposed a "due obedience" measure that would prevent the prosecution of hundreds of military officers who had been in middle and lower ranks during the "dirty war." Alfonsín himself said that he did not like the law. But despite opposition from human rights activists, the proposal passed, releasing hundreds of officers from the threat of prosecution, including Major Barreiro, whose arrest had started the Easter uprising. The president and the legislature felt they had no choice. As one judicial authority said, the country could "not live with an army in this situation" of tension and danger.[10] Americas Watch concluded in a report, *Truth and Partial Justice in Argentina* (p. 83):

> We see a government and a Congress legislating under duress; under the ominous threat, by a powerfully armed elite, to eliminate the country's democratic process and to return to the brutal practices of the past.

Dr. Jorge Berges and two fellow policemen convicted in the Camps case appealed their convictions, relying on the new law. They argued that they had acted on orders from General Camps. The Argentine Supreme Court upheld the due obedience law, releasing Dr. Berges and two others from their prison terms. Marcelo Parrilli, a human rights lawyer, contended that the ruling would "free hundreds of assassins." He said, "This is a historic ruling, because from now on, Argentina is the only nation in the world where the use of torture is legal."[11] That sharp criticism has a strong foundation: the U.N. Convention against Torture, ratified by Argentina in 1986, says that "no order from a superior or from a public authority can be alleged as justification for torture."

President Alfonsín took a different view:

110

I believe I have acted as would a good father in thinking of the future. By being lenient instead of taking punitive measures, we have demonstrated that Argentines want peace, reconciliation and for all to live together under democracy.[12]

Although the due obedience law barred prosecution of military officers for torture, murder, and arbitrary arrest, three crimes were exempted: rape, theft, and the falsification of civil status. The third offense included the crime of giving false identities and secretly adopting children of the disappeared.

The atrocious practice of kidnapping and giving away children has left in its wake uncounted personal tragedies and continued struggles to right those wrongs. The Grandmothers of the Plaza de Mayo continue to search for their missing grandchildren. Forty-one of the perhaps two hundred children who disappeared have been identified so far. New scientific methods have been developed to prove the genetic link between grandchildren and their grandparents. A National Genetic Data Bank has been established in Buenos Aires, collecting blood samples from grandparents, aunts, and uncles who are still seeking the missing and who fear that their kin will not be found in their lifetimes. Mary-Claire King, a geneticist at the University of California who worked on developing the new test, explained, "As children grow up and learn they were kidnapped in infancy, they can find out who they are."

It is often difficult to find the children, as the harrowing case of Liliana Rosetti illustrates. On December 12, 1976, a pregnant Liliana Rosetti was abducted as she left the medical school where she studied in La Plata, the capital city of the province of Buenos Aires. Her mother and mother-in-law tried to find her. In April 1977 a military official suggested that she might be at the Los Olmos women's prison, about ten miles from La Plata. The two mothers asked a woman at a nearby bus stop whether the bus went to Los Olmos. By coincidence, the woman they asked turned out to be Hilda Delgadillo, the prison midwife. She told them that a woman in jail had just given birth to twin boys, and that she had said that her aunts were twins. Liliana had aunts who were twins. The midwife also reported that the mother had named one of the boys Martin, the name Liliana and her husband had chosen. A doctor and a prison chaplain later confirmed the birth of twins on April 22, 1977, at Los Olmos, but the doctor was unable to identify the mother, and the chaplain died of natural causes. Hilda Delgadillo disappeared.

In 1980 the Grandmothers of the Plaza de Mayo received a tip that twin boys were living in a suburb of Buenos Aires with Samuel Miara and were not his sons. The missing twins' grandmothers went to Miara's house, pretending to be women looking for an English teacher. They spoke with the boys. Liliana's mother later said, "I was overwhelmed. Their noses were exactly like Liliana's."[13] After President Alfonsín's election, Liliana's husband, who had been in hiding abroad, returned to Argentina. He began legal proceedings to recover his sons. Blood tests were ordered, but before they were taken the Miara family had disappeared. Early in 1987 another tip located the Miara family in Paraguay. Argentina has sought to extradite the Miaras for blood tests, but Paraguay, under the dictatorial rule of General Alfredo Stroessner, did not cooperate. (Whether the new military regime will be any more cooperative remains to be seen.) The Paraguayan official charged with extraditing Mr. Miara has said that it is "madness of the Argentines to try to punish those responsible for the dirty war. It's a political campaign and they want to persecute [Mr. Miara] as a police chief."[14] But Liliana Rosetti's family is confident that the twins are Liliana's and determined to have them returned.

Despite the retreat from punishing the junior army officers for most offenses, and notwithstanding threats from the military, Argentina has made great strides in human rights. The past abuses have been painstakingly documented. The top leaders have been convicted and are serving their sentences. Perhaps thirty or more top-ranking military leaders are awaiting trial. Still, Las Madres de la Plaza de Mayo march; as Hebe Bonafini said, they "will not give up the battle until all the guilty are judged."

Other countries emerging from repressive governments have been far less successful than Argentina in prosecuting torturers and murderers. In both Brazil and Uruguay, the military insisted on an amnesty as part of the price for moving toward democracy. In Brazil, São Paulo's archbishop had a team of twenty-five investigators and lawyers investigating abuses during the military rule. After the military government left, the evidence was published as the report mentioned earlier, *Brasil: Nunca Mais*.[15]

Uruguay's Parliament adopted an amnesty for human rights violations during the military government's reign (from 1973 to 1984) just one day before Argentina adopted the *punto final* law. Thirty-eight pending cases were suddenly dropped as a result. Uruguayan human rights activists launched a drive for a national vote to overturn the amnesty, and succeeded in obtaining signatures of one out of four voters (555,701 people) on a petition to hold a referendum for that purpose. At the time of this writing, the electoral court is planning to hold the referendum in March or April 1989. The people of Uruguay thus will have an opportunity to cast their votes on this vital issue.

In Guatemala, after bitter struggles within the leadership of the armed forces, the military rulers gradually, partially, and grudgingly yielded to civilian control. But they continue to stand by, highly visible and making noises about potential interventions if the civilian leadership goes "too far." Four days before the inauguration of the democratically elected president, Mario Vincio Cerezo Arevalo, the military government decreed an amnesty for past offenses. Unlike Argentina's President Alfonsín, President Cerezo said that he would respect the self-amnesty. A bill to repeal the amnesty was introduced in Congress in 1986, but it was roundly defeated.

As a result, there is no prospect in Guatemala of bringing to justice the brutes whose reign of terror led to thousands of tortured, raped, and murdered victims. As yet there is no strong investigative effort to find out what happened to the *desaparecidos*. Judge Olegario Labbe Morales, appointed by the Supreme Court to investigate, has confined his investigation to locating those still living. Since most of the *desaparecidos* are believed to have been murdered, his investigation leaves a gaping void—what happened to those who cannot be found, and if they were murdered, who killed them and why? Moreover, human rights abuses, including killings and disappearances apparently attributable to the armed forces, continue in Guatemala. President Cerezo seems to be unable to control the military.

In the Philippines, where people power ousted Ferdinand Marcos, human rights violators still hold important positions in the military. The seventy-thousand-man Civilian Home Defense Force, which was responsible for the worst violations, has not been abolished despite the recommendation of President Aquino's Presidential Committee on Human Rights. General Fidel Ramos, chief of staff of the armed forces, opposed that recommendation. The general's support for President Aquino had been critical to the peaceful overthrow of the Marcos government. To his credit, Ramos has been steadfast in supporting democracy in the face of threats from other military forces. When a military group attempted a coup on August 27, 1987—the fifth attempt since Marcos left—General Ramos led the loyal military in crushing the rebellion. Unlike what happened in Argentina, the Philippine army members turned their guns on their comrades, resulting in over forty deaths. Still, the armed forces in that troubled country remain restive and divided. The civilian government needs their support to maintain democracy. But the failure to purge and punish the human rights abusers may leave little to prevent the military from further violations.

When the military establishment is able to defy or control the civilian government, human rights abuses are a continuing threat. Agonizing questions arise in countries like the Philippines, Argentina, Brazil, and El Salvador. How can a civilian government put powerful armies under the rule of law and civilian control? What does a nation do when the human rights abusers are still soldiers on duty? Costa Rica found one solution by abolishing its military altogether. As a result, it is one of the few Latin American nations to remain a stable democracy for over forty years. But this solution is unlikely to appeal to many nations or to be practical for countries such as El Salvador or the Philippines, faced with guerrilla warfare. Short of abolishing the military, a government can act to reduce its power. President Alfonsín has pruned defense spending by a third and decreased the draft. He has also moved the military out of the major cities, where it had acted much like an occupation force, to the nation's frontiers. Nevertheless, the military's power was a sufficient threat to lead to the due obedience legislation.

The problems are different where the repressive government has refused to yield to demands for democracy and respect for human rights. The victims of human rights abuses and other opponents of the regime may turn to revolution to change the government. As you can see, when there is a revolution from within, there is a decent chance of punishing the ousted officials for human rights crimes. But a new regime may generate human rights violations of its own, turning out no better than the one that was replaced. This has been the recent fate of Iran and Cuba.

It is by no means universally agreed that there have been violations under Nicaragua's Sandinistas or Robert Mugabe's government in Zimbabwe, which is moving toward a one-party state. There is strong evidence, however, that the new governments in both places have not shown sufficient respect for human rights. Both appear to be superior to the powers they replaced. And both have confronted pressures, external and internal, that account in some measure for their handling, or mishandling, of rights concerns. The fact remains that there are no good reasons or adequate excuses for the violations of the basic rights of freedom from detention without charges, unfair trials, and torture that have occurred in both Nicaragua and Zimbabwe. In Zimbabwe the abuses have included summary executions as well.

Both countries have been beset with the miseries of armed conflict since the new governments took over. Most Americans are familiar with the campaigns of the contras in Nicaragua, in which the United States has been deeply and controversially implicated. Many of the Nicaraguan contras are former supporters of the ousted Somoza government and continue to rely on lethal force as a political weapon. This does not excuse Sandinista abuses. It merely adds to the complexities of a mixed and sorrowful picture.

In Nicaragua, the new government made an effort to punish members of the regime of General Anastasio Somoza Debayle, who had violated human rights. That effort fell short of adhering to international standards. Like all detainees, human rights abusers are entitled to a fair trial. But Nicaragua stacked the decks by setting up a separate court system—the Special Tribunals—to try more than six thousand civilian and military members of the ousted Somoza government. The defendants were accused of serious abuses under Somoza—torture, killings, and other brutalities. To hear these cases, the Sandinista junta appointed panels, each composed of three individuals of "good moral standing" —two lay persons and one with some legal background, either a lawyer or a law student. The Inter-American Commission on Human Rights of the Organization of American States found that these Special Tribunals violated the right to a fair trial under the American Convention on Human Rights, because the accused were subject "to the verdict of political enemies and to the judgment of people more inclined to be severe than fair, because of their victory," and because the defendants were charged not with their personal activities but with the general abuses of the Somoza regime.

Such criticism did not stop the Nicaraguan government from establishing another, similar court system, this time called the Popular Anti-Somocista Tribunals, to try those charged with crimes involving national security such as aiding the contras. Supporters of the Sandinistas argue that these trials are far better than the summary executions more typical of many revolutionary regimes, especially since there is no possibility of a death sentence. That may be, but the trials still miss the mark set by the international standards for fairness.

In Zimbabwe, formerly Rhodesia, the white minority government surrendered to black majority rule after an agreement had been brokered by Great Britain. The new government did not prosecute the whites who had denied the black majority rights for many years. Instead, the newly elected prime minister, Robert Mugabe, focused on his rival, Joshua Nkomo, and his supporters, the members of the Ndebele tribe. Soon the new government was accused of torture with methods that included whips, rubber hoses, electric shock, and suffocation by immersing the victim's head in a canvas bag filled with water. A former Rhodesian policeman said, "Nothing the police are doing now is new. The police have learned all their bad habits from the Rhodesian police. The beatings, the electric shock."[16]

On several occasions the Zimbabwean courts have dismissed criminal charges because the only evidence offered was a confession that had been coerced. But the reports of torture have not been formally investigated, and the torturers have not been punished. Prime Minister Mugabe has ridiculed the allegations of torture. He has said, "Anyone who gets a little scratch on his ear or head is now regarded as having been tortured." When Amnesty International reported widespread torture in Zimbabwe, Mugabe said that the organization had become "Amnesty Lies International."

What can the international community do to aid in the struggle for justice against human rights violators? They should not be given refuge. Those found in the United States should be returned (extradited is the legal term) for trial, as was done in the case of General Carlos Guillermo Suarez-Mason, Argentina's most wanted military fugitive. Suarez-Mason had served as chief of Argentina's First Army Corps during the Junta. He was found and arrested in Foster City, California, in 1987. Argentina applied to extradite him for trial on forty-three counts of murder and twenty-four counts of false imprisonment. On April 27, 1988, a federal judge granted the Argentine request, finding that Suarez-Mason had been "directly in control" of the army's actions. He returned to Argentina on May 9, 1988, to face trial.[17]

Dolly Filartiga, a Paraguayan living in exile, tried a different approach when she discovered that an official who had tortured and murdered her brother was living in Brooklyn. She and her father filed a suit in federal court seeking $10 million. The official, Americo Norberto Pena-Irala, argued that the United

117

States did not have jurisdiction to decide on claims against him for acts committed in Paraguay. The federal court disagreed, finding under an old federal law that the courts have jurisdiction "whenever an alleged torturer is found and served with process by an alien within our borders," because "official torture is now prohibited by the law of nations."[18]

A proposed law has been introduced in the United States Congress called the Torture Victim Protection Act. It would clearly authorize suits by aliens and American citizens who have suffered from gross human rights abuses in other countries. The law would also allow deportation from the United States of any alien who, in his official capacity, took part in torture. This proposed law raises some questions. Would other nations adopt similar laws and authorize lawsuits against Americans traveling abroad for human rights abuses? Would the law have any practical effect if torturers simply avoided travel to the United States? While it would leave many problems for the future, the proposed law seems to be worthwhile. At a minimum, it would underscore our national stance that torturers are barbarians and outlaws who cannot find a haven in the United States and are subject to liability for damages if they come here.

CHAPTER 8

The United States: Human Rights at Home

> . . . *I have a dream that one day this nation will rise up and live out the true meaning of its creed—we hold these truths to be self-evident, that all men are created equal.*
>
> *I have a dream that one day on the red hills of Georgia, the sons of former slaves and the sons of former slave owners will be able to sit down together at the table of brotherhood.*
>
> *I have a dream that one day even the state of Mississippi, a state sweltering with the heat of injustice, sweltering with the heat of oppression, will be transformed into an oasis of freedom and justice.*
>
> *I have a dream that my four little children will one day live in a nation where they will not be judged by the color of their skin, but by the content of their character.*
>
> *I have a dream today! . . .*
>
> MARTIN LUTHER KING, JR., August 1963[1]

So far, we've been looking at human rights from an international perspective, focusing on contemporary human rights problems abroad. As we've seen, the United States has been a world leader in the international human rights movement. But human rights begin at home. We must take a careful look at out own record.

There is much that is good and, alas, too much that is not good. The United States has certainly not been a paragon. Our greatest flaw has been racism, although, largely because of the work of dedicated human rights activists at home, our racial problems have improved in recent decades. Much remains to be done if we are true to our stated ideals and international standards.

Today we look with horror at the system of apartheid in South

119

Africa and wonder how anyone can justify treating people less than equally just because of the color of their skin. It is hard to believe that not very long ago an American version of apartheid—segregation or, more familiarly, Jim Crow—was the law of the land in many states, mostly in the South, and in the nation's capital, Washington, D.C. On December 10, 1948, when the Universal Declaration of Human Rights was adopted, equality for blacks was only a distant dream in the United States of America. By law, blacks were born in separate hospitals, attended separate schools, borrowed books from separate libraries, used separate rest rooms, drank from separate water fountains, and were buried in separate cemeteries.

Today it is also difficult to believe that in many places blacks were once excluded from voting. As late as 1961, no blacks were registered to vote in two counties of Alabama, where they comprised 80 percent of the population. Blacks were denied the right to vote through devices such as poll taxes—taxes that had to be paid in order to vote—and literacy tests that were applied so that no black could pass. A typical case was that of a black schoolteacher in Selma, Alabama, who flunked the test although she had to help the white registrar read the questions, saying, "Those words are *constitutionality* and *interrogatory*."[2] Under the "grandfather clauses," anyone whose grandfathers had voted—meaning whites, since the grandfathers of blacks had been slaves and barred from voting—was exempted from literacy tests.

Discrimination was rampant throughout the United States, not only in the South, and the law gave no help to the victims. Employers hired whites in preference to blacks and paid blacks lower wages for doing the same job. Landlords refused to rent to blacks, and homeowners refused to sell to them. Many hotels, restaurants, and country clubs denied blacks admission. The American military forces that fought in World War II were segregated. It was not until 1948 that President Truman ordered that the armed forces be integrated.

After the United Nations was established, American blacks asked for its assistance in the struggle for equal rights. In 1947 the

NAACP filed a document entitled "An Appeal to the World" with the United Nations, accusing the United States of violating the human rights of its black citizens. The appeal asked for international pressure urging the United States "to be just to its own people." With the opposition of the United States, the appeal was defeated. Two years later, in 1951, the Civil Rights Congress, led by Paul Robeson and William L. Patterson, presented to the U.N. General Assembly a petition entitled "We Charge Genocide: The Crime of Government Against the Negro People." Patterson later explained that the purposes of the petition were "to expose the nature and depth of racism in the United States; and to arouse the moral conscience of progressive mankind against the inhuman treatment of black nationals by those in political places." But no nation was willing to sponsor the proposal.

The Soviet Union has often denounced the United States for racial discrimination—in the General Assembly, in the debate over the Universal Declaration of Human Rights, and in the drafting of the covenants. For example, on May 11, 1949, a Soviet delegate said, "Guided by the principles of the United Nations Charter, the General Assembly must condemn the policy and practice of racial discrimination in the United States." When the issue was raised during the debate over the Universal Declaration, Eleanor Roosevelt told the United Nations of the progress that had been made and noted that she herself had spent a good part of her life "fighting discrimination and working for educational and other measures for the benefit of the Negro citizens of the United States."[3] On one occasion she proposed that the Soviets send a team to observe the racial problems in the United States, provided that an American team was allowed to do the same in the Soviet Union. The Soviets backed off. And that is surely too bad. Nothing better serves human rights than to have the superpowers competing with each other and exposing each other's failings.

International political concerns have affected how American officials view the problem of racial discrimination. In 1946, Secretary of State Dean Acheson reported, "The continuance of racial discrimination in the United States remains a source of constant embarrassment to this government in the day-to-day conduct of its foreign relations; and it jeopardizes the effective maintenance of our moral leadership of the free and democratic nations of the world." Not the least of the problems segregation created for foreign relations was the fact that African diplomats stationed in Washington, D.C., were often denied food, lodging, and entertainment because of their race. But the battle for human rights in America was principally fought by and for Americans.

The battle was fought by many thousands of individuals, of differing races and religious beliefs, from many different backgrounds, including lawyers, ministers, rabbis, priests, homemakers, teachers, artists, students, and farmers. Many were beaten and spent time in jail. Some were permanently scarred by their injuries. Some died. The battle had begun before the Second World War, but it gained momentum after the war.

The first serious blows to segregation were struck by the United States Supreme Court. After years of litigation carefully planned by the NAACP Legal Defense Fund under the leadership of Thurgood Marshall, on May 17, 1954, the Supreme Court announced its decision in the case of *Brown v. Board of Education*. The court held that segregated public schools violated the Fourteenth Amendment to the Constitution, which guarantees to all citizens the "equal protection of the laws." Rejecting the concept of "separate but equal" facilities for both races, the Supreme Court said, "To separate black children in grade and high schools from others of similar age and qualifications solely because of their race generates a feeling of inferiority as to their status in the community that may affect their hearts and minds in a way unlikely ever to be undone."

The United States government had supported the NAACP Legal Defense Fund by filing a brief in that case, asking the Supreme Court to find segregation unlawful. That brief discussed at length the problems that racial discrimination created for American foreign policy.

Brown was hailed as the most important Supreme Court decision of the century. The *United Nations Review* called the case "momentous." But the decision only ordered the desegregation of the four school systems at issue in the case, those in Kansas, South Carolina, Virginia, and Delaware. A companion case decided the same day finally desegregated the public schools in Washington, D.C.

Many school districts refused to recognize the Supreme Court's decision as binding. As a result, numerous lawsuits had to be brought to enforce *Brown*. In Little Rock, Arkansas, not even a court order was enough. In 1957, when nine black students were scheduled to enroll, Governor Orval Faubus predicted, "Blood will run in the streets if Negro pupils should attempt to enter Central High School."[4] On the first day of classes, Governor Faubus had the Arkansas National Guard surround the school to prevent the black students from attending. When a white mob yelling "Lynch her! Lynch her!" attacked fifteen-year-old Elizabeth Eckford, the Arkansas National Guard just watched. She escaped, thanks to a reporter and a white bystander.[5]

To enforce the federal court's order, President Dwight D. Eisenhower was forced to order in a thousand paratroopers and to nationalize the Arkansas National Guard. Even this dramatic confrontation did not resolve the problem. The first year of integration was very difficult for the black students, who were tripped, kicked, shoved, and called names by some of their classmates throughout the year. Soon after Ernest Green became the first black to graduate (on May 29, 1958), Governor Faubus was nominated for his third term, with 69 percent of the vote. Rather than continue integration, the state decided to close Little Rock's schools. A full school year later, in August 1959, the schools were forced to reopen on an integrated basis; the Supreme Court held that closing the public schools was an unconstitutional evasion of the court-ordered desegregation.

Fierce opposition to integration continued. In 1962 the federal government again intervened, this time to protect an American veteran, James Meredith, who had spent nine years in the United States Army, when he sought to attend the University of Mississippi.

President John F. Kennedy had to resort to a force of federal marshals to gain admittance for him.

As the battle for school desegregation illustrates, the process of integration through litigation was slow. However, the victory in *Brown* inspired many blacks who were no longer willing to submit to the humiliations of segregation and believed that they would prevail before the Supreme Court. The massive actions that became known as the civil rights movement began on December 1, 1955, when a weary seamstress, Rosa Parks, refused to give up her seat on a crowded bus for a white man in Montgomery, Alabama's capital, thereby violating the state's segregation laws. Following standard practice, the bus driver had asked all four blacks in the fifth row of the bus to move to the back where they would have to stand, so that one white man could sit down without having to share the same row with a black person. Three of the blacks moved, but not Rosa Parks. The driver said, "Well, if you don't stand up, I'm going to have to call the police and have you arrested." Rosa Parks said, "You may do that."[6]

Rosa Parks was a member of the local NAACP, and knew that the black community had been organizing to oppose segregation on the buses, a daily indignity for many blacks. The community was looking for a test case, and she presented the perfect one—a middle-aged woman tired from a long day's work politely refusing to give up her seat—unlike an earlier case of a fifteen-year-old girl who was charged with assault for resisting when the police asked her to leave the bus.

With Rosa Parks's arrest, the Montgomery bus boycott was born. The next day 35,000 leaflets were distributed, calling for a one-day boycott. The leaflets said:

> Negroes have rights, too, for if Negroes did not ride the buses, they could not operate. Three-fourths of the riders are Negroes, yet we are arrested, or have to stand over empty seats. If we do not do something to stop these arrests, they will continue. The next time it may be you, or your daughter, or mother.

> This woman's case will come up on Monday. We are, therefore, asking every Negro to stay off the buses Monday in protest of the arrest and trial. Don't ride the buses to work, to town, to school, or anywhere on Monday.[7]

Practically all blacks boycotted the buses on Monday, but Rosa Parks was found guilty of violating the segregation ordinance, fined ten dollars, and charged another four dollars in court costs.

That night a community meeting was held to decide what to do next. A little-known minister in his first pulpit had been asked to become president of the Montgomery Improvement Association (MIA). His name was Martin Luther King, Jr., and he was twenty-six years old. He told the crowd that filled the church and the nearby streets:

> There comes a time that people get tired. We are here this evening to say to those who have mistreated us so long that we are tired—tired of being segregated and humiliated; tired of being kicked about by the brutal feet of oppression. . . . One of the great glories of democracy is the right to protest for right. . . . We will not retreat one inch in our fight to secure and hold onto our American citizenship.[8]

Another MIA member, the Reverend Ralph Abernathy, listed the group's demands: courteous treatment on the buses; first come, first served seating, with whites in front and blacks in back; and the hiring of black bus drivers on bus routes serving blacks. He asked the crowd to vote on whether to continue the boycott. The crowd stood in support of the boycott. The MIA's demands did not include an end to segregation. King said, "That's a matter for the legislature and the courts. We feel we have a plan within the existing law."[9]

The blacks in Montgomery boycotted the public bus system, walking to work or using a well-organized car pool system, for over a year. Their seemingly modest demands ran into the brick wall of staunch opposition to integration. The bus company's attorney, Jack Crenshaw, said, "If we granted the Negroes these demands they would go about boasting of a victory over the white people, and this we will not stand for."[10] Violence erupted; bombs exploded at the homes of Dr. King and E. D. Nixon, the former president of the local NAACP chapter, who had been instrumental in planning the boycott. Since it was clear that the city leaders were unwilling to compromise, the MIA filed suit in federal court, arguing that the laws requiring segregation on the buses were unconstitutional.

Nearly a year after the boycott began, on November 13, 1956, the Supreme Court upheld a lower court ruling that invalidated Alabama's segregation laws. But Montgomery was not convinced; the city asked the Supreme Court to reconsider the decision. The boycott continued for more than another month while the Supreme Court pondered the request. On December 20, 1956, the Supreme Court's order denying Montgomery's request finally reached the city officials. Even so, integration of the bus lines was not easy; snipers fired at the buses, and bombs exploded at five black churches and at the homes of three black pastors. For a while, evening bus service was suspended because of snipers. Still, the buses were integrated. The success of the Montgomery bus boycott inspired similar boycotts in Birmingham, Mobile, and Tallahassee.

A new tactic was born on February 1, 1960, in Greensboro, North Carolina, when four black college freshmen, Joseph McNeil, Ezell Blair, Franklin McCain, and David Richmond, decided to buy some toothpaste and school supplies at the local F. W. Woolworth's and to take seats to eat at the lunch counter. The local custom was that only whites could sit at the counters; blacks would be served standing. When the four students asked for coffee, the white waitress replied, "I'm sorry, but we don't serve colored here." McCain responded, "I beg your pardon. You just served me at a counter two feet away. Why is it that you serve me at one counter and deny me at another? Why not stop serving me at all the counters?"[11] Although the waitress continued to refuse to serve them, the students sat there until the store closed, about half an hour later.

The "sit-in" captured the imagination of students throughout the nation. Within just two weeks, sit-ins had spread to fourteen cities in five southern states. By the end of 1960 more than seventy thousand students had engaged in sit-ins protesting segregation in about a hundred cities throughout the South. They participated in "stand-ins" in segregated movie theaters, "read-ins" in segregated libraries, "sleep-ins" in the lobbies of segregated hotels, and "wade-ins" on segregated beaches. Many were arrested for trespassing under new laws passed soon after the first sit-in, and some were beaten by the police or by angry mobs.

But there was progress. For example, after 2,500 people marched on Nashville's city hall on April 19, 1960, Diane Nash, a twenty-two-year-old student leader, asked the mayor, "Do you feel it is wrong to discriminate against a person solely on the basis of their race or color?" Mayor West replied, "Yes."[12] The next day, the headline of the *Nashville Tennessean* was, "Mayor says Integrate Counters."[13] The store owners complied.

The sit-in effort was not limited to the South. To add to the costs of segregation, students picketed Woolworth's branch stores in Boston, Madison, and Boulder, among other places, and called for a nationwide boycott. Woolworth's business fell 9 percent across the nation.

In Philadelphia, after spending a day picketing a five-and-ten-cent store, the Reverend Leon Sullivan went home exhausted, but glad that he had aided a good cause. His wife was less enthusiastic; as he later said, "Grace asked me why I was picketing to help people eat at a lunch counter in Georgia when colored people in Philadelphia couldn't even be salesmen on bakery trucks or soft drink trucks." She told him, "If you really want to do something worthwhile, help your people right here at home. Get them jobs."[14] In his next sermon, he suggested a "selective patronage" campaign; blacks would boycott companies that refused to hire blacks or otherwise discriminated against them.

In 1961 the Freedom Rides began. The Supreme Court had held in 1946 that segregated seating of interstate passengers was unconstitutional, but fifteen years later black passengers often were beaten, jailed, or thrown out if they tried to sit on the front seats of the buses or use bus terminal facilities. James Farmer, national director of the Congress of Racial Equality (CORE), observed, "Those Supreme Court decisions had become merely scraps of paper gathering dust with cobwebs over them. They were not being enforced."[15] So CORE decided to challenge segregation in interstate transportation. Farmer has since explained:

> What we had to do was to make it more dangerous politically for the federal government *not* to enforce federal law than it would be for them to enforce federal law. . . . We decided the way to do it was to have an interracial group ride through the South. This was not civil disobedience really, because we would be merely doing what the Supreme Court said we had a right to do.[16]

Farmer expected violence. He later said, "We felt we could count on the racists of the South to create a crisis so that the federal government would be compelled to enforce the law."[17]

The first Freedom Ride began on May 4, 1961, when thirteen people, seven black and six white, left Washington, D.C., by bus, in order to arrive in New Orleans on May 17, the seventh anniversary of the *Brown* decision. When the two buses bearing the Freedom Riders traveled through Alabama, they were met by mobs. One bus exploded into flames after it was firebombed. The passengers on the other bus were assaulted by a violent mob in Birmingham. Alabama's governor, John Patterson, had no sympathy for the Freedom Riders. He told reporters, "When you go somewhere looking for trouble, you usually find it."[18]

The original Freedom Riders flew from Birmingham to New Orleans, but a new group picked up where they had left off. As Farmer predicted, federal protection proved necessary for the

Freedom Riders. During the summer of 1961 hundreds of them traveled through the Deep South. The Freedom Rides stirred the president to petition the Interstate Commerce Commission for an order prohibiting segregation in all buses and stations used by interstate passengers. An order to that effect was issued on September 22, 1961.

In 1964 a coalition of civil rights groups launched an effort to register blacks to vote in Mississippi, and called their project "Freedom Summer." Segregation was fiercest in Mississippi. One commentator, Juan Williams of the *Washington Post*, noted:

> Forty-five percent of Mississippi's people were black, a higher percentage than in any other state. Mississippi also led the nation in beatings, lynchings, and mysterious disappearances. Only five percent of black Mississippians were registered to vote, the lowest rate in the United States. With majorities in many counties, blacks might well have controlled local politics through the ballot box. But segregationists were not about to let blacks vote; many would sooner kill them.[19]

The day after the first volunteers arrived, June 21, 1964, three civil rights workers failed to return from investigating the burning of a black church in Lawndale, Mississippi. Their bodies were found six weeks later buried in an earthen dam. The sole native Mississippian of the three, James Cheney, a twenty-one-year-old black CORE worker, had been brutally beaten. National attention focused on the murders of Cheney and his white colleagues, Michael Schwerner, age twenty-four, a CORE worker, and Andrew Goodman, age twenty, a volunteer.

The FBI found that the three young civil rights workers had been arrested for speeding by Deputy Sheriff Cecil Price, who kept them in the Neshoba County Jail in Philadelphia, Mississippi, for several hours while the local Ku Klux Klan gathered. Price then released them, but his car soon overtook theirs. He drove them to a deserted area and turned them over to a lynch mob. Although the state did not prosecute anyone for murder, the federal government charged eighteen individuals with conspiracy to deprive the murdered men of their civil rights. The trial was held in 1967 before an all-white jury, and seven men were convicted and sentenced to terms of from three to ten years. Price received a six-year sentence for his part in the murders.[20]

Punishing human rights violators was vital to establishing the rule of law in the United States, just as it is important in Argentina, Uruguay, and other places. The trial of Price and his confederates marked the first time that murderers were convicted for any crime in a civil rights slaying in Mississippi. There had been numerous murders of blacks exercising their civil rights, including the 1962 assassination of Medgar Evers, the NAACP field secretary for Mississippi, but no one had ever been punished for such a crime. The *Tupelo Journal* hailed the convictions, declaring that the state had "actually reached a turning point in race relations. But we are still not far around the corner."[21] The *New York Times* observed, "As a result, white terrorists can no longer strike out at Negroes and their white sympathizers with an unshakable belief that they will be acquitted on any charge brought against them."[22]

Television played a vital role in the civil rights movement. It showed the nation scenes of blacks and whites being beaten just for exercising their human rights—the right not to be subjected to discrimination, the right to ride a bus as equal human beings, the right to vote, the right to protest. The noted legal scholar Alexander Bickel wrote, "Here were grown men and women furiously confronting their enemy: two, three, a half-dozen scrubbed, starched, scared and incredibly brave colored children. The moral bankruptcy, the shame of the thing was evident."[23] Civil rights activists used the media to show the brutality of segregation.

One of the harshest scenes was recorded in Birmingham, Alabama, in 1963, which was then called the "Johannesburg of America." Under the orders of Eugene "Bull" Connor, the chief of police and a virulent opponent of desegregation, the police turned fire hoses and police dogs on nonviolent marchers, many of them children. Throughout the nation Americans saw the

130

Police use truncheons to break up an August 1983 demonstration of women in Santiago, Chile, who demanded an investigation into the whereabouts of their missing relatives, "los desaparecidos." *(UPI/Bettmann Newsphotos)*

Carmen Gloria Quintana, survivor of a burning by government soldiers in Chile that killed her companion, Rodrigo Rojas de Negri, in July 1986. A button showing Rodrigo Rojas appears on her blouse. She is pictured at home in April 1987, on the first day of her return to Chile following months of medical treatment in Canada. *(Impact Visuals)*

Nelson and Winnie Mandela on their wedding day in 1958. Six years later he was sentenced to life imprisonment in South Africa for sabotage. Today (early 1989) Mandela is still in custody, yet he has a tremendous impact on worldwide human rights. *(Eli Weinberg IDAF/Impact Visuals)*

Young man with a passbook, 1985. Passbooks, which have since been outlawed in South Africa, restricted where blacks could live and work. *(United Nations Photo/155572)*

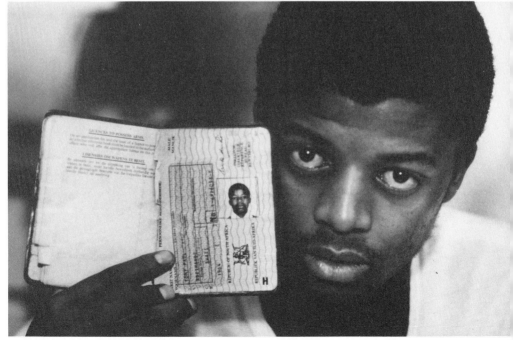

Ezakheni, a "resettlement" village in Kwazulu "homeland," Natal. Millions of black South Africans have been forcibly resettled in such villages since 1948—the largest forced movement of people in peacetime history. *(United Nations Photo/151707)*

Segregated facilities.

Left: Cape Town.
(United Nations Photo/151902)

Right: Johannesburg.
(United Nations Photo/151613)

Coffins of demonstrators killed by the South African police during the celebration of International Day for the Elimination of Racial Discrimination in March 1985. This day commemorates the anniversary of the March 21, 1960, Sharpeville massacre, when police fired upon and killed people demonstrating against the pass laws. *(United Nations Photo/155584)*

Eleanor Roosevelt, chairwoman of the United Nations Human Rights Commission, with a copy of the Universal Declaration of Human Rights, November 1949. *(United Nations Photo)*

KENYA  TIMES

TUESDAY, JANUARY 12, 1988   THE BADGE OF PATRIOTISM   No. 1479   PRICE 3/00

Two US citizens arrested in court

By JEREMIAH AURAH

TWO Americans were yesterday arrested by the Kenyan security personnel after they were found in possession of subversive documents.

The two came into the country over the weekend posing as a tourist and a businessman, respectively.

Mr Robert Howard Kirschner, 47, and Mr Marvin E. Frankel, 67, were arrested at the Nairobi Law Courts in possession of documents bear-

Mr Tinis :.. Issued

Robert Kirschner

into the courts and take notes or the proceedings without prior accreditation as required by the regulations.

Howard, who posed as a businessman together with his colleague, who posed as a

Marvin Frankel

On Saturday January 9, 1988, and Sunday January 10, 1988, two Americans, Mr Robert Howard Kirschner and Mr Marvin E. Frankel arrived into the country. The two gentlemen, according to their

January 12, 1988, newspaper account of the arrest of Marvin Frankel and Dr. Robert Kirschner, a forensic pathologist, in Kenya. Frankel and Kirschner were arrested while taking notes as international observers during an inquest into the death of Peter Karanja, a Kenyan business-man who died while in police custody. Kirschner was accused of "posing as a businessman," Frankel, of "posing as a tourist," and both were accused of "carrying subversive documents."

Mona Mahmudnizhad (1965–83), a Baha'i who was executed by the Iranian government at the age of seventeen because she refused to recant her faith. *(Courtesy of the Baha'i Office of Public Information)*

The House of the Bab in Shiraz, the holiest Baha'i shrine in Iran, being destroyed by Revolutionary Guards in 1979. *(Courtesy of the Baha'i Office of Public Information)*

Student demonstrators in Manila, the Philippines, ward off riot police during a protest rally on the twelfth anniversary of the declaration of martial law. *(UPI/Bettmann Newsphotos)*

February 15, 1986: In front of the Presidential Palace, jubilant Filipinos hold posters of Corazon Aquino and Salvador Laurel as the crowd celebrates the overthrow of President Marcos. *(Reuters/Bettmann Newsphotos)*

September 4, 1957: Arkansas National Guardsmen turn away Elizabeth Eckford, fifteen, as she attempts to enter Central High School in Little Rock. The soldiers, called out to prevent the desegregation of the school because it might set off a riot between blacks and whites, stopped the black students in defiance of a federal judge's order that the school was to be integrated. *(UPI/Bettmann Newsphotos)*

Dr. Martin Luther King, with portraits of slain Mississippi civil rights workers Andrew Goodman, James Chaney, and Michael Schwerner behind him, speaks to members of CORE and SNCC outside Convention Hall in Atlantic City, New Jersey, on August 24, 1964. *(UPI/Bettmann Newsphotos)*

Marvin Frankel (right) meeting with Andrei Sakharov and Elena Bonner at their apartment in Moscow in October 1987.

Soviet dissident Anatoly Shcharansky (now Natan Sharansky) and his wife Avital, reunited after twelve years, smile during airport news conference following his arrival in Israel on February 11, 1986. *(Reuters/Bettmann Newsphotos)*

contradiction between the "land of the free" and the land of segregation and discrimination.

In response to the civil rights movement, the Civil Rights Act of 1964 and the Voting Rights Act of 1965 were passed by the Congress and signed by President Johnson. The Civil Rights Act banned discrimination in employment, public accommodations and facilities, and education. The Voting Rights Act barred literacy tests and replaced local registrars with federal registrars under certain circumstances. In 1968 the Fair Housing Act outlawed discrimination in housing.

Of course, racial discrimination has not been entirely eradicated. There are still employers who won't hire blacks and landlords who won't rent to blacks. But today federal and state laws prohibit racial discrimination rather than sanction it. After the passage of the Voting Rights Act, over a million blacks registered to vote and have thereby achieved a significant measure of political power. Elected southern officials know the power of black votes and pay attention. The ranks of those officials themselves contain increasing numbers of black men and women. Black mayors preside over large American cities—including Cleveland, Philadelphia, Los Angeles, Chicago, Washington, Atlanta, and Newark. Jesse Jackson's spectacular campaign for the Democratic nomination for president in 1988 suggested how far we've come and the distance yet to go.

To be sure, the legacy of generations of second-class treatment cannot be erased overnight, not even in a few years. Today, black Americans still earn less and have a shorter life expectancy than their white counterparts. But the good fight continues. And things get better.

Many of those who fought in the battle for civil rights in America later turned their efforts to the movement for international human rights. Patricia Derian, who participated in the 1962 formation of Mississippians for Public Education, an organization designed to keep the public schools and parks open after integration, became the first assistant secretary of state for human rights. Jack Greenberg, director of the NAACP Legal Defense Fund during the 1960s and 1970s, now shares the leadership of Columbia Law School's human rights program. James Peck, a Freedom Rider who survived a brutal beating in Birmingham, has worked for Amnesty International. The Reverend Leon Sullivan, the author of "selective patronage" to combat racial discrimination at home, has applied the same concept to South Africa, asking Americans to stop investing in companies that refused to implement the "Sullivan principles" requiring equal opportunity for South African black employees of multinational corporations.

Blacks are not the only Americans who have suffered from discrimination. During World War II, Japanese Americans living on the West Coast were relocated to concentration camps in inland areas. In 1988 Congress finally passed a law giving some financial compensation to the people who had suffered this outrage. Before the Civil Rights Act of 1964, discrimination on the basis of religion and national origin was common in employment, public accommodations, and housing. Sex discrimination was also rampant. In fact, it was only because a political maneuver backfired that sex discrimination was included in the 1964 Civil Rights Act. The act, as originally drafted, did not mention sex at all. An amendment adding sex as a protected characteristic was proposed by a southern senator in what many believed was a ploy to defeat the act. The amendment was approved, and the act passed.

Today the most blatant discrimination is that against AIDS victims and carriers. Schools have barred people with AIDS, ambulance drivers have refused to carry them, and some doctors and dentists refuse to treat them. They are afraid of exposure to a disease that may always be fatal, although scientists believe that the disease is not transmitted through "casual contact"—contact that does not involve the exchanges of bodily fluids such as blood and semen. Further, the groups at highest risk for AIDS—homosexual men and intravenous drug users—were often treated like pariahs before AIDS entered the scene. Some have gone so far as to suggest that AIDS is a punishment of the afflicted for their conduct.

One area where the United States record is generally good is

132

freedom of speech and of the press, guaranteed by the First Amendment to the Constitution, but even here we are far from perfect. Under the McCarran-Walter Act of 1952 foreign visitors may be denied entrance to the United States because of their political views. In October 1986 the United States refused to admit Patricia Lara, a reporter for *El Tiempo*, Colombia's leading newspaper, because our officials believed she "might engage in subversive activities." Lara had come to attend a dinner for recipients of an award "for distinguished contributions to the advancement of inter-American understanding and freedom of information" at Columbia University. Upon arriving at Kennedy International Airport she was detained by the Immigration and Naturalization Service because her name was listed in that agency's "Lookout Book," which "looks out" for people who are to be barred from the United States. The President of Columbia University, Michael Sovern, called Lara's detention an "anathema to a free society." A representative of the Colombian embassy said, "She is a respected journalist, and in Colombia, where we have free press, she has never been denied the right to write or the right to report."[24] Arthur Helton of the Lawyers Committee for Human Rights represented Lara. The government, however, succeeded in barring her.

Among other distinguished people who have been barred under the same law are Gabriel García Márquez, the Colombian Nobel laureate in literature; Dario Fo, an Italian playwright; and Hortensia Allende, the widow of President Salvador Allende of Chile.

Significant progress in changing this regrettable law took place in December 1987 when President Reagan signed an amendment that temporarily prohibits the exclusion or deportation of aliens "because of any past, current or expected belief, statements or associations which, if engaged in by a United States citizen in the United States, would be protected under the Constitution." The amendment expires in March 1989. It is expected that the Congress will have reexamined this issue by then and will decide if the amendment should be made permanent.

The American record on political refugees is mixed. Article 14 of the Universal Declaration of Human Rights states, "Everyone has the right to seek and to enjoy in other countries asylum from persecution." Our own Statue of Liberty says, "Give me your tired, your poor, your huddled masses yearning to breathe free." Most Americans (except Native Americans and those descended from blacks who were brought here in chains to serve as slaves) are descendants of immigrants who came to these shores for religious and political liberty as well as economic opportunity. Early in this century racial and ethnic prejudice led to restrictions on immigration. Economic concerns led to legal barriers. The hostility toward immigrants increased during the Depression, when one of every five Americans was out of work.

Prejudice also played a role in keeping the doors tightly shut on Jewish refugees fleeing Nazi Germany. Perhaps the most dramatic example of America's closed door policy was that of the *St. Louis*, a ship carrying 939 German Jewish refugees, which was refused permission to land in the United States in 1939. Nazi propagandists asked: how could the world criticize Germany for its treatment of the Jews when other countries rejected them? Although France, Belgium, the Netherlands, and England said they would shelter them, this handful of refugees was returned to Europe, where most of them were murdered during the Nazi occupation.

Since World War II, the United States has been decidedly more hospitable, admitting over two million refugees. But more than 90 percent of the refugees have been people fleeing communist nations: 800,000 from Cuba and 750,000 from Indochina alone. A large proportion of those seeking refuge from right-wing governments have been turned away. The Refugee Act of 1980 was adopted to provide a politically neutral test for granting asylum: the applicant must have a "well-founded fear of persecution" in his or her homeland "on account of race, religion, nationality, membership in a particular social group, or political opinion." But applicants from communist countries still continue to receive preference. For example, in 1986 all but three of the 153 individuals from Latin America who were granted asylum were from Cuba.

Many claims have been rejected because the Immigration and Naturalization Service said that to win asylum, the alien had to show a "clear probability of persecution." In 1987 the Supreme Court rejected that standard, holding that the Refugee Act required that the alien show only that "persecution is a reasonable possibility." It is too early to tell whether this new standard will make a significant difference in the granting of asylum.

Prior to July 1981, most asylum applicants were released on parole pending a determination of their claims. Since then, however, hundreds have been detained in prison or in prisonlike conditions. This policy of detention deters many would-be applicants with clear cases from pursuing their claims, or even entering the United States. One Afghan refugee said:

> From this jail and the mental torture I have been put through, it has become clear to me that what I had heard about the United States and what we had hoped for and what they promised us and announced to the world is not anything other than a dream and propaganda. The United States will never extend a helping hand to me. I feel that I will never be free or granted political asylum. Since there is no hope for me here, I give up my case and request that I be sent back to our beloved and invaded country under the Russian torture. Although it is very clear that I will be killed in Afghanistan, I am sure that by my death our people who suffer under Russian atrocities will recognize the United States' true humanitarian feelings. Before I die, I will tell them that there is no hope for their safety and that it would be better to be killed by the Russians before leaving the country and coming to a foreign land where they will face jail, torture and be treated like animals.[25]

To deter immigration, the United States Coast Guard has intercepted boats from Haiti and sent the Haitians back to their native land. Despite well-documented reports of human rights abuses by the Haitian government, the United States argued that the Haitians were merely economic refugees. But there is a strong argument that the practice of thus returning refugees to their native lands is a violation of international human rights law. Article 33 of the Covenant Relating to the Status of Refugees states, "No Contracting State shall expel or return [*refouler*] a refugee in any manner whatsoever to the frontiers of territories where his life or freedom would be threatened on account of his race, religion, nationality, membership of a particular social group or political opinion." The Lawyers Committee has tried unsuccessfully to have this Coast Guard program declared unlawful. That effort failed on fairly technical grounds. The treatment of Haitians remains a blot on our human rights record against which continued protest is needed.

In addition to the battle for political and civil liberties, important struggles involve economic and social rights. Article 11 of the International Covenant on Economic, Social, and Cultural Rights recognizes "the right of everyone to an adequate standard of living for himself and his family, including adequate food, clothing and housing, and to the continuous improvement of living conditions." Today in America, as many as 3 million Americans may be homeless. It is impossible to walk down the streets of Manhattan, Los Angeles, or any large city without noticing someone who appears to live on the street. Perhaps the most prominent NGOs in this area are the Coalitions for the Homeless. Both the national and the New York coalitions are led by Robert Hayes, who left a job at a prestigious law firm to devote himself to this cause. After observing homeless people on his way to work, he began talking to them to find out why they lived outside. Then he visited a men's shelter, which was overcrowded, filthy, and dangerous, and found that there were thousands more homeless men who could not fit in the shelter.

In October 1979 the coalition filed a class action suit in New York State Court, arguing that the New York State Constitution provides a right to shelter. The coalition won an injunction, and New York City agreed to provide shelter. Today the coalition is involved with monitoring the quality and quantity of housing provided. The state and city provide single individuals with shelter in barracks where hundreds sleep, but many who are homeless still prefer sleeping in the streets and the subways. Families are housed in hotels that have become infamous for their squalid conditions at inflated prices. The coalition has also worked to enable the homeless to vote and receive government benefits such as Social Security disability payments and food stamps without having to provide a permanent address.

Today, when the Soviets discuss human rights with Americans, they raise the issue of homelessness in the richest country in the world. Under Mikhail S. Gorbachev they are willing to admit to some shortcomings in their own country and are making some changes in the area of human rights. This creates a challenge for Americans—to admit to our own problems and to work toward solving them.

CHAPTER 9

U.S. v. U.S.S.R.: Competition

I think there will be a lot of water passing through the Mississippi and the Volga before the U.S. Congress and the Administration recognize the American people's right to the protection of their social and economic rights. But all that has been guaranteed in the Soviet Union.
MIKHAIL S. GORBACHEV, November 1987[1]

It may seem a little surprising that the United States and the U.S.S.R. have never fought a war against each other. During the latter half of the twentieth century these two superpowers have tended to deal with each other as "enemies." Our huge military establishments appear to be aimed at each other—even though the occasions when Soviet or American fighting men have been in combat since World War II have always involved other adversaries.

The two giant nations lead (or control) blocs of nations opposed to each other in fundamental respects—in governmental philosophy, social organization, economic order. The Soviet dictatorship, in power since 1917, is the latest stage in a long history of authoritarian government in Russia. Despite the revolutionary change to a professedly Marxist regime, the legacy of the Russian czars—with their secret police, repression of dissent, and often paranoid view of the world outside—continues to be a factor in Soviet culture. There is a huge gulf and a grim rivalry between the Soviets and the capitalist democracies, still led, in significant respects, by the United States.

The antagonism between the Soviet bloc and what we call the

West is a central fact of life for most aspects of international affairs, including human rights. For the most part, when we Americans think of the Soviets in connection with human rights, we say that the U.S.S.R. is guilty of gross violations. Most of the democratic nations in the world would agree. Though no individual or country is qualified to pose as impartial judge of its own case, we tend to imagine that a neutral observer from another planet would agree with the United States and condemn the Soviets. But the happy judgment that we're right and they're wrong is by no means a sufficient resolution of human rights issues as they arise between the United States and the U.S.S.R. It is vital here, as elsewhere, to seek accommodations that are more complicated than a simple identification of the good guys on one side and the bad guys on the other.

We can hardly think of the U.S.S.R. in relation to our human rights values without being aware that the Soviets have indeed committed massive violations. A history of rigged political trials, the millions murdered under Josef Stalin, ghastly prisons of the Gulag made gruesomely real for us by Aleksandr Solzhenitsyn, confinement of dissenters in psychiatric hospitals—these are major horrors in the Soviet Union's monstrous record.

Some of these violations have become bones of contention between the United States and other democracies on one side and the Soviets on the other. Among the steadiest and currently best known of these has been the effort of Soviet Jews to leave the U.S.S.R.—an effort that has produced a harrowing record of governmental abuse, personal bravery, tragedy, anguish, and triumph. The story has deep and varied roots, and reflects a long history of virulent and cruel anti-Semitism from the days of the czars, the pogroms, and the Pale of Settlement (the Russian version of the ghetto). In the early years following the Bolshevik revolution there was a brief respite, and Russian Jews enjoyed an era of equal treatment under law, individual opportunity, and freedom from abuse. They rose to high positions in government (the highest being that of Leon Trotsky, eventually to become Stalin's archenemy and assassination victim), the arts, and the

professions. Anti-Semitism and other forms of racism were officially outlawed, though they continued in the attitudes and behavior
of people steeped in Russian traditions.

The brief interlude ended in what appeared to be a generalized
megalomania that afflicted Josef Stalin and led to murders and
tragedies on an unimaginable scale. Stalin himself reverted to the
old anti-Semitism, finding plots by Jewish doctors against his life
and other imaginary conspiracies by Jews. Anti-Semitic literature
and public pronouncements came back into vogue. Nonsensical
but potent fabrications like *The Protocols of the Elders of Zion*[2] were
published again and treated seriously. Although the Soviet Union
voted to establish the state of Israel in 1948, after the 1967 war
the Soviets took a pro-Arab line and severed relations with Israel.
"Anti-Zionism" became the new name for the same old anti-
Semitism. Within the U.S.S.R. discrimination in schools, jobs, and
professions reappeared. In that environment, substantial numbers of Jews despaired of their lives as Soviet citizens and yearned
to leave their native land—many wishing to go to Israel, others to
the United States or elsewhere.

Beginning around 1970, a pattern emerged in thousands of
cases. In a closed society never receptive to requests for emigration, a Soviet Jew would apply for permission to leave for Israel,
normally with his or her immediate family. The first consequence
of the application would be dismissal from employment, especially
if the applicant was a relatively high-ranking scientist or artist or
other kind of professional. Usually the telephone line would be
cut. Harassment by the KGB (the security police) would begin.
Prosecution on trumped-up charges—often the grab bag crime of
"hooliganism"—would lead to prison or distant exile. Whatever
else happened, permission to emigrate would be denied or postponed
for years or decades. The applicants labeled themselves with a
new term in the human rights vocabulary: they became *refuseniks*.

For many in this group—and probably for an unknown number
of Soviet Jews who did not seek to emigrate—the combination of
mistreatment at home and the emergence of Israel as a viable
state led to a new or renewed interest in Jewishness. Reared in

141

a Marxist country where atheism remains the preferred stance on religion, a substantial number became adherents to the Jewish faith and practitioners of its ritual. Others developed or deepened their interest in Jewish culture—learning Hebrew or Yiddish and Jewish history, taking an interest in Jewish food, art, and contemporary Israeli affairs.

Jewish groups outside the U.S.S.R., led by those in the United States, mounted pressure campaigns against the Soviets and their own governments to seek the release of the *refuseniks* and fair treatment for the 2 million or so Soviet Jews seemingly prepared to remain within the U.S.S.R. As has been noted earlier, trade sanctions and inducements were employed in an effort to lower the emigration barriers. The repressive Soviet position was steadily denounced in international forums—notably in the Helsinki Review meetings. Private organizations—of physicians, scientists, artists, lawyers, and others—added to the carrot-and-stick approach of offering or withholding exchange relationships as inducements to favorable change.

Most of the *refuseniks* remained unknown as individuals to the outside world. But a handful, some of whom we've referred to earlier, became world-famous leaders of the group. People like Vladimir and Maria Slepak, Josef Begun, Ida Nudel, Aleksandr Lerner, Lev Alpert, Alexander Yoffe, and Natan Sharansky were international media figures. Caught between the aggressions of their own government and the limited powers of outside supporters, their combative roles led to macabre tests of their courage and endurance. One day the Slepaks might be giving an interview to a foreign correspondent. The next, Vladimir was on trial for "malicious hooliganism" for a public protest, soon to be shipped to Siberia for five years or so of punitive exile.

Having already denied Sharansky a visa, the Soviets granted one to his fiancée, Avital Stieglitz—on the condition that she leave for Israel within ten days. Sharansky was in jail at the time, one of eighteen Jews arrested on the eve of President Nixon's visit to the Soviet Union. He was freed two days before her visa expired, and they were married the following day, July 4, 1974.

Once she left, Avital Sharansky became a tireless crusader travel-ing the world on behalf of her husband and other Jews. That battle must have seemed hopeless at times—as on July 14, 1978, when Sharansky was convicted of treason and sentenced to thir-teen years in prison. The eight and a half years he served were marked by cruelty and life-threatening health conditions. Finally, on February 11, 1986, he was released. Like others who make history, Natan Sharansky has tended to find the right words. When he and Avital were at last together again, meeting at the airport in Frankfurt, Germany, after twelve years of separation, his first words to her, in Hebrew, were *Silchi li she'icharti k'zat*— "Sorry I'm a little late."[3] He has since become an Israeli, and changed his first name to Natan. His provocative style and his energies have not changed. The struggle for Soviet Jewry remains the central cause of his life.

The case of Soviet Jews epitomizes both the possibilities and the limits of international human rights causes in our time. Dur-ing the relatively relaxed period of détente in the 1970s the Soviets responded to international pressure and allowed increasing num-bers of Jews to emigrate. In 1979 the annual total reached a peak of 51,320. The U.S.S.R. invaded Afghanistan in December of that year. The United States and the rest of the "free world" were outraged. The United States boycotted the Olympic Games held in Moscow in 1980, embargoed sales of grain and other agricul-tural products to the Soviet Union, and suspended licenses for technological exports. Jewish emigration plummeted, coming close to zero by the mid-eighties. Then, after the advent of Mikhail Gorbachev in 1985 and the new policies of *glasnost* (openness) and *perestroika* (restructuring) within the U.S.S.R., accompanied by strong efforts to promote a thaw in relations with the West, doors opened again for the *refuseniks*. In 1987 the Slepaks, Nudel, Begun, Alpert, and Aleksandr Lerner were released. The exodus continued into 1988.

I visited Lerner and the Slepaks in July 1974 and again in October 1987, weeks before their long-awaited release. In 1974 Lerner, world-renowned cyberneticist, told me two of his major

143

reasons for wanting to be freed to go to Israel. First, because he hoped to pursue there his ideas for the production of artificial human hearts. Second, because he had come to feel that the U.S.S.R., though it had heaped him with honors and material comforts before he announced his desire to leave, was "a pseudosociety, with a pseudogovernment, built on pseudoideas, a place after all where you can't live." In late 1987 the Slepaks said they no longer joined in human rights movements within the U.S.S.R.—efforts for which they had sacrificed so much over the years—because it was no longer their country, no longer a place in which they had any more of themselves to invest. Those resigned thoughts were sad for the U.S.S.R. and sad for the Slepaks. They were reminders of the emptiness that stands in the place of patriotism when governments are engines of abuse rather than inspiration for their people.

While the *refuseniks* became a subject of special international attention, theirs was by no means the only human rights issue in the Soviet Union. The story of Andrei Sakharov and Elena Bonner, sketched in Chapter 1, has all the elements of the noblest Greek tragedies, particularly *Antigone,* a play about the indomitable individual against the implacable state. Their saga, and the things they stand for, continues to unfold. It appears, finally, that they have regained their freedom to speak, to publish their views, even to travel.

The struggle symbolized by the Sakharovs will go on. The 1988 summit meetings in Moscow, when President Reagan challenged the Soviets on human rights, were a dramatic episode in the long process. The United States should and will continue to press this vital concern. The Soviets will make counterdemands on us. People in both countries will benefit from the contest.

Let's look at some of the valid points the Soviets score against us. One is the failure of the United States to ratify most of the treaties proclaiming and undertaking to honor human rights. The Soviet Union has ratified far more of these than we have. Most prominently, they have ratified both the International Covenant on Economic, Social, and Cultural Rights and the International

Covenant on Civil and Political Rights. President Carter signed both in 1977 and sent them to the Senate for ratification, where they have been stalled ever since. The Soviet Union ratified the Genocide Convention in 1954; the United States Senate finally consented to ratification in 1987, and adopted necessary legislation to implement its obligations under the convention in 1988.

The U.S.S.R., unlike the United States, has also ratified the International Convention on the Elimination of All Forms of Racial Discrimination, the International Convention on the Suppression and Punishment of the Crime of Apartheid, the Convention on the Elimination of All Forms of Discrimination against Women, the Convention on the Nonapplicability of Statutory Limitations to War Crimes and Crimes Against Humanity, the Convention for the Suppression of the Traffic in Persons and of the Exploitation or the Prostitution of Others, and the Convention on the Nationality of Married Women. Both have ratified the Slavery Convention of 1926 as amended, the 1953 Protocol amending the 1926 Slavery Convention, and the Convention on the Political Rights of Women. The only modern international human rights treaty that the United States has ratified and the U.S.S.R. has not is the Protocol Relating to the Status of Refugees. There are other agreements—such as the Optional Protocol that contains the teeth for the International Covenant on Civil and Political Rights—that neither has signed. The fact remains that the Soviets have an impressive lead.

Some people say that the Soviets sign because they are cynical; they know that they will not comply. But this simple-minded view is no excuse for us. For one thing, the case for Soviet violations is not clear. They deny most charges of violations, and charges are not convictions under any system. More important, by ratifying the treaties, they agree to be tested by the agreed international standards. Soviet defects can't justify our refusal to do likewise.

Why don't we sign? There are various reasons—none, in my opinion, very good ones. For example, to take one of the best, the Covenant on Civil and Political Rights contains provisions inconsistent with the American Constitution, requiring that nations joining the covenant adopt prohibitions against propaganda for aggressive war or racism. The idea of forbidding such propaganda is widely approved around the world, and it is difficult to say for sure that it's clearly wrong or unwise. But one *can* say that it's contrary to the principles of free speech in the First Amendment to the U.S. Constitution. Our commitment to free speech means that we permit propaganda most of us detest in the belief that truth and liberty are both best served when people can say just about anything, leaving listeners to make up their minds about what's right and wrong. So we couldn't go along with the covenant in this respect. But that's not a valid ground for refusing to join. Covenants, like other kinds of treaties, can be signed with "reservations," and we could make a reservation for this specific problem. It is not very likely that we'd suffer serious criticism for insisting on *more* freedom of speech than the covenant allows or requires.

There are other details in the arguments against the covenants, but none justify the unfortunate stand of the United States. For the most part, the failure to ratify reflects a long-standing strain of isolationism in our thinking about the world. Believing—correctly—that our actual performance in human rights is splendid, we don't want to be subjected to "meddling" from outsiders. The contradiction in this is especially unfortunate, since in practice we do honor the great majority of the provisions that we refuse to honor in form by ratification. By not ratifying, we actually give our critics and adversaries debating points against us despite the merits of our behavior. And we diminish the strength of our own voice in criticizing others. It is the rights, not the documents, that matter most, and we can hope that the Senate will finally realize this before too long, and vote for ratification.

Of course, the signing of covenants is a long way from the end of human rights problems. There is always considerable room for *interpretation*—for differences of opinion as to what the documents mean. These differences may be genuine. Sometimes they are pretextual—coverups for simple failures or refusals to honor the obligations. And sometimes, without even the pretense of a difference in interpretation, governments engage in flat-out violations of the rights they've agreed to respect. Our disagreements with the Soviets about emigration illustrate such problems.

The Covenant on Civil and Political Rights says, "Everyone shall be free to leave any country, including his own." That right could not be intended that broadly, without any limits whatever. And so the article goes on to say the right to emigrate "shall . . . be subject to . . . restrictions . . . which are provided by law, are necessary to protect national security, public order, public health or morals or the rights or freedoms of others, and are consistent with the other rights recognized in the present Covenant." Thus, an individual who has been charged with criminal activity and is out on bail pending trial may be denied the right to leave the country and so avoid trial and possible conviction. Similarly, it is arguable that if an individual knows military secrets, there may be good reason to prevent that person from leaving and possibly delivering those secrets to a hostile power. The United States does not actually have any restriction of this sort. On the other hand, the Soviet Union has often used this reason to deny individuals the right to leave.

In this claim of military secrets, and by a broad pattern of restrictions, the U.S.S.R., which has signed the Civil and Political Covenant, has shown itself to be far less respectful of the right to emigrate than the United States, which has not signed. Thousands of Soviet citizens have been barred from leaving the country without even the pretense of a reason that is valid under the covenant. For instance, the Soviet government has required that people wishing to emigrate produce a letter of invitation from a close relative living abroad, and that they have the consent of parents and other close relatives planning to remain in the U.S.S.R., even when there is no basis for supposing that these relatives need or are entitled to support from those seeking to emigrate.

The Soviet government has also blown the problem of military secrets to fantastic proportions. Scientists who last did secret work twenty or thirty years ago have been prevented from leaving on this ground. In almost every such case it is clear that the "secrets" have long since ceased to be classified information. In the fast-moving universe of science and technology, secrets rarely survive beyond ten years or so. Premier Gorbachev acknowledged that early in the era of *glasnost*. Still, many were barred from leaving because of this rule. On the other hand, the pressures of international disapproval as well as the insistent demands from within have opened the gates at long last for emigrés who once may have known secrets, as in the case of Aleksandr Lerner and Vladimir Slepak, mentioned earlier, and Naum Meiman, who was allowed to leave shortly after them.

Naum Meiman, a distinguished Soviet Jewish mathematician, applied to emigrate in August 1974. He had done some calculations, very possibly secret, in connection with the nuclear weapons program in the early 1950s. Nobody doubted that by 1974 the things he knew or had learned were no longer secret. But the Soviets said otherwise. Meanwhile, Meiman's wife, Inna, was stricken with cancer. Her only hope of survival lay in experimental cancer treatments in the United States. For three years the Meimans pleaded for her release to go for treatment in the United States. Finally, in January 1987, she was allowed to leave. But it was too late. She was dead three weeks later.

The wanton cruelty and Meiman's agony did not end with that. Approaching his eightieth birthday, he continued to seek permission and continued to be denied. His only living relatives—a married daughter, her husband and child—were in the United States. Meiman demanded to know whose judgment it was that he still had secrets. But that decision was itself kept secret, and there was no one to whom Meiman could talk and plead his case. As he said, both sadly and angrily, when I visited with him late in 1987, "I don't know who decided my fate." But whoever had decided, the word came out that Meiman would *never* be allowed to leave.

That chilling report could have meant a personal grudge, the stubborn closed mind of some bureaucrat, or any sort of real or imagined reason. It presented this sick, aged, weary man with a

148

hopeless prospect. Still, he persisted in his demands, and protests from around the world continued to beat against the Soviet walls. And then, early in 1988, with as little explanation as there had been for the refusals, Meiman got permission to leave.

That heartbreaking story of a single individual supports charges from the western world that the Soviet government has been capable of unspeakable, seemingly mindless cruelty. At the same time it reminds us that we are right to believe we should never give up, and that we must try to understand the gulf between us and other nations in order to deal effectively with them.

Why, after all, are we so much more willing than the Soviets to honor the right to emigrate? In an unusual interview with an American TV newscaster toward the end of 1987, Gorbachev gave part of the answer. In response to a question about Soviet hostility to emigration, he first pointed to a difference in perspective. "I understand the concern of the American side to some extent, since that is a nation that was formed . . . largely as a result of emigration processes. And therefore our views are different." He went on to a more adversarial argument, saying that what Americans were doing was "organizing" a "brain drain." He further said, "We will never accept a condition when the people are being exhorted from outside to leave their country."

From our side, we don't worry about our people being "exhorted" to move away and go live in the Soviet Union or anywhere else. But we believe that the Soviets have reason to fear that allowing too many people out, and allowing word to come back about the difference between life in the U.S.S.R. and elsewhere in the world, could undermine morale in the U.S.S.R. and subvert their claim to a better way of life than that in the West. Like most arguments, this one is not open and shut. Some Soviet citizens who have emigrated, even some Jews, have chosen to return to their homeland. Some find it hard to adapt to a regime in which they have to make many decisions that were made for them by the government in the U.S.S.R. Life in the United States can be hard for those accustomed to the cradle-to-grave security of the Soviet system. Ofra Bikel, creator of the documentary *The Russians Are Here*, observed, "American freedom can be a tough thing, it can be the freedom to fail, the freedom to be kicked out of your apartment for not paying the rent." One writer interviewed in her film had not found success in the United States; he said, "I miss the KGB, which paid attention to me. They were the first to read my works and read them carefully. It was great to have such close attention. I felt important."[4] The great majority, however, do not choose to go back. In the end, whatever balance we strike on a complex question like this, each government will continue to be convinced of its own superiority.

But there is reason to hope that all of us, on both sides, will benefit from the continued dialogue and debate. The most dramatic cases may be those where prisoners are freed or people are allowed to leave the country. But there are broader, less spectacular subjects on which mutual criticism seems healthful. The Soviets boast that they have no unemployment, no homeless, and no racism like ours. They probably misstate, or at least exaggerate, on all counts. With respect to unemployment, while there is no "official" joblessness, there are work problems in the U.S.S.R., in some ways more oppressive than ours. A disfavored writer or a Jew wishing to work as a teacher of Hebrew may be unable or unwilling to work at an officially approved place. Despite the claim of full employment, there are people who have difficulty finding jobs. Because unemployment is not supposed to exist, such people may be prosecuted for the communist crime of "parasitism" and thrown in jail for their departure from the officially stated ideal.

As for homelessness, although they have no visibly homeless people, the Soviets are far from the millennium in housing their people. Newlyweds or people who want to marry have enormous difficulty finding places to live. Multiple families share cramped, dingy apartments. Lack of space has tended to keep families notably small. Urban couples with more than one child are exceptional.

Finally, even apart from their notorious mistreatment of such minorities as Jews and Gypsies, the Soviets' record with respect to

150

minorities is not exemplary. True, they have lionized an occasional black like Paul Robeson or Oliver Tambo, head of the African National Congress, when such people have been in conflict with their own governments. But only a handful of blacks, usually as students, have ever lived for any time in the U.S.S.R. And reports are mixed at best as to whether these small numbers have in fact enjoyed the easy acceptance that a nonracist society would offer.

But there are more profitable ways for us to exploit Soviet criticisms than to point at their failings. We can take heed of our own deficiencies. We can remind our Soviet competitors that criticisms of our failings are freely voiced within our country as well as from the outside. We can press for the continuation and expansion of the openness—*glasnost*—begun under Gorbachev. We can, above all, proceed to improve life for our homeless, our unemployed, and our still numerous victims of racial discrimination.

There are signs that this approach can bear fruit within the U.S.S.R. as well as here. The great promise of Gorbachev, which still remains to be kept, lies in the public recognition of deep Soviet imperfections. This extends to human rights violations. Now Soviet critics not only condemn the crimes of Stalin, but concede that there are serious wrongs in their society to this day. By word and deed—in their treatment of Sakharov, the *refuseniks*, and others—the Soviets acknowledge evils and the need for correction.

Neither they nor we can expect paradise overnight. The two systems, so markedly different, will remain in conflict. We will continue to need active pressure, sticks as well as carrots, to insist that the Soviets honor human rights and their formal promises to do so. There will be similar occasions for the Soviets to return the favor in dealing with us.

Insofar as the contention between these superpowers is over human rights, there is a prospect that human beings in both countries—and elsewhere—will be the beneficiaries. Taunted by the U.S.S.R., we may ratify the covenants sooner than we otherwise might have. If we bait each other about prison conditions, prisoners in our state penitentiaries as well as in Siberia may be treated more humanely. People there may be able to speak more freely, vote in genuine elections, and worry less about the surveillance of the KGB. People here may be better housed and respected. That is a vision, a glimpse of a possible future, and not necessarily an idle dream.

CHAPTER 10

The Human Rights That Are Universal

The General Assembly Proclaims this Universal Declaration of Human Rights as a common standard of achievement for all peoples and nations, to the end that every individual and every organ of society, keeping this Declaration in mind, shall strive by teaching and education to promote respect for these rights and freedoms and by progressive measures, national and international, to secure their universal and effective recognition and observance, both among the peoples of Member States themselves and among the peoples of territories under their jurisdiction.
Universal Declaration of Human Rights,
December 10, 1948

The Universal Declaration of Human Rights and the two main covenants represent centuries of aspiration, invested with the creative energies and the blood of our ancestors. They say a great deal about the past and the hopes of our civilized world.

When it promulgated the declaration on December 10, 1948, the United Nations General Assembly called on member countries "to cause it to be disseminated, displayed, read and expounded principally in schools and other educational institutions." People everywhere are entitled to know and act upon these universal rights. In many countries people have paid with their freedom and their lives for seeking to spread the message of the declaration. All of us who live in the "free world" must try to know and to understand the protections and the aspirations embodied in the declaration, the covenants, and other international charters of human rights.

153

This book is meant to contribute to that knowledge and understanding. In the light of the history, the blood, and the sacrifices that led to these papers, it should be of interest to look more closely at the specific rights. In the Appendix you will find excerpts from the preamble and five of the main documents: the Universal Declaration, the Convention on the Prevention and Punishment of the Crime of Genocide, the International Convention on the Elimination of All Forms of Racial Discrimination, the International Covenant on Economic, Social, and Cultural Rights, and the International Covenant on Civil and Political Rights (as well as its Optional Protocol). The words are vital and carefully chosen. Words of this nature take a lot of interpreting and can be subjects of considerable disagreement. Interpreting the U.S. Constitution, relatively few pages in length, has filled libraries with judicial decisions, books, and articles on what the words mean and how the meanings may change with changing times and circumstances. Problems of international law, including human rights, are similar to a degree. Scholars and judges have shaped and expanded the meanings of words in both the declaration and the covenants. They are well worth study and appreciation.

It pays to stop for just a moment over a slightly technical but quite important point of information. The Universal Declaration is not a treaty or a "binding" international agreement. It cannot in itself be enforced as a matter of strict international law. The later covenants embody that relatively more substantial legal status and are, in principle at least, enforceable. "Binding" or not, the Universal Declaration (adopted unanimously by the 1948 General Assembly, with the Soviet bloc abstaining then, but later accepting the declaration in the Helsinki Final Act of 1975)[1] is properly viewed as a milestone in human rights history. The rights it declares are not empty ideals, but prescribed goals and standards against which the behavior of every nation may meaningfully be tested. The covenants, though the United States has failed thus far to ratify them, are likely to be of increasing importance. It is useful to know all three of these basic documents and the higher standards to which they can lead us.

Here we will look at the declaration for its broad outlines and for important points about the origins, the basic premises, and the potential lines of future development. In the preamble we hear immediately echoes of the American Declaration of Independence and the French Declaration of the Rights of Man. The commitment to "equal and inalienable rights" is like our declaration and significantly different at the same time. The idea of equality is not sullied by an acceptance of slavery (as it was in our own Constitution until after the Civil War), which is explicitly denounced in Article 4 of the Universal Declaration. The goal in the second "whereas" clause of "a world in which human beings shall enjoy freedom of speech and belief and freedom from fear and want" is the affirmation of the Four Freedoms proclaimed by President Franklin Roosevelt on the eve of American entry into World War II. The earlier reference in the same clause to "barbarous acts which have outraged the conscience of mankind" embodies the memory, sharp and fresh in 1948, of what the Nazis and Japanese had wrought. The fifth "whereas" clause, on the equal rights of men *and women* introduces a different sector of the struggle for human rights. This sense of something old and new, along with things that scarcely exist yet except as aspirations, comes through over and over again.

The first twenty-one articles of the Universal Declaration, like the later Covenant on Civil and Political Rights, are reminiscent of the Bill of Rights in the American Constitution in their essential emphasis on freedom from hurtful or oppressive treatment by government. These articles are for the most part protections *against* government power rather than demands for the helpful exercise of that power. They include the right not to be tortured (Article 5), not to be arbitrarily arrested (Article 9), not to be condemned as a criminal except after a fair and public trial (Articles 10 and 11), and an array of basic freedoms—of religion, thought, expression, and peaceful assembly (Articles 18–20).

Among the omissions Americans will notice is the right to a jury trial and the prohibition (found in our First Amendment) against any law "respecting an establishment of religion"—which means, greatly oversimplifying it, a prohibition against any established church and against government support or favoritism for any or all religions. While the separation of church and state has surely proved vital for pluralistic America, the Universal Declaration in effect tells us it is not essential everywhere to an acceptable list of the basic human rights. In a number of countries where religious freedom appears to be respected, there exist relationships between government and religion that would constitute forbidden "establishments" under the American First Amendment. In the same way, however precious we deem the right to a jury trial, many countries manage to administer fair systems of both civil and criminal justice without juries. These examples remind us that no single country's prescription of rights would work for the whole world. Nevertheless there is a wide consensus on the basic rights in the Universal Declaration.

It is also instructive for Americans to note that the Universal Declaration and the covenants contain a substantial number of protections and freedoms that are not provided for in our own Bill of Rights. In many cases these are rights that our courts have evolved, although the Constitution does not mention them explicitly. Among the best known of these is the presumption of innocence. It is stated in the Universal Declaration (Article 11) and honored in the United States although it is not included in our Bill of Rights. Another is the right of privacy, protecting a still incompletely defined zone of personal choices and relationships that include, for instance, the right to decide whether or not to use birth control devices. Other rights that are not specifically mentioned in the Constitution that the Supreme Court has recognized include the right to travel (Article 13) and the right to marry (Article 16).

The Universal Declaration places much greater emphasis on equality than our Constitution does. In direct, clear language, Article 2 says, "Everyone is entitled to all the rights and freedoms set forth in this Declaration without distinction of any kind, such as race, colour, sex, language, religion, political or other opinion, national or social origin, property, birth or other status." In contrast, the constitutional protection against discrimination has evolved from the Fourteenth Amendment's guarantee of "equal protection of the laws." Under this provision, the Supreme Court has held racial discrimination unconstitutional. On the other hand, sex discrimination is subject to less stringent scrutiny, and the proposed Equal Rights Amendment to the U.S. Constitution, which would clearly have barred discrimination on the basis of sex, failed to win ratification. By and large, the federal and state governments have stepped in to fill this gap by passing civil rights laws and thereby promoting equality.

As the years roll on it may be expected that the meanings of these large concepts will expand and become more precise. Lawyers and others will perceive the interplay between the words of the international charters and the experience within individual nations. Looking again at Article 12, it would not be surprising to find international lawyers trying to spell out the meaning of "arbitrary interference with . . . [a person's] home or correspondence" studying and citing cases from our Supreme Court decided under our Fourth Amendment, which says, "The right of the people to be secure in their persons, houses, papers, and effects against unreasonable searches and seizures shall not be violated."

As you proceed to Article 22 of the Universal Declaration and those following it, plus the implementing provisions of the Covenant on Economic, Social, and Cultural Rights, you come to broad categories of human rights missing from our Constitution and almost wholly absent from the guaranties our courts have inferred from the Constitution. Governmental assurances like "the right to social security" (Article 22), "the right to work" (Article 23), "the right to rest and leisure" (Article 24), to an "adequate" standard of living (Article 25), and the others found in the last third of the Universal Declaration differ in essential nature from the protections *against* government found in our eighteenth-century Constitution. These are positive entitlements, demands upon government to act affirmatively for the welfare and material security of the people.

Although President Franklin Roosevelt spoke of the "freedom

from want," that freedom was totally absent from our Constitution. Today, however, many economic rights have been guaranteed by statutes, on the state as well as the federal level. Americans tend to think that basic rights are only those embodied in a constitution, but that is a misconception. Rights can be achieved in other ways, for example, by legislative enactment and executive order. The question of rights, after all, is not simply what the national constitution says, but what is actually done by the government to further the cause of human rights. Many tyrannical governments have constitutions that have broader protections for human rights—for civil and political rights as well as economic rights—than ours, but they pay only lip service to the words of their constitutions.

In the American federal system, the states have traditionally been responsible for economic and social legislation. Many state constitutions guarantee economic and social rights. Perhaps the most widely accepted of the declaration's economic rights that is commonly found in most state constitutions is the entitlement to an education. This is another of the rights for which the United States was among the world's leaders. Article 26 of the Universal Declaration says in part, "Education shall be free, at least in the elementary and fundamental stages. Elementary education shall be compulsory." Every state and the District of Columbia provide for free public education from first to twelfth grades, and education is usually compulsory between ages six and sixteen. Many states also provide low-cost college and graduate school educations for their residents, and both federal and state governments offer scholarships and guaranteed loans to disadvantaged students. More recently, the federal government has provided for free education for handicapped children.

It was not until the Great Depression that the federal government began to get involved in meeting the economic needs of Americans. President Franklin Roosevelt described the depth of the national problem in his second inaugural address when he said, "I see one third of a nation ill-housed, ill-clad, ill-nourished." He devoted most of his energies in his first two terms to providing "freedom from want." Going down the list of freedoms in the Covenant on Economic, Social, and Cultural Rights, it is clear that many of those rights were and continue to be protected by Roosevelt's New Deal programs: the Fair Labor Standards Act provides a minimum wage (originally twenty-five cents an hour) and a maximum on hours (forty per week) (Article 7) and forbids child labor (Article 10, Section 3); the National Labor Relations Act protects the right to form trade unions and bargain collectively, among other rights of labor and management (Article 8); and the Social Security Act provides old-age pensions among other forms of social security (Article 9). Since these original portions of the New Deal, other federal programs have been adopted that protect other human rights. For example, the Occupational Safety and Health Administration (OSHA) was created to provide safe and healthful working conditions (Article 7, Section B).

The issue of economic rights has been hotly debated in this century. The New Deal programs were very controversial when adopted and are still disputed by some individuals. Although some economic rights—like the right to an education—are widely accepted as obligations of the state or federal governments, others are not. The right to health care (Article 12 of the Covenant on Economic, Social, and Cultural Rights) has been the subject of intense national debate. Through Medicaid and Medicare, both passed in 1965, the federal and state governments provide assistance to the poor and the elderly. But many Americans, particularly the "working poor," have no health insurance and therefore cannot afford necessary health care. In the 1970s, Senator Edward Kennedy introduced a bill for national health insurance for all Americans, but that proposal does not yet have the support it needs to become the law of the land. Most other western countries—England, for one—provide for national health insurance. Yet for many Americans it smacks of "socialism." While the right to an education is essential to the American dream that anyone can succeed here, the right to health insurance suggests a kind of collectivist interdependence that some believe is "un-American."

This is, of course, only a fleeting reference to a long and complicated story that will continue to unfold over the years ahead. The fact is that the United States joined—in fact, led—in the adoption of the Universal Declaration, economic and social rights and all. As noted in Chapter 3, Eleanor Roosevelt, speaking for the United States, agreed to the inclusion of social and economic rights as a compromise with the Soviet bloc. It might have been supposed that the richest country in the world, as we undoubtedly were in 1948, would not hesitate to endorse rights to minimum food, clothing, shelter, and other bare decencies. In any event, it may have been thought that as mere aspirations, not legally enforceable, the array of economic, social, and cultural "rights" could not be objectionable.

As a general matter, economic and social rights are truly of a different order from civil or political rights. Violations of the right not to be tortured or killed by officials are readily defined and identified. The right "to a standard of living adequate for . . . health . . . , including food, clothing, housing and medical care" (Article 25 of the Universal Declaration) is a good deal more complex. How do you define that right in a poor country like Bangladesh? Is it different in a rich nation like the United States or West Germany? How can this right be enforced? The covenant calls upon each state party "to take steps . . . to the maximum of its available resources, with a view to achieving progressively the full realization of the rights recognized in the present Covenant by all appropriate means." Each nation's obligation is limited to "the maximum of its available resources."

It may well be that the United States is right in placing higher store by the civil and political than the economic and social rights. Still, our professed ideals should have led us to join in the international commitment to share among ourselves sufficiently to assure all of us an "adequate" standard of living. Lawyers and politicians may argue about what is "adequate." But we all know that the homeless and hungry lack adequate housing and food. The universal aspirations for shared enjoyment of the world's economic, social, and cultural goods must win our enthusiastic support rather than our aloof skepticism and ambivalence.

The United States' ratification of the covenants and other human rights treaties to which we are not yet a party would serve as a symbol of what is a vital reality—that we are, in truth, a leader in the quest for human rights. We must continue to lead; we must continue our quest. Though the United States has made great strides toward advancing human rights, we still have a long way to go. Our poverty and hunger, the strains of racism in our culture, our brutal prisons, our mistreatment of certain immigrants, our grossly imperfect courts—a host of wrongs remain to be righted. But we must continue to struggle toward our goals. The vindication of human rights at home and around the world should be at the top of our agenda as a nation, and a high priority for each of us individually.

NOTES

Chapter 1: Human Rights—Victims and Heroes

1. John Simpson and Jana Bennett, *The Disappeared and the Mothers of the Plaza* (New York: St. Martin's Press, 1985), p. 157.
2. Simpson and Bennett, pp. 154–55.
3. Jean-Pierre Bousquet, *Las Locas de la Plaza de Mayo* (Buenos Aires: Fundación para la Democracia en Argentina, 1983), p. 48.
4. Simpson and Bennett, p. 162; *Nunca Más: The Report of the Argentine National Commission on the Disappeared* (New York: Farrar, Straus & Giroux, 1986), p. 343.
5. *Nunca Más*, p. 343.
6. Some of the story has been published in Sakharov's writings. See listings in the Bibliography.
7. Nelson Mandela, *The Struggle Is My Life* (New York: Pathfinder Press, 1986), pp. 195–96.
8. Jorge Valls, *Twenty Years and Forty Days* (New York: Americas Watch Committee, 1986), p. iv.
9. Sharansky published his own story in a 1988 book, *Fear No Evil* (New York: Farrar, Straus & Giroux).
10. *New York Times*, Oct. 21, 1987, p. A7.

Chapter 2: Lawless Governments

1. Anne Frank, *The Diary of a Young Girl* (New York: Pocket Books, 1952), p. 48.

2. J. N. Westwood, *Endurance and Endeavor: Russian History, 1812–1980*, 2nd ed. (New York: Oxford University Press, 1981), p. 296.
3. *Nunca Más: The Report of the Argentine National Commission On the Disappeared* (New York: Farrar, Straus & Giroux, 1986), p. 4.
4. Raúl Alfonsín, "Building Democracy," *Yale Journal of International Law*, vol. 12 (1987), pp. 121–22.
5. "Review and Outlook: Persecuting the Baha'is," *Wall Street Journal*, Nov. 12, 1987.

Chapter 3: Out of the Ashes

1. Adolf Hitler, *Mein Kampf* (New York: Reynal & Hitchcock, 1939), p. 405.
2. Hitler, p. 640.
3. See Joseph P. Lash, *Eleanor: The Years Alone* (New York: Norton, 1972).
4. Eleanor Roosevelt, *The Autobiography of Eleanor Roosevelt* (New York: Harper, 1961), pp. 302–3.
5. For an account of that fascinating, arduous process see Eleanor Roosevelt, *Autobiography*, pp. 314–23, and Lash, *Eleanor*, pp. 55–58.
6. Sir Zafrulla Khan, the foreign minister of Pakistan, disagreed with that interpretation of the Koran and voted for the declaration. He said, "I understand the Koran to say, 'He who can believe shall believe; he who cannot believe, shall disbelieve; the only unforgivable sin is to be a hypocrite' " (Eleanor Roosevelt, *Autobiography*, p. 322).

Chapter 4: Governments as Human Rights Guardians

1. *United Nations Chronicle*, Feb. 1987, p. 120.
2. John Simpson and Jana Bennett, *The Disappeared and the Mothers of the Plaza* (New York: St. Martin's Press, 1985), p. 214.

3. Nelson Mandela, *The Struggle Is My Life* (New York: Pathfinder Press, 1986), p. 129.
4. *Human Rights Internet Reporter* 10 (Jan.–Apr. 1985), pp. 319–20.
5. *New York Times*, March 13, 1987, p. A35.
6. *United Nations Chronicle*, Dec. 1977, p. 9.
7. *Time*, Nov. 7, 1977, p. 36.
8. *New York Times*, Mar. 6, 1987, p. A6.
9. William Korey, *Human Rights and the Helsinki Accord* (New York: Foreign Policy Association, 1983), p. 52.

Chapter 5: The United States and Human Rights Abroad

1. *New York Times*, Feb. 20, 1987, p. A1.
2. *New York Times*, Apr. 25, 1981, p. 6.
3. Winston Churchill, *The Second World War*, vol. 3: *The Grand Alliance* (Boston: Houghton Mifflin, 1950), p. 370.
4. Lawyers Committee for Human Rights, *The Philippines: A Country in Crisis* (New York: Lawyers Committee for Human Rights, Dec. 1983), p. 4.
5. *New York Times*, Oct. 7, 1988, p. A12.
6. *Nation*, Oct. 12, 1974, p. 323.
7. U.S. Congress, House of Representatives Committee on Foreign Affairs, Subcommittee on International Organizations and Movements, *Human Rights in the World Community: A Call for U.S. Leadership*, Mar. 27, 1974, p. 9.
8. *Congressional Quarterly*, July 19, 1986.

Chapter 6: Worldwide Volunteers

1. Jonathan Power, *Amnesty International: The Human Rights Story* (New York: McGraw-Hill, 1981), p. 9.
2. Power, p. 21.
3. Amnesty International, U.S. Section, Bulletin No. 6 (Fall 1985), p. 3.

4. Ibid.

5. Power, p. 32.

6. The Dreyfus Affair involved the court-martial and conviction of a French Jewish army officer, Alfred Dreyfus, for alleged espionage in the 1890s. Through a long struggle for his vindication, his family and friends established that the conviction was built on false evidence. Much of it was contrived by high military officials. The indications of anti-Semitism as the basis for the travesty were strong and clear. Dreyfus was ultimately vindicated, but only after he had suffered for many years, including a period of imprisonment in a solitary cell on Devil's Island.

7. The Robert Bernstein quotations are from *Current Biography*, July 1987, pp. 5 and 6.

8. *American Lawyer*, Sept. 1987, pp. 97, 98.

9. In January 1989, Stroessner was deposed in a military coup. Whether the new military regime will be better remains to be seen.

10. *Life*, July 17, 1970, p. 27.

11. *Life*, July 17, 1970, p. 2A.

12. Greathead, R. Scott, *Human Rights Advocacy in the Philippines: A Report of a Mission of Inquiry of the Association of the Bar of the City of New York*, Nov. 1, 1985, p. 12.

13. William Zabel, Diane Orentlicher, and David Nechman, *Human Rights and the Administration of Justice in Chile: Report of a Delegation of the Association of the Bar of the City of New York and the International Bar Association*, Mar. 31, 1987, p. 8.

Chapter 7: Punishing Human Rights Violators

1. *New York Times*, Dec. 31, 1983, p. 7.

2. *In These Times*, May 20–26, 1987, p. 9.

3. *Nunca Más: The Report of the Argentine National Commission on the Disappeared* (New York: Farrar, Straus & Giroux, 1986), p. xxii; Americas Watch, *Truth and Partial Justice in Argentina* (New York: Americas Watch, 1987), pp. 36–37.

4. Americas Watch, *Truth and Partial Justice*, pp. 48–49; *New York Times*, Dec. 3, 1986, p. A3.
5. *New York Times*, Mar. 4, 1987, p. A10.
6. *New York Times*, Apr. 19, 1987, p. A17.
7. *New York Times*, Apr. 19, 1987, p. A1.
8. *New York Times*, Apr. 17, 1987, p. A3.
9. *New York Times*, Apr. 17, 1987, p. A1.
10. *New York Times*, May 17, 1987, sec. 4, p. 2.
11. *New York Times*, June 24, 1987, p. A5.
12. *Time*, July 6, 1987, p. 17.
13. *Wall Street Journal*, August 27, 1987, p. 14.
14. Ibid.
15. It has since been published in the United States under the title *Torture in Brazil*. See listing in the Bibliography under "Catholic Church. Archdiocese of São Paulo."
16. Lawyers Committee for Human Rights, *Zimbabwe: Wages of War* (New York: Lawyers Committee for Human Rights, 1986), p. 90.
17. *New York Times*, Apr. 28, 1988, p. 47, and May 12, 1988, p. A16.
18. *Filartiga v. Pena-Irala*, 630 F.2d 876, 878, 884 (1980). After the Second Circuit held that the court had jurisdiction over Pena-Irala, he defaulted, and a judgment was entered against him: $5,175,000 for Dolly Filartiga and $5,210,364 for Joel Filartiga. See *Filartiga v. Pena-Irala*, 577 F. Supp. 860 (E.D.N.Y. 1984).

Chapter 8: The United States: Human Rights at Home

1. David J. Garrow, *Bearing the Cross: Martin Luther King and the Southern Christian Leadership Conference* (New York: Morrow, 1986), pp. 283–84.
2. Juan Williams, *Eyes on the Prize: America's Civil Rights Years, 1954–1965* (New York: Viking, 1986), p. 254.

3. Eleanor Roosevelt, *On My Own* (New York: Harper, 1958), p. 63.
4. Williams, p. 100.
5. Williams, pp. 101–2.
6. Williams, p. 66.
7. Williams, p. 68.
8. Williams, p. 76.
9. Williams, p. 77.
10. Ibid.
11. Williams, p. 127.
12. Williams, p. 138.
13. Williams, p. 139.
14. Leon Howard Sullivan, *Build, Brother, Build* (Philadelphia: Macrae Smith, 1969), p. 68.
15. Williams, p. 145.
16. Williams, p. 147.
17. Ibid.
18. Williams, p. 148.
19. Williams, p. 208.
20. For more information about the conduct and conviction of Cecil Price, see, in addition to the Williams book, *New York Times*, Oct. 21 and Dec. 30, 1967; *Newsweek*, Oct. 23, 1967; *Time*, Oct. 20, 1967; Seth Cagin and Philip Dray, *We Are Not Afraid* (New York: Macmillan, 1988); Mary King, *Freedom Song* (New York: Morrow, 1987).
21. *New York Times*, Oct. 22, 1967, p. 32.
22. *New York Times*, Nov. 5, 1967, sec. 4, p. 6E.
23. Quoted in William E. Leuchtenberg, ed., *The Unfinished Century: America Since 1900* (Boston: Little, Brown, 1973), p. 771.
24. *New York Times*, Oct. 17, 1986, p. B2.
25. Helsinki Watch and Lawyers Committee for Human Rights, *Mother of Exiles: Refugees Imprisoned in America* (New York: Fund for Free Expression, 1986), pp. 72–73.

Chapter 9: U.S. v. U.S.S.R.: Competition

1. *New York Times*, Dec. 1, 1987, p. A12.
2. The *Protocols* was a patently fabricated book that appeared in Russia early in this century. Apparently concocted by the czarist secret police, the book purported to be by a group of Jews plotting to control the world.
3. Natan Sharansky, *Fear No Evil* (New York: Farrar, Straus & Giroux, 1988), p. 415.
4. *New York Times*, Oct. 9, 1986, p. A4.

Chapter 10: The Human Rights That Are Universal

1. As noted in Chapter 3, Saudi Arabia and South Africa also abstained.

BIBLIOGRAPHY

American Association for the International Commission of Jurists. *Guatemala: A New Beginning*. New York: American Association for the International Commission of Jurists, 1987.

Americas Watch. *Human Rights in Nicaragua, 1986*. New York: Americas Watch Committee, 1987.

Americas Watch, *Truth and Partial Justice in Argentina*. New York: Americas Watch, 1987.

Americas Watch and British Parliamentary Human Rights Group, *Human Rights in Guatemala During President Cerezo's First Year*. New York: Americas Watch, 1987.

Amnesty International. *Human Rights in Chile: The Role of the Medical Profession*. New York: Amnesty International, 1986.

Amnesty International. *Report 1986*, and *Financial Supplement 1986*. London: Amnesty International Publications, 1986.

Amnesty International, *Torture in the Eighties*. London: Amnesty International Publications, 1984.

Amnesty International. *Voices for Freedom: An Amnesty International Anthology*. London: Amnesty International Publications, 1986.

Berger, Jason. *A New Deal for the World: Eleanor Roosevelt and American Foreign Policy*. New York: Social Science Monographs, 1981.

Bonner, Elena. *Alone Together*. New York: Knopf, 1986.

Bousquet, Jean-Pierre. *Las Locas de La Plaza de Mayo*. Buenos Aires: Fundación para la Democracia en Argentina, 1983.

Brackman, Arnold C. *The Other Nuremberg: The Untold Story of the Tokyo War Crime Trials*. New York: Morrow, 1987.

Brauer, Carl M. *John F. Kennedy and the Second Reconstruction*. New York: Columbia University Press, 1977.

Brown, Peter G., and Douglas Maclean, ed. *Human Rights and U.S. Foreign Policy: Principles and Applications*. Lexington, Mass.: Lexington Books, 1979.

Cagin, Seth, and Philip Dray. *We Are Not Afraid*. New York: Macmillan, 1988.

Catholic Church. Archdiocese of São Paulo. *Torture in Brazil: The Pervasive Use of Torture by Brazilian Military Governments, 1964–77*. New York: Vintage Books, 1986.

Churchill, Winston. *The Second World War*, vol. 3: *The Grand Alliance*. Boston: Houghton Mifflin, 1950.

Coyle, David Cushman. *The United Nations and How It Works*. New York: Columbia University Press, 1969.

Dorfman, Ariel. *Widows*. New York: Pantheon Books, 1983.

Eichelberg, Clark M. *UN: The First Twenty-five Years*. New York: Harper, 1980.

Everyone's United Nations, annual publication by United Nations Department of Public Information.

Frank, Anne. *The Diary of a Young Girl*. New York: Pocket Books, 1952.

Garling, Marguerite, ed. *The Human Rights Handbook*. New York: Facts on File, 1979.

Garrow, David J. *Bearing the Cross: Martin Luther King and the Southern Christian Leadership Conference*. New York: Morrow, 1986.

Gilbert, Martin. *Shcharansky: Hero of Our Time*. New York: Viking, 1986.

Goodrich, Leland M. *The United Nations in a Changing World*. New York: Columbia University Press, 1974.

Greathead, R. Scott. *Human Rights Advocacy in the Philippines: A Report of a Mission of Inquiry of the Association of the Bar of the City of New York* (Nov. 1, 1985).

Helsinki Watch and Lawyers Committee for Human Rights. *Mother of Exiles: Refugees Imprisoned in America*. New York: Fund for Free Expression, 1986.

Hill, Gerald, and Kathleen Thompson Hill. *Aquino Assassination*. Sonoma, Calif.: Hilltop Publishing, 1983.

Hitler, Adolf. *Mein Kampf.* New York: Reynal & Hitchcock, 1939.

Hoff-Wilson, Joan, and Marjorie Lightman. *Without Precedent: The Life and Career of Eleanor Roosevelt.* Bloomington: Indiana University Press, 1984.

Human Rights Watch. *Annual Report, 1987.*

———. *The Persecution of Human Rights Monitors, December 1986–December 1987.* New York: Human Rights Watch, 1987.

Human Rights Watch and the Lawyers Committee for Human Rights. *The Reagan Administration's Record on Human Rights in 1987.* New York: Human Rights Watch, Dec. 1987.

Humphrey, John P. *Human Rights and the United Nations: A Great Adventure.* Dobbs Ferry, N.Y.: Transnational Publishers, 1984.

Kay, David A., ed. *The Changing United Nations.* New York: Academy of Political Science, 1977.

King, Mary. *Freedom Song.* New York: Morrow, 1987.

Kissinger, Henry. *Years of Upheaval.* Boston: Little, Brown, 1982.

Korey, William. *Human Rights and the Helsinki Accord.* New York: Foreign Policy Association, 1983.

Lake, Anthony. *The "Tar Baby Option": American Foreign Policy Toward Southern Rhodesia.* New York: Columbia University Press, 1976.

Lamson, Peggy. *Roger Baldwin: Founder of the American Civil Liberties Union.* Boston: Houghton Mifflin, 1976.

Lash, Joseph P. *Eleanor: The Years Alone.* New York: Norton, 1972.

Lawyers Committee for Human Rights. *El Salvador: Human Rights Dismissed.* New York: Lawyers Committee for Human Rights, 1986.

———. *Kampuchea: After the Worst.* New York: Lawyers for Committee for Human Rights, 1985.

———. *The Philippines: A Country in Crisis.* New York: Lawyers Committee for Human Rights, Dec. 1983.

———. *"Salvaging Democracy": Human Rights in the Philippines.* New York: Lawyers Committee for Human Rights, 1985.

———. *Seeking Shelter: Cambodians in Thailand.* New York: Lawyers Committee for Human Rights, 1987.

————. *The War Against Children: South Africa's Youngest Victims.* New York: Lawyers Committee for Human Rights, 1986.

————. *Zimbabwe: Wages of War.* New York: Lawyers Committee for Human Rights, 1986.

Lawyers Committee for International Human Rights. *Nicaragua: Revolutionary Justice—A Report on Human Rights and the Judicial System.* New York: Lawyers Committee for International Human Rights, April 1985.

————. *Justice Denied: A Report on Twelve Unresolved Human Rights Cases in El Salvador.* New York: Lawyers Committee for International Human Rights, 1985.

————. *Uruguay: The End of a Nightmare?* New York: Lawyers Committee for International Human Rights, 1984.

Leuchtenberg, William E., ed. *The Unfinished Century: America Since 1900.* Boston: Little, Brown, 1973.

Loescher, Gil, and John Ascanler. *Calculated Kindness: Refugees and America's Half-Open Door, 1945 to the Present.* New York: Free Press, 1986.

Mandela, Nelson. *No Easy Walk to Freedom: Articles, Speeches and Trial Addresses of Nelson Mandela.* London: Heinemann, 1964.

————. *The Struggle Is My Life.* New York: Pathfinder Press, 1986.

Mandela, Winnie. *Part of My Soul Went with Him.* New York: Norton, 1984.

Mendes-Flohr, Paul R., and Jehuda Reinharz. *The Jews in the Modern World.* New York: Oxford University Press, 1980.

Michel, Henry. *The Second World War.* New York: Praeger, 1968.

Mower, A. Glenn, Jr. *The United States, the United Nations and Human Rights: The Eleanor Roosevelt and Jimmy Carter Eras.* Westport, Conn.: Greenwood Press, 1979.

Nunca Más: The Report of the Argentine National Commission on the Disappeared. New York: Farrar, Straus & Giroux, 1986.

Orbach, William S. *The American Movement to Aid Soviet Jews.* Amherst: University of Massachusetts Press, 1979.

Patterson, William L., ed. *We Charge Genocide: The Crime of the Government Against the Negro People.* New York: International Publishers, 1970.

174

Power, Jonathan. *Amnesty International: The Human Rights Story*. New York: McGraw-Hill, 1981.

Ramcharan, B. G., ed. *Human Rights: Thirty Years After the Universal Declaration*. Norwell, Mass.: Kluwer Academic Pubs., 1978.

Robertson, A. H. *Human Rights in the World*, 2nd ed. New York: St. Martin's Press, 1982.

Roosevelt, Eleanor. *The Autobiography of Eleanor Roosevelt*. New York: Harper, 1961.

Roosevelt, Eleanor. *On My Own*. New York: Harper, 1958.

Rubenstein, Joshua. *Soviet Dissidents*. Boston: Beacon Press, 1980.

Rubin, Barry M., and Elizabeth P. Spiro. *Human Rights and U.S. Foreign Policy*. Boulder, Colo.: West View Press, 1979.

Sakharov, Andrei D. *Alarm and Hope*. New York: Vintage, 1978.

————. *Andrei Sakharov and Peace*, ed. Edward D. Lozansky. New York: Avon, 1985.

————. *My Country and the World*. New York: Trilateral Commission, 1975.

————. *On Sakharov*. New York: Random House, 1982.

————. *Progress, Coexistence and Intellectual Freedom*. New York: Norton, 1968.

————. *Sakharov Speaks*. New York: Random House, 1974.

Sharansky, Natan. *Fear No Evil*. New York: Random House, 1988.

Simpson, John, and Jana Bennett. *The Disappeared and the Mothers of the Plaza: The Story of 11,000 Argentinians Who Vanished*. New York: St. Martin's Press, 1985.

Skilling, H. Gordon. *Charter Seventy-seven and Human Rights in Czechoslovakia*. Winchester, Mass.: Allen & Unwin, 1981.

Sohn, Louis B., and Thomas Buegenthal. *Basic Documents on International Protection of Human Rights*. Indianapolis: Bobbs-Merrill, 1973.

Solzhenitsyn, Aleksandr. *The Gulag Archipelago*. New York: Harper, 1975.

Sullivan, Leon Howard. *Build, Brother, Build*. Philadelphia: Macrae Smith, 1969.

Thomas, Gordon, and Max Morgan Witts. *Voyage of the Damned*. Greenwich, Conn.: Fawcett Publications, 1974.

Valladares, Armando. *Against All Hope*. New York: Knopf, 1986.

Valls, Jorge. *Twenty Years and Forty Days: Life in a Cuban Prison*. New York: Americas Watch Committee, 1986.

Vogelgesang, Sandy. *American Dream, Global Nightmare: The Dilemma of U.S. Human Rights Policy*. New York: Norton, 1980.

Westwood, J. N. *Endurance and Endeavor: Russian History, 1812–1980*, 2nd ed. New York: Oxford University Press, 1981.

Williams, Juan. *Eyes on the Prize: America's Civil Rights Years, 1954–1965*. New York: Penguin, 1987.

Woods, Donald. *Biko—Cry Freedom*. New York: Holt, 1987.

Documents

EXCERPTS FROM THE UNITED NATIONS CHARTER

The charter was signed on June 26, 1945, in San Francisco at the conclusion of the UN Conference on International Organization. It entered into force for the United States on October 24, 1945. An important aim was the protection of human rights and language to that effect was incorporated in the charter, pending the preparation and adoption of a universal declaration of rights. Following are excerpts dealing with human rights.

We the Peoples of the United Nations Determined

to save succeeding generations from the scourge of war, which twice in our lifetime has brought untold sorrow to mankind, and

to reaffirm faith in fundamental human rights, in the dignity and worth of the human person, in the equal rights of men and women and of nations large and small . . .

Have Resolved to Combine Our Efforts to Accomplish These Aims . . .

Article 1

The purposes of the United Nations are:

. . . To achieve international co-operation in solving international problems of an economic, social, cultural, or humanitarian character, and in promoting and encouraging respect for human rights and for fundamental freedoms for all without distinction as to race, sex, language, or religion. . . .

Article 55

With a view to the creation of conditions of stability and well-being which are necessary for peaceful and friendly relations among nations based on respect for the principle of equal rights and self-determination of peoples, the United Nations shall promote:

a. higher standards of living, full employment, and conditions of economic and social progress and development;

b. solutions of international economic, social, health, and related problems; and international cultural and educational cooperation; and

c. universal respect for, and observance of, human rights and fundamental freedoms for all without distinction as to race, sex, language, or religion.

Article 56

All Members pledge themselves to take joint and separate action in co-operation with the Organization for the achievement of the purposes set forth in Article 55.

UNIVERSAL DECLARATION OF HUMAN RIGHTS

The declaration was the work of the UN Commission on Human Rights, which met in January 1947 under the chairmanship of Eleanor Roosevelt. The Universal Declaration of Human Rights they drew up was adopted and proclaimed by the General Assembly on December 10, 1948. It was the first effort to set common standards of achievement in human rights for all peoples of all nations.

Preamble

Whereas recognition of the inherent dignity and of the equal and inalienable rights of all members of the human family is the foundation of freedom, justice and peace in the world,

Whereas disregard and contempt for human rights have resulted in barbarous acts which have outraged the conscience of mankind, and the advent of a world in which human beings shall enjoy freedom of speech and belief and freedom from fear and want has been proclaimed as the highest aspiration of the common people,

Whereas it is essential, if man is not to be compelled to have recourse, as a last resort, to rebellion against tyranny and oppression, that human rights should be protected by the rule of law,

Whereas it is essential to promote the development of friendly relations between nations,

Whereas the peoples of the United Nations have in the Charter reaffirmed their faith in fundamental human rights, in the dignity and worth of the human person and in the equal rights of men and women and have determined to promote social progress and better standards of life in larger freedom,

Whereas Member States have pledged themselves to achieve, in cooperation with the United Nations, the promotion of universal respect for and observance of human rights and fundamental freedoms,

Whereas a common understanding of these rights and freedoms is of the greatest importance for the full realization of this pledge,

Now, therefore,

The General Assembly

Proclaims this Universal Declaration of Human Rights as a common standard of achievement for all peoples and all nations, to the end that every individual and every organ of society, keeping this Declaration constantly in mind, shall strive by teaching and education to promote respect for these rights and freedoms and by progressive measures, national and international, to secure their universal and effective recognition and observance, both among the peoples of Member States themselves and among the peoples of territories under their jurisdiction.

Article 1

All human beings are born free and equal in dignity and rights. They are endowed with reason and conscience and should act towards one another in a spirit of brotherhood.

Article 2

Everyone is entitled to all the rights and freedoms set forth in this Declaration, without distinction of any kind, such as race, colour, sex, language, religion, political or other opinion, national or social origin, property, birth or other status.

Furthermore, no distinction shall be made on the basis of the political, jurisdictional or international status of the country or territory to which a person belongs, whether it be independent, trust, non-self-governing or under any other limitations of sovereignty.

Article 3

Everyone has the right to life, liberty and the security of person.

Article 4

No one shall be held in slavery or servitude; slavery and the slave trade shall be prohibited in all their forms.

Article 5

No one shall be subjected to torture or to cruel, inhuman or degrading treatment or punishment.

Article 6

Everyone has the right to recognition everywhere as a person before the law.

Article 7

All are equal before the law and are entitled without any discrimination to equal protection of the law. All are entitled to equal protection against any discrimination in violation of this Declaration and against any incitement to such discrimination.

Article 8

Everyone has the right to an effective remedy by the competent national tribunals for acts violating the fundamental rights granted him by the constitution or by law.

Article 9

No one shall be subjected to arbitrary arrest, detention or exile.

Article 10

Everyone is entitled in full equality to a fair and public hearing by an independent and impartial tribunal, in the determination of his rights and obligations and of any criminal charge against him.

Article 11

1. Everyone charged with a penal offence has the right to be presumed innocent until proved guilty according to law in a public trial at which he has had all the guarantees necessary for his defence.

2. No one shall be held guilty of any penal offence on account of any act or omission which did not constitute a penal offence, under national or international law, at the time when it was committed. Nor shall a heavier penalty be imposed than the one that was applicable at the time the penal offence was committed.

Article 12

No one shall be subjected to arbitrary interference with his privacy, family, home or correspondence, nor to attacks upon his honour and reputation. Everyone has the right to the protection of the law against such interference or attacks.

Article 13

1. Everyone has the right to freedom of movement and residence within the borders of each State.

2. Everyone has the right to leave any country, including his own, and to return to his country.

Article 14

1. Everyone has the right to seek and to enjoy in other countries asylum from persecution.

2. This right may not be invoked in the case of prosecutions genuinely arising from non-political crimes or from acts contrary to the purposes and principles of the United Nations.

Article 15

1. Everyone has the right to a nationality.
2. No one shall be arbitrarily deprived of his nationality nor denied the right to change his nationality.

Article 16

1. Men and women of full age, without any limitation due to race, nationality or religion, have the right to marry and to found a family. They are entitled to equal rights as to marriage, during marriage and at its dissolution.
2. Marriage shall be entered into only with the free and full consent of the intending spouses.
3. The family is the natural and fundamental group unit of society and is entitled to protection by society and the State.

Article 17

1. Everyone has the right to own property alone as well as in association with others.
2. No one shall be arbitrarily deprived of his property.

Article 18

Everyone has the right to freedom of thought, conscience and religion; this right includes freedom to change his religion or belief, and freedom, either alone or in community with others and in public or private, to manifest his religion or belief in teaching, practice, worship and observance.

Article 19

Everyone has the right to freedom of opinion and expression; this right includes freedom to hold opinions without interference and to seek, receive and impart information and ideas through any media and regardless of frontiers.

Article 20

1. Everyone has the right to freedom of peaceful assembly and association.

2. No one may be compelled to belong to an association.

Article 21

1. Everyone has the right to take part in the government of his country, directly or through freely chosen representatives.

2. Everyone has the right of equal access to public service in his country.

3. The will of the people shall be the basis of the authority of government; this will shall be expressed in periodic and genuine elections which shall be by universal and equal suffrage and shall be held by secret vote or by equivalent free voting procedures.

Article 22

Everyone, as a member of society, has the right to social security and is entitled to realization, through national effort and international cooperation and in accordance with the organization and resources of each State, of the economic, social and cultural rights indispensable for his dignity and the free development of his personality.

Article 23

1. Everyone has the right to work, to free choice of employment, to just and favourable conditions of work and to protection against unemployment.

2. Everyone, without any discrimination, has the right to equal pay for equal work.

3. Everyone who works has the right to just and favourable remuneration ensuring for himself and his family an existence worthy of human dignity, and supplemented, if necessary, by other means of social protection.

4. Everyone has the right to form and to join trade unions for the protection of his interests.

Article 24

Everyone has the right to rest and leisure, including reasonable limitation of working hours and periodic holidays with pay.

Article 25

1. Everyone has the right to a standard of living adequate for the health and well-being of himself and of his family, including food, clothing, housing and medical care and necessary social services, and the right to security in the event of unemployment, sickness, disability, widowhood, old age or other lack of livelihood in circumstances beyond his control.

2. Motherhood and childhood are entitled to special care and assistance. All children, whether born in or out of wedlock, shall enjoy the same social protection.

Article 26

1. Everyone has the right to education. Education shall be free, at least in the elementary and fundamental stages. Elementary education shall be compulsory. Technical and professional education shall be made generally available and higher education shall be equally accessible to all on the basis of merit.

2. Education shall be directed to the full development of the human personality and to the strengthening of respect for human rights and fundamental freedoms. It shall promote understanding, tolerance and friendship among all nations, racial or religious groups, and shall further the activities of the United Nations for the maintenance of peace.

3. Parents have a prior right to choose the kind of education that shall be given to their children.

Article 27

1. Everyone has the right freely to participate in the cultural life of the community, to enjoy the arts and to share in scientific advancement and its benefits.

2. Everyone has the right to the protection of the moral and material interests resulting from any scientific, literary or artistic production of which he is the author.

Article 28

Everyone is entitled to a social and international order in which the rights and freedoms set forth in this Declaration can be fully realized.

Article 29

1. Everyone has duties to the community in which alone the free and full development of his personality is possible.

2. In the exercise of his rights and freedoms, everyone shall be subject only to such limitations as are determined by law solely for the purpose of securing due recognition and respect for the rights and freedoms of others and of meeting the just requirements of morality, public order and the general welfare in a democratic society.

3. These rights and freedoms may in no case be exercised contrary to the purposes and principles of the United Nations.

Article 30

Nothing in this Declaration may be interpreted as implying for any State, group or person any right to engage in any activity or to perform any act aimed at the destruction of any of the rights and freedoms set forth herein.

CONVENTION ON THE PREVENTION AND PUNISHMENT OF THE CRIME OF GENOCIDE

Drawn up in the immediate wake of World War II, this convention forbids states or individuals to commit acts with the specific intent to destroy, wholly or partially, a national, ethnic, racial, or religious group. The convention was adopted by the UN General Assembly in 1948; the United States signed it and it was submitted to the Senate for advice and consent to ratification in 1949 and resubmitted in 1970. Eighty-four nations are parties to the convention, including, as of 1988, the United States.

The Contracting Parties,

Having considered the declaration made by the General Assembly of the United Nations in its resolution 96 (I) dated 11 December 1946 that genocide is a crime under international law, contrary to the spirit and aims of the United Nations and condemned by the civilized world;

Recognizing that at all periods of history genocide has inflicted great losses on humanity; and

Being convinced that, in order to liberate mankind from such an odious scourge, international co-operation is required,

Hereby agree as hereinafter provided:

Article 1

The Contracting Parties confirm that genocide, whether committed in time of peace or in time of war, is a crime under international law which they undertake to prevent and to punish.

Article 2

In the present Convention, genocide means any of the following acts committed with intent to destroy, in whole or in part, a national, ethnical, racial or religious group, as such:

(*a*) Killing members of the group;

(*b*) Causing serious bodily or mental harm to members of the group;

(*c*) Deliberately inflicting on the group conditions of life calculated to bring about its physical destruction in whole or in part;

(*d*) Imposing measures intended to prevent births within the group;

(*e*) Forcibly transferring children of the group to another group.

Article 3

The following acts shall be punishable:

(*a*) Genocide;

(*b*) Conspiracy to commit genocide;

(*c*) Direct and public incitement to commit genocide;

(*d*) Attempt to commit genocide;

(*e*) Complicity in genocide.

186

Article 4

Persons committing genocide or any of the other acts enumerated in article 3 shall be punished, whether they are constitutionally responsible rulers, public officials or private individuals.

Article 5

The Contracting Parties undertake to enact, in accordance with their respective Constitutions, the necessary legislation to give effect to the provisions of the present Convention and, in particular, to provide effective penalties for persons guilty of genocide or of any of the other acts enumerated in article 3.

Article 6

Persons charged with genocide or any of the other acts enumerated in article 3 shall be tried by a competent tribunal of the State in the territory of which the act was committed, or by such international penal tribunal as may have jurisdiction with respect to those Contracting Parties which shall have accepted its jurisdiction.

Article 7

Genocide and the other acts enumerated in article 3 shall not be considered as political crimes for the purpose of extradition.

The Contracting Parties pledge themselves in such cases to grant extradition in accordance with their laws and treaties in force.

Article 8

Any Contracting Party may call upon the competent organs of the United Nations to take such action under the Charter of the United Nations as they consider appropriate for the prevention and suppression of acts of genocide or any of the other acts enumerated in article 3.

Article 9

Disputes between the Contracting Parties relating to the interpretation, application or fulfillment of the present Convention, including those relating to the responsibility of a State for genocide or for any of the other acts enumerated in article 3, shall be submitted to the International Court of Justice at the request of any of the parties to the dispute.

Article 10

The present Convention, of which the Chinese, English, French, Russian and Spanish texts are equally authentic, shall bear the date of 9 December 1948.

Article 11

The present Convention shall be open until 31 December 1949 for signature on behalf of any Member of the United Nations and of any non-member State to which an invitation to sign has been addressed by the General Assembly.

The present Convention shall be ratified, and the instruments of ratification shall be deposited with the Secretary-General of the United Nations.

After 1 January 1950 the present Convention may be acceded to on behalf of any Member of the United Nations and of any non-member State which has received an invitation as aforesaid.

Instruments of accession shall be deposited with the Secretary-General of the United Nations.

Article 12

Any Contracting Party may at any time, by notification addressed to the Secretary-General of the United Nations, extend the application of the present Convention to all or any of the territories for the conduct of whose foreign relations that Contracting Party is responsible.

Article 13

On the day when the first twenty instruments of ratification or accession have been deposited, the Secretary-General shall draw up a *procès-verbal* and transmit a copy thereof to each Member of the United Nations and to each of the non-member States contemplated in article 11.

The present Convention shall come into force on the ninetieth day following the date of deposit of the twentieth instrument of ratification or accession.

Any ratification or accession effected subsequent to the latter date shall become effective on the ninetieth day following the deposit of the instrument of ratification or accession.

Article 14

The present Convention shall remain in effect for a period of ten years as from the date of its coming into force.

It shall thereafter remain in force for successive periods of five years for such Contracting Parties as have not denounced it at least six months before the expiration of the current period.

Denunciation shall be effected by a written notification addressed to the Secretary-General of the United Nations.

Article 15

If, as a result of denunciations, the number of Parties to the present Convention should become less than sixteen, the Convention shall cease to be in force as from the date on which the last of these denunciations shall become effective.

Article 16

A request for the revision of the present Convention may be made at any time by any Contracting Party by means of a notification in writing addressed to the Secretary-General.

The General Assembly shall decide upon the steps, if any, to be taken in respect of such request.

Article 17

The Secretary-General of the United Nations shall notify all Members of the United Nations and the non-member States contemplated in article 11 of the following:

(*a*) Signatures, ratifications and accessions received in accordance with article 11;

(*b*) Notifications received in accordance with article 12;

(*c*) The date upon which the present Convention comes into force in accordance with article 13;

(*d*) Denunciations received in accordance with article 14;

(*e*) The abrogation of the Convention in accordance with article 15;

(*f*) Notifications received in accordance with article 16.

Article 18

The original of the present Convention shall be deposited in the archives of the United Nations.

A certified copy of the Convention shall be transmitted to each Member of the United Nations and to each of the non-member States contemplated in article 11.

Article 19

The present Convention shall be registered by the Secretary-General of the United Nations on the date of its coming into force.

INTERNATIONAL CONVENTION ON THE ELIMINATION OF ALL FORMS OF RACIAL DISCRIMINATION

The convention forbids racial and ethnic discrimination in all fields of public life. Its terms, for the most part, parallel U.S. constitutional and statutory law and policy. The convention was adopted by the UN General Assembly in 1965 and signed by Ambassador Arthur Goldberg for the United States in 1966. One hundred and one nations have adhered to the convention. President Carter transmitted it to the U.S. Senate for advice and consent to ratification on February 23, 1978.

The States Parties to this Convention,

Considering that the Charter of the United Nations is based on the principles of the dignity and equality inherent in all human beings, and that all Member States have pledged themselves to take joint and separate action, in co-operation with the Organization, for the achievement of one of the purposes of the United Nations which is to promote and encourage universal respect for and observance of human rights and fundamental freedoms for all, without distinction as to race, sex, language or religion.

Considering that the Universal Declaration of Human Rights proclaims that all human beings are born free and equal in dignity and rights and that everyone is entitled to all the rights and freedoms set out therein, without distinction of any kind, in particular as to race, colour or national origin,

Considering that all human beings are equal before the law and are entitled to equal protection of the law against any discrimination and against any incitement to discrimination,

Considering that the United Nations has condemned colonialism and all practices of segregation and discrimination associated therewith, in whatever form and wherever they exist, and that the Declaration on the Granting of Independence to Colonial Countries and Peoples of 14 December 1960 (General Assembly resolution 1514 (XV)) has affirmed and solemnly proclaimed the necessity of bringing them to a speedy and unconditional end,

Considering that the United Nations Declaration on the Elimination of All Forms of Racial Discrimination of 20 November 1963 (General Assembly resolution 1904 (XVIII)) solemnly affirms the necessity of speedily eliminating racial discrimination throughout the world in all its forms and manifestations and of securing understanding of and respect for the dignity of the human person,

Convinced that any doctrine of superiority based on racial differentiation is scientifically false, morally condemnable, socially unjust and dangerous, and that there is no justification for racial discrimination, in theory or in practice, anywhere,

Reaffirming that discrimination between human beings on the grounds of race, colour or ethnic origin is an obstacle to friendly and peaceful relations among nations and is capable of disturbing peace and security among peoples and the harmony of persons living side by side even within one and the same State,

Convinced that the existence of racial barriers is repugnant to the ideals of any human society,

Alarmed by manifestations of racial discrimination still in evidence in some areas of the world and by governmental policies based on racial superiority or hatred, such as policies of *apartheid*, segregation or separation,

Resolved to adopt all necessary measures for speedily eliminating racial discrimination in all its forms and manifestations, and to prevent and combat racist doctrines and practices in order to promote understanding between races and to build an international community free from all forms of racial segregation and racial discrimination,

Bearing in mind the Convention concerning Discrimination in respect of Employment and Occupation adopted by the International Labour Organisation in 1958, and the Convention against Discrimination in

Education adopted by the United Nations Educational, Scientific and Cultural Organization in 1960,

Desiring to implement the principles embodied in the United Nations Declaration on the Elimination of All Forms of Racial Discrimination and to secure the earliest adoption of practical measures to that end,

Have agreed as follows:

PART I

Article 1

1. In this Convention, the term "racial discrimination" shall mean any distinction, exclusion, restriction or preference based on race, colour, descent, or national or ethnic origin which has the purpose or effect of nullifying or impairing the recognition, enjoyment or exercise, on an equal footing, of human rights and fundamental freedoms in the political, economic, social, cultural or any other field of public life.

2. This Convention shall not apply to distinctions, exclusions, restrictions or preferences made by a State Party to this Convention between citizens and non-citizens.

3. Nothing in this Convention may be interpreted as affecting in any way the legal provisions of States Parties concerning nationality, citizenship or naturalization, provided that such provisions do not discriminate against any particular nationality.

4. Special measures taken for the sole purpose of securing adequate advancement of certain racial or ethnic groups or individuals requiring such protection as may be necessary in order to ensure such groups or individuals equal enjoyment or exercise of human rights and fundamental freedoms shall not be deemed racial discrimination, provided, however, that such measures do not, as a consequence, lead to the maintenance of separate rights for different racial groups and that they shall not be continued after the objectives for which they were taken have been achieved.

Article 2

1. States Parties condemn racial discrimination and undertake to pursue by all appropriate means and without delay a policy of eliminating racial discrimination in all its forms and promoting understanding among all races, and, to this end:

192

(*a*) Each State Party undertakes to engage in no act or practice of racial discrimination against persons, groups of persons or institutions and to ensure that all public authorities and public institutions, national and local, shall act in conformity with this obligation;

(*b*) Each State Party undertakes not to sponsor, defend or support racial discrimination by any persons or organizations;

(*c*) Each State Party shall take effective measures to review governmental, national and local policies, and to amend, rescind or nullify any laws and regulations which have the effect of creating or perpetuating racial discrimination wherever it exists;

(*d*) Each State Party shall prohibit and bring to an end, by all appropriate means, including legislation as required by circumstances, racial discrimination by any persons, group or organization;

(*e*) Each State Party undertakes to encourage, where appropriate, integrationist multi-racial organizations and movements and other means of eliminating barriers between races, and to discourage anything which tends to strengthen racial division.

2. States Parties shall, when the circumstances so warrant, take, in the social, economic, cultural and other fields, special and concrete measures to ensure the adequate development and protection of certain racial groups or individuals belonging to them, for the purpose of guaranteeing them the full and equal enjoyment of human rights and fundamental freedoms. These measures shall in no case entail as a consequence the maintenance of unequal or separate rights for different racial groups after the objectives for which they were taken have been achieved.

Article 3

States Parties particularly condemn racial segregation and *apartheid* and undertake to prevent, prohibit and eradicate all practices of this nature in territories under their jurisdiction.

Article 4

States Parties condemn all propaganda and all organizations which are based on ideas or theories of superiority of one race or group of persons of one colour or ethnic origin, or which attempt to justify or promote racial hatred and discrimination in any form, and undertake to adopt immediate and positive measures designed to eradicate all incitement to, or acts of, such discrimination and, to this end, with due regard to the principles embodied in the Universal Declaration of Human Rights and the rights expressly set forth in article 5 of this Convention, *inter alia*:

(*a*) Shall declare an offence punishable by law all dissemination of ideas based on racial superiority or hatred, incitement to racial discrimination, as well as all acts of violence or incitement to such acts against any race or group of persons of another colour or ethnic origin, and also the provision of any assistance to racist activities, including the financing thereof;

(*b*) Shall declare illegal and prohibit organizations, and also organized and all other propaganda activities, which promote and incite racial discrimination, and shall recognize participation in such organizations or activities as an offence punishable by law;

(*c*) Shall not permit public authorities or public institutions, national or local, to promote or incite racial discrimination.

Article 5

In compliance with the fundamental obligations laid down in article 2 of this Convention, States Parties undertake to prohibit and to eliminate racial discrimination in all its forms and to guarantee the right of everyone, without distinction as to race, colour, or national or ethnic origin, to equality before the law, notably in the enjoyment of the following rights:

(*a*) The right to equal treatment before the tribunals and all other organs administering justice;

(*b*) The right to security of person and protection by the State against violence or bodily harm, whether inflicted by government officials or by any individual group or institution;

(*c*) Political rights, in particular the rights to participate in elections—to vote and to stand for election—on the basis of universal and equal suffrage, to take part in the Government as well as in the conduct of public affairs at any level and to have equal access to public service;

(*d*) Other civil rights, in particular:

    (i)   The right to freedom of movement and residence within the border of the State;

    (ii)   The right to leave any country, including one's own, and to return to one's country;

    (iii)   The right to nationality;

    (iv)   The right to marriage and choice of spouse;

    (v)   The right to own property alone as well as in association with others;

    (vi)   The right to inherit;

    (vii) The right to freedom of thought, conscience and religion;

    (viii) The right to freedom of opinion and expression;

    (ix)   The right to freedom of peaceful assembly and association;

(*e*) Economic, social and cultural rights, in particular:

    (i)   The rights to work, to free choice of employment, to just and favourable conditions of work, to protection against unemployment, to equal pay for equal work, to just and favourable remuneration;

    (ii)   The right to form and join trade unions;

    (iii)   The right to housing;

    (iv)   The right to public health, medical care, social security and social services;

    (v)   The right to education and training;

    (vi)   The right to equal participation in cultural activities;

(*f*)   The right of access to any place of service intended for use by the general public, such as transport, hotels, restaurants, cafés, theatres and parks.

Article 6

States Parties shall assure to everyone within their jurisdiction effective protection and remedies, through the competent national tribunals and other State institutions, against any acts of racial discrimination which violate his human rights and fundamental freedoms contrary to this Convention, as well as the right to seek from such tribunals just and adequate reparation or satisfaction for any damage suffered as a result of such discrimination.

Article 7

States Parties undertake to adopt immediate and effective measures, particularly in the fields of teaching, education, culture and information, with a view to combating prejudices which lead to racial discrimination and to promoting understanding, tolerance and friendship among nations and racial or ethnical groups, as well as to propagating the purposes and principles of the Charter of the United Nations, the Universal

Declaration of Human Rights, the United Nations Declaration on the Elimination of All Forms of Racial Discrimination, and this Convention.

PART II

Article 8

1. There shall be established a Committee on the Elimination of Racial Discrimination (hereinafter referred to as the Committee) consisting of eighteen experts of high moral standing and acknowledged impartiality elected by States Parties from among their nationals, who shall serve in their personal capacity, consideration being given to equitable geographical distribution and to the representation of the different forms of civilization as well as of the principal legal systems.

2. The members of the Committee shall be elected by secret ballot from a list of persons nominated by the States Parties. Each State Party may nominate one person from among its own nationals.

3. The initial election shall be held six months after the date of the entry into force of this Convention. At least three months before the date of each election the Secretary-General of the United Nations shall address a letter to the States Parties inviting them to submit their nominations within two months. The Secretary-General shall prepare a list in alphabetical order of all persons thus nominated, indicating the States Parties which have nominated them, and shall submit it to the States Parties.

4. Elections of the members of the Committee shall be held at a meeting of States Parties convened by the Secretary-General at United Nations Headquarters. At that meeting, for which two thirds of the States Parties shall constitute a quorum, the persons elected to the Committee shall be those nominees who obtain the largest number of votes and an absolute majority of the votes of the representatives of States Parties present and voting.

5. (*a*) The members of the Committee shall be elected for a term of four years. However, the terms of nine of the members elected at the first election shall expire at the end of two years; immediately after the first election the names of these nine members shall be chosen by lot by the Chairman of the Committee.

(*b*) For the filling of casual vacancies, the State Party whose expert has ceased to function as a member of the Committee shall appoint another expert from among its nationals, subject to the approval of the Committee.

6. States Parties shall be responsible for the expenses of the members of the Committee while they are in performance of Committee duties.

Article 9

1. States Parties undertake to submit to the Secretary-General of the United Nations, for consideration by the Committee, a report on the legislative, judicial, administrative or other measures which they have adopted and which give effect to the provisions of this Convention: (*a*) within one year after the entry into force of the Convention for the State concerned; and (*b*) thereafter every two years and whenever the Committee so requests. The Committee may request further information from the States Parties.

2. The Committee shall report annually, through the Secretary-General, to the General Assembly of the United Nations on its activities and may make suggestions and general recommendations based on the examination of the reports and information received from the States Parties. Such suggestions and general recommendations shall be reported to the General Assembly together with comments, if any, from States Parties.

Article 10

1. The Committee shall adopt its own rules of procedure.

2. The Committee shall elect its officers for a term of two years.

3. The secretariat of the Committee shall be provided by the Secretary-General of the United Nations.

4. The meetings of the Committee shall normally be held at United Nations Headquarters.

Article 11

1. If a State Party considers that another State Party is not giving effect to the provisions of this Convention, it may bring the matter to the attention of the Committee. The Committee shall then transmit the communication to the State Party concerned. Within three months, the receiving State shall submit to the Committee written explanations or statements clarifying the matter and the remedy, if any, that may have been taken by that State.

2. If the matter is not adjusted to the satisfaction of both parties, either by bilateral negotiations or by any other procedure open to them, within six months after the receipt by the receiving State of the initial communication, either State shall have the right to refer the matter again to the Committee by notifying the Committee and also the other State.

3. The Committee shall deal with a matter referred to it in accordance with paragraph 2 of this article after it has ascertained that all available domestic remedies have been invoked and exhausted in the case, in conformity with the generally recognized principles of international law. This shall not be the rule where the application of the remedies is unreasonably prolonged.

4. In any matter referred to it, the Committee may call upon the States Parties concerned to supply any other relevant information.

5. When any matter arising out of this article is being considered by the Committee, the States Parties concerned shall be entitled to send a representative to take part in the proceedings of the Committee, without voting rights, while the matter is under consideration.

Article 12

1. (*a*) After the Committee has obtained and collated all the information it deems necessary, the Chairman shall appoint an *ad hoc* Conciliation Commission (hereinafter referred to as the Commission) comprising five persons who may or may not be members of the Committee. The members of the Commission shall be appointed with the unanimous consent of the parties to the dispute, and its good offices shall be made available to the States concerned with a view to an amicable solution to the matter on the basis of respect for this Convention.

(*b*) If the States Parties to the dispute fail to reach agreement within three months on all or part of the composition of the Commission, the members of the Commission not agreed upon by the States Parties to the dispute shall be elected by secret ballot by a two-thirds majority vote of the Committee from among its own members.

2. The members of the Commission shall serve in their personal capacity. They shall not be nationals of the States Parties to the dispute or of a State not Party to this Convention.

3. The Commission shall elect its own Chairman and adopt its own rules of procedure.

4. The meetings of the Commission shall normally be held at United Nations Headquarters or at any other convenient place as determined by the Commission.

5. The secretariat provided in accordance with article 10, paragraph 3, of this Convention shall also service the Commission whenever a dispute among States Parties brings the Commission into being.

6. The States Parties to the dispute shall share equally all the expenses of the members of the Commission in accordance with estimates to be provided by the Secretary-General of the United Nations.

7. The Secretary-General shall be empowered to pay the expenses of the members to the Commission, if necessary, before reimbursement by the States Parties to the dispute in accordance with paragraph 6 of this article.

8. The information obtained and collated by the Committee shall be made available to the Commission, and the Commission may call upon the States concerned to supply any other relevant information.

Article 13

1. When the Commission has fully considered the matter, it shall prepare and submit to the Chairman of the Committee a report embodying its findings on all questions of fact relevant to the issue between the parties and containing such recommendations as it may think proper for the amicable solution of the dispute.

2. The Chairman of the Committee shall communicate the report of the Commission to each of the States Parties to the dispute. These States shall, within three months, inform the Chairman of the Committee whether or not they accept the recommendations contained in the report of the Commission.

3. After the period provided for in paragraph 2 of this article, the Chairman of the Committee shall communicate the report of the Commission and the declarations of the States Parties concerned to the other States Parties to this Convention.

Article 14

1. A State Party may at any time declare that it recognizes the competence of the Committee to receive and consider communications from individuals or groups of individuals within its jurisdiction claiming to be victims of a violation by that State Party of any of the rights set forth in this Convention. No communication shall be received by the

Committee if it concerns a State Party which has not made such a declaration.

2. Any State Party which makes a declaration as provided for in paragraph 1 of this article may establish or indicate a body within its national legal order which shall be competent to receive and consider petitions from individuals and groups of individuals within its jurisdiction who claim to be victims of a violation of any of the rights set forth in this Convention and who have exhausted other available local remedies.

3. A declaration made in accordance with paragraph 1 of this article and the name of any body established or indicated in accordance with paragraph 2 of this article shall be deposited by the State Party concerned with the Secretary-General of the United Nations, who shall transmit copies thereof to the other States Parties. A declaration may be withdrawn at any time by notification to the Secretary-General, but such a withdrawal shall not affect communications pending before the Committee.

4. A register of petitions shall be kept by the body established or indicated in accordance with paragraph 2 of this article, and certified copies of the register shall be filed annually through appropriate channels with the Secretary-General on the understanding that the contents shall not be publicly disclosed.

5. In the event of failure to obtain satisfaction from the body established or indicated in accordance with paragraph 2 of this article, the petitioner shall have the right to communicate the matter to the Committee within six months.

6. (a) The Committee shall confidentially bring any communication referred to it to the attention of the State Party alleged to be violating any provision of this Convention, but the identity of the individual or groups of individuals concerned shall not be revealed without his or their express consent. The Committee shall not receive anonymous communications.

(b) Within three months, the receiving State shall submit to the Committee written explanations or statements clarifying the matter and the remedy, if any, that may have been taken by that State.

7. (a) The Committee shall consider communications in the light of all information made available to it by the State Party concerned and by the petitioner. The Committee shall not consider any communication from a petitioner unless it has ascertained that the petitioner has exhausted all available domestic remedies. However, this shall not be the rule where the application of the remedies is unreasonably prolonged.

(b) The Committee shall forward its suggestions and recommendations, if any, to the State Party concerned and to the petitioner.

8. The Committee shall include in its annual report a summary of such communications and, where appropriate, a summary of the explanations and statements of the States Parties concerned and of its own suggestions and recommendations.

9. The Committee shall be competent to exercise the functions provided for in this article only when at least ten States Parties to this Convention are bound by declarations in accordance with paragraph 1 of this article.

Article 15

1. Pending the achievement of the objectives of the Declaration on the Granting of Independence to Colonial Countries and Peoples, contained in General Assembly resolution 1514 (XV) of 14 December 1960, the provisions of this Convention shall in no way limit the right of petition granted to these peoples by other international instruments or by the United Nations and its specialized agencies.

2. (*a*) The Committee established under article 8, paragraph 1, of this Convention shall receive copies of the petitions from, and submit expressions of opinion and recommendations on these petitions to, the bodies of the United Nations which deal with matters directly related to the principles and objectives of this Convention in their consideration of petitions from the inhabitants of Trust and Non-Self-Governing Territories and all other territories to which General Assembly resolution 1514 (XV) applies, relating to matters covered by this Convention which are before these bodies.

(*b*) The Committee shall receive from the competent bodies of the United Nations copies of the reports concerning the legislative, judicial, administrative or other measures directly related to the principles and objectives of this Convention applied by the administering Powers within the Territories mentioned in subparagraph (*a*) of this paragraph, and shall express opinions and make recommendations to these bodies.

3. The Committee shall include in its report to the General Assembly a summary of the petitions and reports it has received from United Nations bodies, and the expressions of opinion and recommendations of the Committee relating to the said petitions and reports.

4. The Committee shall request from the Secretary-General of the United Nations all information relevant to the objectives of this Convention and available to him regarding the Territories mentioned in paragraph 2 (*a*) of this article.

Article 16

The provisions of this Convention concerning the settlement of disputes or complaints shall be applied without prejudice to other procedures for settling disputes or complaints in the field of discrimination laid down in the constituent instruments of, or in conventions adopted by, the United Nations and its specialized agencies, and shall not prevent the States Parties from having recourse to other procedures for settling a dispute in accordance with general or special international agreements in force between them.

PART III

Article 17

1. This Convention is open for signature by any State Member of the United Nations or member of any of its specialized agencies, by any State Party to the Statute of the International Court of Justice, and by any other State which has been invited by the General Assembly of the United Nations to become a Party to this Convention.

2. This Convention is subject to ratification. Instruments of ratification shall be deposited with the Secretary-General of the United Nations.

Article 18

1. This Convention shall be open to accession by any State referred to in article 17, paragraph 1, of the Convention.

2. Accession shall be effected by the deposit of an instrument of accession with the Secretary-General of the United Nations.

Article 19

1. This Convention shall enter into force on the thirtieth day after the date of the deposit with the Secretary-General of the United Nations of the twenty-seventh instrument of ratification or instrument of accession.

2. For each State ratifying this Convention or acceding to it after the deposit of the twenty-seventh instrument of ratification or instrument of accession, the Convention shall enter into force on the thirtieth day after the date of the deposit of its own instrument of ratification or instrument of accession.

Article 20

1. The Secretary-General of the United Nations shall receive and circulate to all States which are or may become Parties to this Convention reservations made by States at the time of ratification or accession. Any State which objects to the reservation shall, within a period of ninety days from the date of the said communication, notify the Secretary-General that it does not accept it.

2. A reservation imcompatible with the object and purpose of this Convention shall not be permitted, nor shall a reservation the effect of which would inhibit the operation of any of the bodies established by this Convention be allowed. A reservation shall be considered imcompatible or inhibitive if at least two thirds of the States Parties to this Convention object to it.

3. Reservations may be withdrawn at any time by notification to this effect addressed to the Secretary-General. Such notification shall take effect on the date on which it is received.

Article 21

A State Party may denounce this Convention by written notification to the Secretary-General of the United Nations. Denunciation shall take effect one year after the date of receipt of the notification by the Secretary-General.

Article 22

Any dispute between two or more States Parties with respect to the interpretation or application of this Convention, which is not settled by negotiation or by the procedures expressly provided for in this Convention, shall, at the request of any of the parties to the dispute, be referred to the International Court of Justice for decision, unless the disputants agree to another mode of settlement.

Article 23

1. A request for the revision of this Convention may be made at any time by any State Party by means of a notification in writing addressed to the Secretary-General of the United Nations.

2. The General Assembly of the United Nations shall decide upon the steps, if any, to be taken in respect of such a request.

Article 24

The Secretary-General of the United Nations shall inform all States referred to in article 17, paragraph 1, of this Convention of the following particulars:

(*a*) Signatures, ratifications and accessions under articles 17 and 18;
(*b*) The date of entry into force of this Convention under article 19;
(*c*) Communications and declarations received under articles 14, 20 and 23;
(*d*) Denunciations under article 21.

Article 25

1. This Convention, of which the Chinese, English, French, Russian and Spanish texts are equally authentic, shall be deposited in the archives of the United Nations.
2. The Secretary-General of the United Nations shall transmit certified copies of this Convention to all States belonging to any of the categories mentioned in article 17, paragraph 1, of the Convention.

INTERNATIONAL COVENANT ON ECONOMIC, SOCIAL, AND CULTURAL RIGHTS

The covenant affirms a series of standards in economic, social, and cultural activities. Formulated as statements of goals to be achieved progressively rather than immediately, the covenant was adopted by the UN General Assembly in 1966 and fifty-four nations are parties. The United States has signed it and President Carter transmitted it to the Senate for advice and consent to ratification on February 23, 1978.

Preamble

The States Parties to the present Covenant,
Considering that, in accordance with the principles proclaimed in the Charter of the United Nations, recognition of the inherent dignity and of the equal and inalienable rights of all members of the human family is the foundation of freedom, justice and peace in the world,
Recognizing that those rights derive from the inherent dignity of the human person,

Recognizing that, in accordance with the Universal Declaration of Human Rights, the ideal of free human beings enjoying freedom from fear and want can only be achieved if conditions are created whereby everyone may enjoy his economic, social and cultural rights, as well as his civil and political rights,

Considering the obligation of States under the Charter of the United Nations to promote universal respect for, and observance of, human rights and freedoms,

Realizing that the individual, having duties to other individuals and to the community to which he belongs, is under a responsibility to strive for the promotion and observance of the rights recognized in the present Covenant,

Agree upon the following articles:

PART I

Article 1

1. All peoples have the right of self-determination. By virtue of the right they freely determine their political status and freely pursue their economic, social and cultural development.

2. All peoples may, for their own ends, freely dispose of their natural wealth and resources without prejudice to any obligations arising out of international economic co-operation, based upon the principle of mutual benefit, and international law. In no case may a people be deprived of its own means of subsistence.

3. The States Parties to the present Covenant, including those having responsibility for the administration of Non-Self-Governing and Trust Territories, shall promote the realization of the right of self-determination, and shall respect that right, in conformity with the provisions of the United Nations Charter.

PART II

Article 2

1. Each State Party to the present Covenant undertakes to take steps, individually and through international assistance and co-operation especially economic and technical, to the maximum of its available resources,

with a view to achieving progressively the full realization of the rights recognized in the present Covenant by all appropriate means, including particularly the adoption of legislative measures.

2. The States Parties to the present Covenant undertake to guarantee that the rights enunciated in the present Covenant will be exercised without discrimination of any kind as to race, colour, sex, language, religion, political or other opinion, national or social origin, property, birth or other status.

3. Developing countries, with due regard to human rights and their national economy, may determine to what extent they would guarantee the economic rights recognized in the present Covenant to nonnationals.

Article 3

The States Parties to the present Covenant undertake to ensure the equal right of men and women to the enjoyment of all economic, social and cultural rights set forth in this Covenant.

Article 4

The States Parties to the present Covenant recognize that in the enjoyment of those rights provided by the State in conformity with the present Covenant, the State may subject such rights only to such limitations as are determined by law only in so far as this may be compatible with the nature of these rights and solely for the purpose of promoting the general welfare in a democratic society.

Article 5

1. Nothing in the present Covenant may be interpreted as implying for any State, group or person, any right to engage in any activity or to perform any act aimed at the destruction of any of the rights or freedoms recognized herein, or at their limitation to a greater extent than is provided for in the present Covenant.

2. No restriction upon or derogation from any of the fundamental human rights recognized or existing in any country in virtue of law, conventions, regulations or custom shall be admitted on the pretext that the present Covenant does not recognize such rights or that it recognizes them to a lesser extent.

PART III

Article 6

1. The States Parties to the present Covenant recognize the right to work, which includes the right of everyone to the opportunity to gain his living by work which he freely chooses or accepts, and will take appropriate steps to safeguard this right.

2. The steps to be taken by a State Party to the present Covenant to achieve the full realization of this right shall include technical and vocational guidance and training programmes, policies and techniques to achieve steady economic, social and cultural development and full and productive employment under conditions safeguarding fundamental political and economic freedoms to the individual.

Article 7

The States Parties to the present Covenant recognize the right of everyone to the enjoyment of just and favourable conditions of work, which ensure, in particular:

(a) Remuneration which provides all workers as a minimum with:

(i) Fair wages and equal remuneration for work of equal value without distinction of any kind, in particular women being guaranteed conditions of work not inferior to those enjoyed by men, with equal pay for equal work; and
(ii) A decent living for themselves and their families in accordance with the provisions of the present Covenant;

(b) Safe and healthy working conditions;
(c) Equal opportunity for everyone to be promoted in his employment to an appropriate higher level, subject to no considerations other than those of seniority and competence;
(d) Rest, leisure and reasonable limitation of working hours and periodic holidays with pay, as well as remuneration for public holidays.

Article 8

1. The States Parties to the present Covenant undertake to ensure:

(a) The right of everyone to form trade unions and join the trade union of his choice subject only to the rules of the organization concerned, for the promotion and protection of his economic and social interests. No restrictions may be placed on the exercise of this right other than those prescribed by law and which are necessary in a democratic society in the interests of national security or public order or for the protection of the rights and freedom of others;

(b) The right of trade unions to establish national federations or confederations and the right of the latter to form or join international trade-union organizations;

(c) The right of trade unions to function freely subject to no limitations other than those prescribed by law and which are necessary in a democratic society in the interests of national security of public order or for the protection of the rights and freedoms of others;

(d) The right to strike, provided that it is exercised in conformity with the laws of the particular country.

2. This article shall not prevent the imposition of lawful restrictions on the exercise of these rights by members of the armed forces, or of the police, or of the administration of the State.

3. Nothing in this article shall authorize States Parties to the International Labour Convention of 1948 on Freedom of Association and Protection of the Rights to Organize to take legislative measures which would prejudice, or apply the law in such a manner as would prejudice, the guarantees provided for in that Convention.

Article 9

The States Parties to the present Covenant recognize the right of everyone to social security including social insurance.

Article 10

The States Parties to the present Covenant recognize that:

1. The widest possible protection and assistance should be accorded to the family, which is the natural and fundamental group unit of society, particularly for its establishment and while it is responsible for

the care and education of dependent children. Marriage must be entered into with the free consent of the intending spouses;

2. Special protection should be accorded to mothers during a reasonable period before and after childbirth. During such period working mothers should be accorded paid leave or leave with adequate social security benefits;

3. Special measures of protection and assistance should be taken on behalf of all children and young persons without any discrimination for reasons of parentage or other conditions. Children and young persons should be protected from economic and social exploitation. Their employment in work harmful to their morals or health or dangerous to life or likely to hamper their normal development should be punishable by law. States should also set age limits below which the paid employment of child labour should be prohibited and punishable by law.

Article 11

1. The States Parties to the present Covenant recognize the right of everyone to an adequate standard of living for himself and his family, including adequate food, clothing and housing, and to the continuous improvement of living conditions. The States Parties will take appropriate steps to ensure the realization of this right, recognizing to this effect the essential importance of international co-operation based on free consent.

2. The States Parties to the present Covenant, recognizing the fundamental right of everyone to be free from hunger, shall take, individually and through international co-operation, the measures, including specific programmes, which are needed:

(a) To improve methods of production, conservation and distribution of food by making full use of technical and scientific knowledge, by disseminating knowledge of the principles of nutrition and by developing or reforming agrarian systems in such a way as to achieve the most efficient development and utilization of natural resources; and

(b) Take into account the problems of both food-importing and food-exporting countries, to ensure an equitable distribution of world food supplies in relation to need.

Article 12

1. The States Parties to the present Covenant recognize the right of everyone to the enjoyment of the highest attainable standard of physical and mental health.

209

2. The steps to be taken by the States Parties to the present Covenant to achieve the full realization of this right shall include those necessary for:

(a) The provision for the reduction of the stillbirth-rate and of infant mortality and for the healthy development of the child;

(b) The improvement of all aspects of environmental and industrial hygiene;

(c) The prevention, treatment and control of epidemic, endemic, occupational and other diseases;

(d) The creation of conditions which would assure to all medical service and medical attention in the event of sickness.

Article 13

1. The States Parties to the present Covenant recognize the right of everyone to education. They agree that education shall be directed to the full development of the human personality and the sense of its dignity, and shall strengthen the respect for human rights and fundamental freedoms. They further agree that education shall enable all persons to participate effectively in a free society, promote understanding, tolerance and friendship among all nations and all racial, ethnic or religious groups, and further the activities of the United Nations for the maintenance of peace.

2. The States Parties to the present Covenant recognize that, with a view to achieving the full realization of this right:

(a) Primary education shall be compulsory and available free to all;

(b) Secondary education in its different forms, including technical and vocational secondary education, shall be made generally available and accessible to all by every appropriate means, and in particular by the progressive introduction of free education;

(c) Higher education shall be made equally accessible to all, on the basis of capacity, by every appropriate means, and in particular by the progressive introduction of free education;

(d) Fundamental education shall be encouraged or intensified as far as possible for those persons who have not received or completed the whole period of their primary education;

(e) The development of a system of schools at all levels shall be actively pursued, an adequate fellowship system shall be established, and the material conditions of teaching staff shall be continuously improved.

3. The States Parties to the present Covenant undertake to have respect for the liberty of parents and, when applicable, legal guardians, to choose for their children schools other than those established by the public authorities which conform to such minimum educational standards as may be laid down or approved by the State and to ensure the religious and moral education of their children in conformity with their own convictions.

4. No part of this article shall be construed so as to interfere with the liberty of individuals and bodies to establish and direct educational institutions, subject always to the observance of the principles set forth in paragraph 1 and to the requirement that the education given in such institutions shall conform to such minimum standards as may be laid down by the State.

Article 14

Each State Party to the present Covenant which, at the time of becoming a Party, has not been able to secure in its metropolitan territory or other territories under its jurisdiction compulsory primary education, free of charge, undertakes, within two years, to work out and adopt a detailed plan of action for the progressive implementation, within a reasonable number of years, to be fixed in the plan, of the principle of compulsory education free of charge for all.

Article 15

1. The States Parties to the present Covenant recognize the right of everyone:

(a) To take part in cultural life;
(b) To enjoy the benefits of scientific progress and its applications;
(c) To benefit from the protection of the moral and material interests resulting from any scientific, literary or artistic production of which he is the author.

2. The steps to be taken by the States Parties to the present Covenant to achieve the full realization of this right shall include those necessary for the conservation, the development and the diffusion of science and culture.

3. The States Parties to the present Covenant undertake to respect the freedom indispensable for scientific research and creative activity.

4. The States Parties to the present Covenant recognize the benefits to be derived from the encouragement and development of international contacts and co-operation in the scientific and cultural fields.

PART IV

Article 16

1. The States Parties to the present Covenant undertake to submit in conformity with this part of the Covenant reports on the measures which they have adopted and the progress made in achieving the observance of the rights recognized herein.

2. (a) All reports shall be submitted to the Secretary-General of the United Nations who shall transmit copies to the Economic and Social Council for consideration in accordance with the provisions of the present Covenant.

(b) The Secretary-General of the United Nations shall also transmit to the specialized agencies copies of the reports, or any relevant parts therefrom, from States Parties to the present Covenant which are also members of these specialized agencies in so far as these reports, or parts therefrom, relate to any matters which fall within the responsibilities of the said agencies in accordance with their constitutional instruments.

Article 17

1. The States Parties to the present Covenant shall furnish their reports in stages, in accordance with a programme to be established by the Economic and Social Council within one year of the entry into force of the present Covenant after consultation with the States Parties and the specialized agencies concerned.

2. Reports may indicate factors and difficulties affecting the degree of fulfilment of obligations under the present Covenant.

3. Where relevant information has previously been furnished to the United Nations or to any specialized agency by any State Party to the present Covenant it will not be necessary to reproduce that information but a precise reference to the information so furnished will suffice.

Article 18

Pursuant to its responsibilities under the Charter in the field of human rights and fundamental freedoms, the Economic and Social Council may make arrangements with the specialized agencies in respect of their reporting to it on the progress made in achieving the observance of the provisions of the present Covenant falling within the scope of their activities. These reports may include particulars of decisions and recommendations on such implementation adopted by their competent organs.

Article 19

The Economic and Social Council may transmit to the Commission on Human Rights for study and general recommendation or as appropriate for information the reports concerning human rights submitted by States in accordance with articles 16 and 17, and those concerning human rights submitted by the specialized agencies in accordance with article 18.

Article 20

The States Parties to the present Covenant and the specialized agencies concerned may submit comments to the Economic and Social Council on any general recommendation under article 19 or reference to such general recommendation in any report of the Commission or any documentation referred to therein.

Article 21

The Economic and Social Council may submit from time to time to the General Assembly reports with recommendations of a general nature and a summary of the information received from the States Parties to the present Covenant and the specialized agencies on the measures taken and the progress made in achieving general observance of the rights recognized in the present Covenant.

Article 22

The Economic and Social Council may bring to the attention of other organs of the United Nations, their subsidiary organs and specialized agencies concerned with furnishing technical assistance, any matters arising out of the reports referred to in this part of the present Covenant which may assist such bodies in deciding each within its field of compe tence, on the advisability of international measures likely to contribute to the effective progressive implementation of the present Covenant.

Article 23

The States Parties to the present Covenant agree that international action for the achievement of the rights recognized in the present Covenant includes such methods as the conclusion of conventions, the adoption of recommendations, the furnishing of technical assistance and the holding of regional meetings and technical meetings for the purpose of consultation and study organized in conjunction with the Governments concerned.

Article 24

Nothing in the present Covenant shall be interpreted as impairing the provisions of the Charter of the United Nations and of the constitutions of the specialized agencies which define the respective responsibilities of the various organs of the United Nations and of the specialized agencies in regard to the matters dealt with in the present Covenant.

Article 25

Nothing in the present Covenant shall be interpreted as impairing the inherent right of all peoples to enjoy and utilize fully and freely their natural wealth and resources.

PART V

Article 26

1. The present Covenant is open for signature by any State Member of the United Nations or member of any of its specialized agencies, by any State Party to the Statute of the International Court of Justice, and by any other State which has been invited by the General Assembly of the United Nations to become a party to the present Covenant.

2. The present Covenant is subject to ratification. Instruments of ratification shall be deposited with the Secretary-General of the United Nations.

3. The present Covenant shall be open to accession by any State referred to in paragraph 1 of this article.

4. Accession shall be effected by the deposit of an instrument of accession with the Secretary-General of the United Nations.

214

5. The Secretary-General of the United Nations shall inform all States which have signed the present Covenant or acceded to it of the deposit of each instrument of ratification or accession.

Article 27

1. The present Covenant shall enter into force three months after the date of the deposit with the Secretary-General of the United Nations of the thirty-fifth instrument of ratification or instrument of accession.

2. For each State ratifying the present Covenant or acceding to it after the deposit of the thirty-fifth instrument of ratification or instrument of accession, the present Covenant shall enter into force three months after the date of the deposit of its own instrument of ratification or instrument of accession.

Article 28

The provisions of the present Covenant shall extend to all parts of federal States without any limitations or exceptions.

Article 29

1. Any State Party to the present Covenant may propose an amendment and file it with the Secretary-General of the United Nations. The Secretary-General of the United Nations shall thereupon communicate any proposed amendments to the States Parties to the present Covenant with a request that they notify him whether they favour a conference of States Parties for the purpose of considering and voting upon the proposal. In the event that at least one third of the States Parties favours such a conference the Secretary-General of the United Nations shall convene the conference under the auspices of the United Nations. Any amendment adopted by a majority of the States Parties present and voting at the conference shall be submitted to the General Assembly of the United Nations for approval.

2. Amendments shall come into force when they have been approved by the General Assembly and accepted by a two-thirds majority of the States Parties to the present Covenant in accordance with their respective constitutional processes.

3. When amendments come into force they shall be binding on those States Parties which have accepted them, other States Parties being still bound by the provisions of the present Covenant and any earlier amendment which they have accepted.

Article 30

Irrespective of the notifications made under article 26, paragraph 5, the Secretary-General of the United Nations shall inform all States referred to in paragraph 1 of the same article of the following particulars:

(a) Signatures, ratifications and accessions under article 26;
(b) The date of the entry into force of the present Covenant under article 27 and the date of the entry into force of any amendments under article 29.

Article 31

1. The present Covenant, of which the Chinese, English, French, Russian and Spanish texts are equally authentic, shall be deposited in the archives of the United Nations.
2. The Secretary-General of the United Nations shall transmit certified copies of the present Covenant to all States referred to in article 26.

INTERNATIONAL COVENANT ON CIVIL AND POLITICAL RIGHTS

Of the four UN treaties, this covenant is the most similar in conception to the U.S. Constitution and Bill of Rights. It consists primarily of limitations upon the power of the State to impose its will on the people under its jurisdiction and, in large measure, guarantees those civil and political rights with which the United States and the Western democratic tradition have always been associated. The covenant was adopted by the UN General Assembly in 1966 and fifty-two nations are parties. The United States has signed it and President Carter transmitted it to the Senate for advice and consent to ratification on February 23, 1978.

Preamble

The States Parties to the present Covenant,
Considering that, in accordance with the principles proclaimed in the Charter of the United Nations, recognition of the inherent dignity and of the equal and inalienable rights of all members of the human family is the foundation of freedom, justice and peace in the world,
Recognizing that these rights derive from the inherent dignity of the human person,

Recognizing that, in accordance with the Universal Declaration of Human Rights, the ideal of free human beings enjoying civil and political freedom and freedom from fear and want can only be achieved if conditions are created whereby everyone may enjoy his civil and political rights, as well as his economic, social and cultural rights,

Considering the obligation of States under the Charter of the United Nations to promote universal respect for, and observance of, human rights and freedoms.

Realizing that the individual, having duties to other individuals and to the community to which he belongs, is under a responsibility to strive for the promotion and observance of the rights recognized in the present Covenant,

Agree upon the following articles:

PART I

Article 1

1. All peoples have the right of self-determination. By virtue of the right they freely determine their political status and freely pursue their economic, social and cultural development.

2. All peoples may, for their own ends, freely dispose of their natural wealth and resources without prejudice to any obligations arising out of international economic co-operation, based upon the principle of mutual benefit, and international law. In no case may a people be deprived of its own means of subsistence.

3. The States Parties to the present Covenant, including those having responsibility for the administration of Non-Self-Governing and Trust Territories, shall promote the realization of the right of self-determination, and shall respect that right, in conformity with the provisions of the United Nations Charter.

PART II

Article 2

1. Each State Party to the present Covenant undertakes to respect and to ensure to all individuals within its territory and subject to its jurisdiction the rights recognized in the present Covenant, without distinction

of any kind, such as race, colour, sex, language, religion, political or other opinion, national or social origin, property, birth or other status.

2. Where not already provided for by existing legislative or other measures, each State Party to the present Covenant undertakes to take the necessary steps, in accordance with its constitutional processes and with the provisions of the present Covenant, to adopt such legislative or other measures as may be necessary to give effect to the rights recognized in the present Covenant.

3. Each State Party to the present Covenant undertakes:

(a) To ensure that any person whose rights or freedoms as herein recognized are violated shall have an effective remedy notwithstanding that the violation has been committed by persons acting in an official capacity;

(b) To ensure that any person claiming such a remedy shall have his right thereto determined by competent judicial, administrative or legislative authorities, or by any other competent authority provided for by the legal system of the State, and to develop the possibilities of judicial remedy;

(c) To ensure that the competent authorities shall enforce such remedies when granted.

Article 3

The State Parties to the present Covenant undertake to ensure the equal right of men and women to the enjoyment of all civil and political rights set forth in the present Covenant.

Article 4

1. In time of public emergency which threatens the life of the nation and the existence of which is officially proclaimed, the States Parties to the present Covenant may take measures derogating from their obligations under the present Covenant to the extent strictly required by the exigencies of the situation, provided that such measures are not inconsistent with their other obligations under international law and do not involve discrimination solely on the ground of race, colour, sex, language, religion or social origin.

2. No derogation from articles 6, 7, 8 (paragraphs 1 and 2), 11, 15, 16 and 18 may be made under this provision.

3. Any State Party to the present Covenant availing itself of the right

of derogation shall inform immediately the other States Parties to the present Covenant, through the intermediary of the Secretary-General of the United Nations, of the provisions from which it has derogated and of the reasons by which it was actuated. A further communication shall be made, through the same intermediary, on the date on which it terminates such derogation.

Article 5

1. Nothing in the present Covenant may be interpreted as implying for any State, group or person any right to engage in any activity or perform any act aimed at the destruction of any of the rights and freedoms recognized herein or at their limitation to a greater extent than is provided for in the present Covenant.

2. There shall be no restriction upon or derogation from any of the fundamental human rights recognized or existing in any State Party to the present Covenant pursuant to law, conventions, regulations or custom on the pretext that the present Covenant does not recognize such rights or that it recognizes them to a lesser extent.

PART III

Article 6

1. Every human being has the inherent right to life. This right shall be protected by law. No one shall be arbitrarily deprived of his life.

2. In countries which have not abolished the death penalty, sentence of death may be imposed only for the most serious crimes in accordance with law in force at the time of the commission of the crime and not contrary to the provisions of the present Covenant and to the Convention on the Prevention and Punishment of the Crime of Genocide. This penalty can only be carried out pursuant to a final judgement rendered by a competent court.

3. When deprivation of life constitutes the crime of genocide, it is understood that nothing in this article shall authorize any State Party to the present Covenant to derogate in any way from any obligation assumed under the provisions of the Convention on the Prevention and Punishment of the Crime of Genocide.

4. Anyone sentenced to death shall have the right to seek pardon or

commutation of the sentence. Amnesty, pardon or commutation of the sentence of death may be granted in all cases.

5. Sentence of death shall not be imposed for crimes committed by persons below eighteen years of age and shall not be carried out on pregnant women.

6. Nothing in this article shall be invoked to delay or to prevent the abolition of capital punishment by any State Party to the present Covenant.

Article 7

No one shall be subjected to torture or to cruel, inhuman or degrading treatment or punishment. In particular, no one shall be subjected without his free consent to medical or scientific experimentation.

Article 8

1. No one shall be held in slavery; slavery and the slave-trade in all their forms shall be prohibited.

2. No one shall be held in servitude.

3. (a) No one shall be required to perform forced or compulsory labour;

(b) The preceding sub-paragraph shall not be held to preclude in countries where imprisonment with hard labour may be imposed as a punishment for a crime, the performance of hard labour in pursuance of a sentence to such punishment by a competent court;

(c) For the purpose of this paragraph the term "forced or compulsory labour" shall not include:

(i) Any work or service, not referred to in sub-paragraph (b), normally required of a person who is under detention in consequence of a lawful order of a court, or of a person during conditional release from such detention;

(ii) Any service of a military character and, in countries where conscientious objection is recognized, any national service required by law of conscientious objectors;

(iii) Any service exacted in cases of emergency or calamity threatening the life or well-being of the community;

(iv) Any work or service which forms part of normal civil obligations.

Article 9

1. Everyone has the right to liberty and security of person. No one shall be subjected to arbitrary arrest or detention. No one shall be deprived of his liberty except on such grounds and in accordance with such procedures as are established by law.

2. Anyone who is arrested shall be informed, at the time of arrest, of the reasons for his arrest and shall be promptly informed of any charges against him.

3. Anyone arrested or detained on a criminal charge shall be brought promptly before a judge or other officer authorized by law to exercise judicial power and shall be entitled to trial within a reasonable time or to release. It shall not be the general rule that persons awaiting trial shall be detained in custody, but release may be subject to guarantees to appear for trial, at any other stage of the judicial proceedings, and, should occasion arise, for execution of the judgement.

4. Anyone who is deprived of his liberty by arrest or detention shall be entitled to take proceedings before a court, in order that such court may decide without delay on the lawfulness of his detention and order his release if the detention is not lawful.

5. Anyone who has been the victim of unlawful arrest or detention shall have an enforceable right to compensation.

Article 10

1. All persons deprived of their liberty shall be treated with humanity and with respect for the inherent dignity of the human person.

2. (a) Accused persons shall, save in exceptional circumstances, be segregated from convicted persons, and shall be subject to separate treatment appropriate to their status as unconvicted persons;

(b) Accused juvenile persons shall be separated from adults and brought as speedily as possible for adjudication.

3. The penitentiary system shall comprise treatment of prisoners the essential aim of which shall be their reformation and social rehabilitation. Juvenile offenders shall be segregated from adults and be accorded treatment appropriate to their age and legal status.

Article 11

No one shall be imprisoned merely on the ground of inability to fulfil a contractual obligation.

Article 12

1. Everyone lawfully within the territory of a State shall, within that territory, have the right to liberty of movement and freedom to choose his residence.

2. Everyone shall be free to leave any country, including his own.

3. The above-mentioned rights shall not be subject to any restrictions except those which are provided by law, are necessary to protect national security, public order (*"ordre public"*), public health or morals or the rights and freedom of others, and are consistent with the other rights recognized in the present Covenant.

4. No one shall be arbitrarily deprived of the right to enter his own country.

Article 13

An alien lawfully in the territory of a State Party to the present Covenant may be expelled therefrom only in pursuance of a decision reached in accordance with law and shall, except where compelling reasons of national security otherwise require, be allowed to submit the reasons against his expulsion and to have his case reviewed by, and be represented for the purpose before, the competent authority or a person or persons especially designated by the competent authority.

Article 14

1. All persons shall be equal before the courts and tribunals. In the determination of any criminal charge against him, or of his rights and obligations in a suit at law, everyone shall be entitled to a fair and public hearing by a competent, independent and impartial tribunal established by law. The press and the public may be excluded from all or part of a trial for reasons of morals, public order (*"ordre public"*) or national security in a democratic society, or when the interest of the private lives of the parties so requires, or to the extent strictly necessary in the opinion of the court in special circumstances where publicity would prejudice the interests of justice; but any judgement rendered in a criminal case or in a suit at law shall be made public except where the interest of juveniles otherwise requires or the proceedings concern matrimonial disputes or the guardianship of children.

2. Everyone charged with a criminal offence shall have the right to be presumed innocent until proved guilty according to law.

3. In the determination of any criminal charge against him, everyone shall be entitled to the following minimum guarantees, in full equality:

(a) To be informed promptly and in detail in a language which he understands of the nature and cause of the charge against him;

(b) To have adequate time and facilities for the preparation of his defence and to communicate with counsel of his own choosing;

(c) To be tried without undue delay;

(d) To be tried in his presence, and to defend himself in person or through legal assistance of his own choosing; to be informed, if he does not have legal assistance, of this right; and to have legal assistance assigned to him, in any case where the interests of justice so require, and without payment by him in any such case if he does not have sufficient means to pay for it;

(e) To examine, or have examined, the witnesses against him and to obtain the attendance and examination of witnesses on his behalf under the same conditions as witnesses against him;

(f) To have the free assistance of an interpreter if he cannot understand or speak the language used in court;

(g) Not to be compelled to testify against himself, or to confess guilt.

4. In the case of juveniles, the procedure shall be such as will take account of their age and the desirability of promoting their rehabilitation.

5. Everyone convicted of a crime shall have the right to his conviction and sentence being reviewed by a higher tribunal according to law.

6. When a person has by a final decision been convicted of a criminal offence and when subsequently his conviction has been reversed or he has been pardoned on the ground that a new or newly discovered fact shows conclusively that there has been a miscarriage of justice, the person who has suffered punishment as a result of such conviction shall be compensated according to law, unless it is proved that the non-disclosure of the unknown fact in time is wholly or partly attributable to him.

7. No one shall be liable to be tried or punished again for an offence for which he has already been finally convicted or acquitted in accordance with the law and penal procedure of each country.

Article 15

1. No one shall be held guilty of any criminal offence on account of any act or omission which did not constitute a criminal offence, under

national or international law, at the time when it was committed. Nor shall a heavier penalty be imposed than the one that was applicable at the time when the criminal offence was committed. If, subsequently to the commission of the offence, provision is made by law for the imposition of a lighter penalty, the offender shall benefit thereby.

2. Nothing in this article shall prejudice the trial and punishment of any person for any act or omission which, at the time when it was committed, was criminal according to the general principles of law recognized by the community of nations.

Article 16

Everyone shall have the right to recognition everywhere as a person before the law.

Article 17

1. No one shall be subjected to arbitrary or unlawful interference with his privacy, family, home or correspondence, nor to unlawful attacks on his honour and reputation.

2. Everyone has the right to the protection of the law against such interference or attacks.

Article 18

1. Everyone shall have the right to freedom of thought, conscience and religion. This right shall include freedom to have or to adopt a religion or belief of his choice, and freedom either individually or in community with others and in public or private, to manifest his religion or belief in worship, observance, practice and teaching.

2. No one shall be subject to coercion which would impair his freedom to have or to adopt a religion or belief of his choice.

3. Freedom to manifest one's religion or beliefs may be subject only to such limitations as are prescribed by law and are necessary to protect public safety, order, health, or morals or the fundamental rights and freedoms of others.

4. The States Parties to the present Covenant undertake to have respect for the liberty of parents and, when applicable, legal guardians, to ensure the religious and moral education of their children in conformity with their own convictions.

Article 19

1. Everyone shall have the right to hold opinions without interference.

2. Everyone shall have the right to freedom of expression; this right shall include freedom to seek, receive and impart information and ideas of all kinds, regardless of frontiers, either orally, in writing or in print, in the form of art, or through any other media of his choice.

3. The exercise of the rights provided for in the foregoing paragraph carries with it special duties and responsibilities. It may therefore be subject to certain restrictions, but these shall be such only as are provided by law and are necessary, (1) for respect of the rights or reputations of others, (2) for the protection of national security or of public order (*"ordre public"*), or of public health or morals.

Article 20

1. Any propaganda for war shall be prohibited by law.

2. Any advocacy of national, racial, or religious hatred that constitutes incitement to discrimination, hostility or violence shall be prohibited by law.

Article 21

The right of peaceful assembly shall be recognized. No restrictions may be placed on the exercise of this right other than those imposed in conformity with the law and which are necessary in a democratic society in the interests of national security or public safety, public order (*"ordre public"*), the protection of public health or morals or the protection of the rights and freedoms of others.

Article 22

1. Everyone shall have the right to freedom of association with others, including the right to form and join trade unions for the protection of his interests.

2. No restrictions may be placed on the exercise of this right other than those prescribed by law and which are necessary in a democratic society in the interests of national security or public safety, public order (*"ordre public"*), the protection of public health or morals or the protection of the rights and freedoms of others. This article shall not prevent the imposition of lawful restrictions on members of the armed forces and of the police in their exercise of this right.

3. Nothing in this article shall authorize States Parties to the International Labour Convention of 1948 on Freedom of Association and Protection of the Right to Organise to take legislative measures which would prejudice, or to apply the law in such a manner as to prejudice, the guarantees provided for in the Convention.

Article 23

1. The family is the natural and fundamental group unit of society and is entitled to protection by society and the State.
2. The right of men and women of marriageable age to marry and to found a family shall be recognized.
3. No marriage shall be entered into without the free and full consent of the intending spouses.
4. States Parties to the present Covenant shall take appropriate steps to ensure equality of rights and responsibilities of spouses as to marriage, during marriage and at its dissolution. In the case of dissolution, provision shall be made for the necessary protection of any children.

Article 24

1. Every child shall have, without any discrimination as to race, colour, sex, language, religion, national or social origin, property or birth, the right to such measures of protection as required by his status as a minor, on the part of his family, the society and the State.
2. Every child shall be registered immediately after birth and shall have a name.
3. Every child has the right to acquire a nationality.

Article 25

Every citizen shall have the right and the opportunity, without any of the distinctions mentioned in article 2 and without unreasonable restrictions:

(a) To take part in the conduct of public affairs, directly or through freely chosen representatives;
(b) To vote and to be elected at genuine periodic elections which shall be by universal and equal suffrage and shall be held by secret ballot, guaranteeing the free expression of the will of the electors;

226

(c) To have access, on general terms of equality, to public service in his country.

Article 26

All persons are equal before the law and are entitled without any discrimination to equal protection of the law. In this respect the law shall prohibit any discrimination and guarantee to all persons equal and effective protection against discrimination on any ground such as race, colour, sex, language, religion, political or other opinion, national or social origin, property, birth or other status.

Article 27

In those States in which ethnic, religious or linguistic minorities exist, persons belonging to such minorities shall not be denied the right, in community with the other members of their group, to enjoy their own culture, to profess and practise their own religion, or to use their own language.

PART IV

Article 28

1. There shall be established a Human Rights Committee (hereafter referred to in the present Covenant as "the Committee"). It shall consist of eighteen members and shall carry out the functions hereinafter provided.
2. The Committee shall be composed of nationals of the States Parties to the present Covenant who shall be persons of high moral character and recognized competence in the field of human rights, consideration being given to the usefulness of the participation of some persons having legal experience.
3. The members of the Committee shall be elected and shall serve in their personal capacity.

Article 29

1. The members of the Committee shall be elected by secret ballot from a list of persons possessing the qualifications prescribed in article

28 and nominated for the purpose by the States Parties to the present Covenant.

2. Each State Party to the present Covenant may nominate not more than two persons. These persons shall be nationals of the nominating State.

3. A person shall be eligible for renomination.

Article 30

1. The initial election shall be held no later than six months after the date of the entry into force of the present Covenant.

2. At least four months before the date of each election to the Committee, other than an election to fill a vacancy declared in accordance with article 34, the Secretary-General of the United Nations shall address a written invitation to the States Parties to the present Covenant to submit their nominations for membership of the Committee within three months.

3. The Secretary-General of the United Nations shall prepare a list in alphabetical order of all the persons thus nominated, with an indication of the States Parties which have nominated them, and shall submit it to the States Parties to the present Covenant no later than one month before the date of each election.

4. Elections of the members of the Committee shall be held at a meeting of the States Parties to the present Covenant convened by the Secretary-General of the United Nations at the Headquarters of the United Nations. At that meeting, for which two thirds of the States Parties to the present Covenant shall constitute a quorum, the persons elected to the Committee shall be those nominees who obtain the largest number of votes and an absolute majority of the votes of the representatives of States Parties present and voting.

Article 31

1. The Committee may not include more than one national of the same State.

2. In the election of the Committee consideration shall be given to equitable geographical distribution of membership and to the representation of the different forms of civilization as well as of the principal legal systems.

Article 32

1. The members of the Committee shall be elected for a term of four years. They shall be eligible for re-election if renominated. However, the terms of nine of the members elected at the first election shall expire at the end of two years; immediately after the first election the names of these nine members shall be chosen by lot by the Chairman of the meeting referred to in paragraph 4 of article 30.

2. Elections at the expiry of office shall be held in accordance with the preceding articles of this part of the present Covenant.

Article 33

1. If, in the unanimous opinion of the other members, a member of the Committee has ceased to carry out his functions for any cause other than absence of a temporary character, the Chairman of the Committee shall notify the Secretary-General of the United Nations who shall then declare the seat of that member to be vacant.

2. In the event of the death or the resignation of a member of the Committee, the Chairman shall immediately notify the Secretary-General of the United Nations who shall declare the seat vacant from the date of death or the date on which the resignation takes effect.

Article 34

1. When a vacancy is declared in accordance with article 33 and if the term of office of the member to be replaced does not expire within six months of the declaration of the vacancy, the Secretary-General of the United Nations shall notify each of the States Parties to the present Covenant which may within two months submit nominations in accordance with article 29 for the purpose of filling the vacancy.

2. The Secretary-General of the United Nations shall prepare a list in alphabetical order of the persons thus nominated and shall submit it to the States Parties to the present Covenant. The election to fill the vacancy shall then take place in accordance with the relevant provisions of this part of the present Covenant.

3. A member of the Committee elected to fill a vacancy declared in accordance with article 33 shall hold office for the remainder of the term of the member who vacated the seat on the Committee under the provisions of that article.

Article 35

The members of the Committee shall, with the approval of the General Assembly of the United Nations, receive emoluments from United Nations resources on such terms and conditions as the General Assembly may decide having regard to the importance of the Committee's responsibilities.

Article 36

The Secretary-General of the United Nations shall provide the necessary staff and facilities for the effective performance of the functions of the Committee under this Covenant.

Article 37

1. The Secretary-General of the United Nations shall convene the initial meeting of the Committee at the Headquarters of the United Nations.
2. After its initial meeting, the Committee shall meet at such times as shall be provided in its rules of procedure.
3. The Committee shall normally meet at the Headquarters of the United Nations or at the United Nations Office at Geneva.

Article 38

Every member of the Committee shall, before taking up his duties, make a solemn declaration in open committee that he will perform his functions impartially and conscientiously.

Article 39

1. The Committee shall elect its officers for a term of two years. They may be re-elected.
2. The Committee shall establish its own rules of procedure, but these rules provide, *inter alia*, that:

(a) Twelve members shall constitute a quorum;
(b) Decisions of the Committee shall be made by a majority vote of the members present.

Article 40

1. The States Parties to the present Covenant undertake to submit reports on the measures they have adopted which give effect to the rights recognized herein and on the progress made in the enjoyment of those rights; (a) within one year of the entry into force of the present Covenant for the States Parties concerned and (b) thereafter whenever the Committee so requests.

2. All reports shall be submitted to the Secretary-General of the United Nations who shall transmit them to the Committee for consideration. Reports shall indicate the factors and difficulties, if any, affecting the implementation of the present Covenant.

3. The Secretary-General of the United Nations may after consultation with the Committee transmit to the specialized agencies concerned copies of such parts of the reports as may fall within their field of competence.

4. The Committee shall study the reports submitted by the States Parties to the present Covenant. It shall transmit its reports and such general comments as it may consider appropriate to the States Parties. The Committee may also transmit to the Economic and Social Council these comments along with the copies of the reports it has received from States Parties to the present Covenant.

5. The States Parties to the present Covenant may submit to the Committee observations on any comments that may be made in accordance with paragraph 4 of this article.

Article 41

1. A State Party to the present Covenant may at any time declare under this article that it recognizes the competence of the Committee to receive and consider communications to the effect that a State Party claims that another State Party is not fulfilling its obligations under the present Covenant. Communications under this article may be received and considered only if submitted by a State Party which has made a declaration recognizing in regard to itself the competence of the Committee. No communication shall be received by the Committee if it concerns a State Party which has not made such a declaration. Communications received under this article shall be dealt with in accordance with the following procedure:

(a) If a State Party to the present Covenant considers that another State Party is not giving effect to the provisions of the present Covenant, it may, by written communication, bring the matter to the attention of that State Party. Within three months after the receipt of the communication, the receiving State shall afford the State which sent the communication an explanation or any other statement in writing clarifying the matter, which should include, to the extent possible and pertinent, reference to domestic procedures and remedies taken, pending, or available in the matter.

(b) If the matter is not adjusted to the satisfaction of both States Parties concerned within six months after the receipt by the receiving State of the initial communication, either State shall have the right to refer the matter to the Committee, by notice given to the Committee and to the other State.

(c) The Committee shall deal with a matter referred to it only after it has ascertained that all available domestic remedies have been invoked and exhausted in the matter, in conformity with the generally recognized principles of international law. This shall not be the rule where the application of the remedies is unreasonably prolonged.

(d) The Committee shall hold closed meetings when examining communications under this article.

(e) Subject to the provisions of sub-paragraph (c), the Committee shall make available its good offices to the States Parties concerned with a view to a friendly solution of the matter on the basis of respect for human rights and fundamental freedoms as recognized in this Covenant.

(f) In any matter referred to it, the Committee may call upon the States Parties concerned, referred to in sub-paragraph (b), to supply any relevant information.

(g) The States Parties concerned, referred to in sub-paragraph (b), shall have the right to be represented when the matter is being considered in the Committee and to make submissions orally and/or in writing.

(h) The Committee shall, within twelve months after the date of receipt of notice under sub-paragraph (b), submit a report:

(i) If a solution within the terms of sub-paragraph (e) is reached, the Committee shall confine its report to a brief statement of the facts and of the solution reached;

(ii) If a solution is not reached, within the terms of sub-paragraph (e), the Committee shall confine its report to a brief statement of the facts; the written submissions and record of the oral submissions made by the States Parties concerned shall be attached to the report.

In every matter the report shall be communicated to the States Parties concerned.

2. The provisions of this article shall come into force when ten States Parties to the present Covenant have made declarations under paragraph 1 of this article. Such declarations shall be deposited by the States Parties with the Secretary-General of the United Nations who shall transmit copies thereof to the other States Parties. A declaration may be withdrawn at any time by notification to the Secretary-General. Such a withdrawal shall not prejudice the consideration of any matter which is the subject of a communication already transmitted under this article; no further communication by any State Party shall be received after the notification of withdrawal of the declaration has been received by the Secretary-General of the United Nations unless the State Party concerned had made a new declaration.

Article 42

1. (a) If a matter referred to the Committee in accordance with article 41 is not resolved to the satisfaction of the States Parties concerned, the Committee may, with the prior consent of the States Parties concerned, appoint an *ad hoc* Conciliation Commission (hereinafter referred to as "the Commission"). The good offices of the Commission shall be made available to the States Parties concerned with a view to an amicable solution of the matter on the basis of respect for the present Covenant;

(b) The Commission shall consist of five persons acceptable to the States Parties concerned. If the States Parties concerned fail to reach agreement within three months on all or part of the composition of the Commission the members of the Commission concerning whom no agreement was reached shall be elected by secret ballot by a two-thirds majority vote of the Committee from among its members.

2. The members of the Commission shall serve in their personal capacity. They shall not be nationals of the States Parties concerned, or of a State not party to the present Covenant, or of a State Party which has not made a declaration under article 41.

3. The Commission shall elect its own Chairman and adopt its own rules of procedure.

4. The meetings of the Commission shall normally be held at the Headquarters of the United Nations or at the United Nations Office at Geneva. However, they may be held at such other convenient places as the Commission may determine in consultation with the Secretary-General of the United Nations and the States Parties concerned.

5. The secretariat provided in accordance with article 36 shall also service the Commissions appointed under this article.

6. The information received and collated by the Committee shall be made available to the Commission and the Commission may call upon the States Parties concerned to supply any other relevant information.

7. When the Commission has fully considered the matter, but in any event not later than twelve months after having been seized of the matter, it shall submit to the Chairman of the Committee a report for communication to the States Parties concerned.

(a) If the Commission is unable to complete its consideration of the matter within twelve months, it shall confine its report to a brief statement of the status of its consideration of the matter.

(b) If an amicable solution to the matter on the basis of respect for human rights as recognized in the present Covenant is reached, the Commission shall confine its report to a brief statement of the facts and of the solution reached.

(c) If a solution within the terms of sub-paragraph (b) is not reached, the Commission's report shall embody its findings on all questions of fact relevant to the issues between the States Parties concerned, as well as its views on the possibilities of amicable solution of the matter. This report shall also contain the written submissions and a record of the oral submissions made by the States Parties concerned.

(d) If the Commission's report is submitted under sub-paragraph (c), the States Parties concerned shall, within three months of the receipt of the report, inform the Chairman of the Committee whether or not they accept the contents of the report of the Commission.

8. The provisions of this article are without prejudice to the responsibilities of the Committee under article 41.

9. The States Parties concerned shall share equally all the expenses of the members of the Commission in accordance with estimates to be provided by the Secretary-General of the United Nations.

10. The Secretary-General of the United Nations shall be empowered to pay the expenses of the members of the Commission, if necessary, before reimbursement by the States Parties concerned in accordance with paragraph 9 of this article.

Article 43

The members of the Committee and of the *ad hoc* conciliation commissions which may be appointed under article 41, shall be entitled to the facilities, privileges and immunities of experts on mission for the

United Nations as laid down in the relevant sections of the Convention on the Privileges and Immunities of the United Nations.

Article 44

The provisions for the implementation of the present Covenant shall apply without prejudice to the procedures prescribed in the field of human rights by or under the constituent instruments and the conventions of the United Nations and of the specialized agencies and shall not prevent the States Parties to the present Covenant from having recourse to other procedures for settling a dispute in accordance with general or special international agreements in force between them.

Article 45

The Committee shall submit to the General Assembly, through the Economic and Social Council, an annual report on its activities.

Part V

Article 46

Nothing in the present Covenant shall be interpreted as impairing the provisions of the Charter of the United Nations and of the constitutions of the specialized agencies which define the respective responsibilities of the various organs of the United Nations and of the specialized agencies in regard to the matters dealt with in the present Covenant.

Article 47

Nothing in the Covenant shall be interpreted as impairing the inherent right of all peoples to enjoy and utilize fully and freely their natural wealth and resources.

PART VI

Article 48

1. The present Covenant is open for signature by any State Member of the United Nations or member of any of its specialized agencies, by any State Party to the Statute of the International Court of Justice, and by any other State which has been invited by the General Assembly of the United Nations to become a party to the present Covenant.

2. The present Covenant is subject to ratification. Instruments of ratification shall be deposited with the Secretary-General of the United Nations.

3. The present Covenant shall be open to accession by any State referred to in paragraph 1 of this article.

4. Accession shall be effected by the deposit of an instrument of accession with the Secretary-General of the United Nations.

5. The Secretary-General of the United Nations shall inform all States which have signed this Covenant or acceded to it of the deposit of each instrument of ratification or accession.

Article 49

1. The present Covenant shall enter into force three months after the date of the deposit with the Secretary-General of the United Nations of the thirty-fifth instrument of ratification or instrument of accession.

2. For each State ratifying the present Covenant or acceding to it after the deposit of the thirty-fifth instrument of ratification or instrument of accession, the present Covenant shall enter into force three months after the date of the deposit of its own instrument of ratification or instrument of accession.

Article 50

The provisions of the present Covenant shall extend to all parts of federal States without any limitations or exceptions.

Article 51

1. Any State Party to the present Covenant may propose an amendment and file it with the Secretary-General of the United Nations. The Secretary-General of the United Nations shall thereupon communicate

any proposed amendments to the States Parties to the present Covenant with a request that they notify him whether they favour a conference of States Parties for the purpose of considering and voting upon the proposal. In the event that at least one third of the States Parties favours such a conference the Secretary-General of the United Nations shall convene the conference under the auspices of the United Nations. Any amendment adopted by a majority of the States Parties present and voting at the conference shall be submitted to the General Assembly of the United Nations for approval.

2. Amendments shall come into force when they have been approved by the General Assembly and accepted by a two-thirds majority of the States Parties to the present Covenant in accordance with their respective constitutional processes.

3. When amendments come into force they shall be binding on those States Parties which have accepted them, other States Parties being still bound by the provisions of the present Covenant and any earlier amendment which they have accepted.

Article 52

Irrespective of the notifications made under article 48, paragraph 5, the Secretary-General of the United Nations shall inform all States referred to in paragraph 1 of the same article of the following particulars:

(a) Signatures, ratifications and accessions under article 48;

(b) The date of the entry into force of the present Covenant under article 49 and the date of the entry into force of any amendments under article 51.

Article 53

1. The present Covenant, of which the Chinese, English, French, Russian and Spanish texts are equally authentic, shall be deposited in the archives of the United Nations.

2. The Secretary-General of the United Nations shall transmit certified copies of the present Covenant to all States referred to in article 48.

OPTIONAL PROTOCOL TO THE INTERNATIONAL COVENANT ON CIVIL AND POLITICAL RIGHTS

The Optional Protocol to the Covenant on Civil and Political Rights was approved by the UN General Assembly on December 16, 1966. It is closely related to the covenant, but is a separate treaty to which only twenty of the parties to the covenant have adhered.

The States Parties to the present Protocol,

Considering that in order further to achieve the purposes of the Covenant on Civil and Political Rights (hereinafter referred to as "the Covenant") and the implementation of its provisions it would be appropriate to enable the Human Rights Committee set up in part IV of the Covenant (hereinafter referred to as "the Committee") to receive and consider, as provided in the present Protocol, communications from individuals claiming to be victims of violations of any of the rights set forth in the Covenant,

Have agreed as follows:

Article 1

A State Party to the Covenant that becomes a party to the present Protocol recognizes the competence of the Committee to receive and consider communications from individuals, subject to its jurisdiction, claiming to be victims of a violation by that State Party of any of the rights set forth in the Covenant. No communication shall be received by the Committee if it concerns a State Party to the Covenant which is not a Party to the present Protocol.

Article 2

Subject to the provision of article 1, individuals claiming that any of their rights enumerated in the Covenant have been violated and who have exhausted all available domestic remedies may submit a written communication to the Committee for consideration.

Article 3

The Committee shall consider inadmissible any communication under this Protocol which is anonymous, or which it considers to be an abuse of the right of submission of such communications or to be incompatible with the provisions of the Covenant.

Article 4

1. Subject to the provisions of article 3, the Committee shall bring any communications submitted to it under the present Protocol to the attention of the State Party to the present Protocol alleged to be violating any provision of the Covenant.

2. Within six months, the receiving State shall submit to the Committee written explanations or statements clarifying the matter and the remedy, if any, that may have been taken by that State.

Article 5

1. The Committee shall consider communications received under the present Protocol in the light of all written information made available to it by the individual and by the State Party concerned.

2. The Committee shall not consider any communication from an individual unless it has ascertained that:

(a) the same matter is not being examined under another procedure of international investigation or settlement;

(b) the individual has exhausted all available domestic remedies. This shall not be the rule where the application of the remedies is unreasonably prolonged.

3. The Committee shall hold closed meetings when examining communications under the present Protocol.

4. The Committee shall forward its views to the State Party concerned and to the individual.

Article 6

The Committee shall include in its annual report under article 45 of the Covenant a summary of its activities under the present Protocol.

Article 7

Pending the achievement of the objectives of General Assembly resolution 1514 (XV) of 14 December 1960 concerning the Declaration on the Granting of Independence to Colonial Countries and Peoples, the provisions of the present Protocol shall in no way limit the right of petition granted to these peoples by the Charter of the United Nations and other international conventions and instruments under the United Nations and its specialized agencies.

Article 8

1. The present Protocol is open for signature by any State which has signed the Covenant.

2. The present Protocol is subject to ratification by any State which has ratified or acceded to the Covenant. Instruments of ratification shall be deposited with the Secretary-General of the United Nations.

3. The present Protocol shall be open to accession by any State which has ratified or acceded to the Covenant.

4. Accession shall be effected by the deposit of an instrument of accession with the Secretary-General of the United Nations.

5. The Secretary-General of the United Nations shall inform all States which have signed the present Protocol or acceded to it of the deposit of each instrument of ratification or accession.

Article 9

1. Subject to the entry into force of the Covenant, the present Protocol shall enter into force three months after the date of the deposit with the Secretary-General of the United Nations of the tenth instrument of ratification or instrument of accession.

2. For each State ratifying the present Protocol or acceding to it after the deposit of the tenth instrument of ratification or instrument of accession, the present Protocol shall enter into force three months after the date of the deposit of its own instrument of ratification or instrument of accession.

Article 10

The provisions of the present Protocol shall extend to all parts of federal States without any limitations or exceptions.

Article 11

1. Any State Party to the present Protocol may propose an amendment and file it with the Secretary-General of the United Nations. The Secretary-General of the United Nations shall thereupon communicate

240

any proposed amendments to the States Parties to the present Protocol with a request that they notify him whether they favour a conference of States Parties for the purpose of considering and voting upon the proposal. In the event that at least one third of the States Parties favours such a conference the Secretary-General of the United Nations shall convene the conference under the auspices of the United Nations. Any amendment adopted by a majority of the States Parties present and voting at the conference shall be submitted to the General Assembly of the United Nations for approval.

2. Amendments shall come into force when they have been approved by the General Assembly and accepted by a two-thirds majority of the States Parties to the present Protocol in accordance with their respective constitutional processes.

3. When amendments come into force they shall be binding on those States Parties which have accepted them, other States Parties being still bound by the provisions of the present Protocol and any earlier amendment which they have accepted.

Article 12

1. Any State Party may denounce the present Protocol at any time by written notification addressed to the Secretary-General of the United Nations. Denunciation shall take effect three months after the date of receipt of the notification by the Secretary-General of the United Nations.

2. Denunciation shall be without prejudice to the continued application of the provisions of the present Protocol to any communication submitted under article 2 before the effective date of denunciation.

Article 13

Irrespective of the notifications made under article 8, paragraph 5, of the present Protocol, the Secretary-General of the United Nations shall inform all States referred to in article 48, paragraph 1, of the Covenant of the following particulars:

(a) Signatures, ratifications and accessions under article 8;
(b) The date of the entry into force of the present Protocol under article 9 and the date of the entry into force of any amendments under article 11;
(c) Denunciations under article 12.

241

Article 14

1. The present Protocol, of which the Chinese, English, French, Russian and Spanish texts are equally authentic, shall be deposited in the archives of the United Nations.

2. The Secretary-General of the United Nations shall transmit certified copies of the present Protocol to all States referred to in article 48 of the Covenant.

APPENDIX B

Human Rights Organizations

The following organizations may be contacted for information and for opportunities to volunteer in specific communities.

Amnesty International
322 Eighth Avenue
New York, NY 10001

The Lawyers Committee for Human Rights
330 Seventh Avenue
New York, NY 10001

Human Rights Watch
36 West 44th Street
New York, NY 10036
    Oversees Helsinki Watch, Americas Watch, Asia Watch, and Africa
    Watch. A Middle East Watch will be started soon.

International League for Human Rights
432 Park Avenue South
Suite 1103
New York, NY 10016

APPENDIX C

Movies, Plays, and Books Concerning Human Rights Issues

Human rights is a relatively new category in bibliographic and reference materials. This list is highly selective. An asterisk indicates a writer who has written several books on the subject in addition to the one or two cited. For more information on films, consult *The Human Rights Film Guide*, by Anne Gelman and Milo Stahlitz (Chicago: Facets Multimedia, 1985).

General

The Hooded Men (film). Canadian Broadcasting Corporation, 1975. Examines torture in many countries, including Argentina, Nicaragua, Northern Ireland, and South Africa.

Meltzer, Milton. *The Human Rights Book* (grades 6 up). New York: Farrar, Straus & Giroux, 1986.

Universal Declaration of Human Rights (film). Produced by Amnesty International, directed by Stephen Johnson, 1975. Animated film presents work of forty-one animators from around the world.

South America

Allende, Isabel. *The House of the Spirits*. New York: Knopf, 1985.

Hauser, Thomas. *The Execution of Charles Horman* (nonfiction). New York: Harcourt Brace Jovanovich, 1978. Reprinted under the title *Missing* (New York: Avon, 1982). Basis of film *Missing* (directed by Constantin Costa-Gavras, 1982). (Chile)

244

The Official Story (film). Directed by Luis Puenzo, 1985. (Argentina)

Timerman, Jacobo. *Prisoner Without a Name, Cell Without a Number* (auto-biography). New York: Knopf, 1981. Basis of film of same title (directed by Linda Yellen, 1983). (Argentina)

South Africa

Carlson, Joel. *No Neutral Ground* (nonfiction). Boston: Charles River Books, 1973.

*Coetzee, J. M. *The Life and Times of Michael K.* (fiction). New York: Viking Penguin, 1984.

———. *Waiting for the Barbarians* (fiction). New York: Viking Penguin, 1980.

Finnegan, William. *Crossing the Line: A Year in the Land of Apartheid* (nonfiction). New York: Harper, 1986.

———. *Dateline Soweto* (nonfiction). New York: Harper, 1988.

*Fugard, Athol. *"Master Harold" and the Boys* (play). New York: Knopf, 1982.

———. *A Lesson from Aloes* (play). New York: Random House, 1981.

*Gordimer, Nadine. *The Essential Gesture* (essays). New York: Viking Penguin, 1988.

———. *July's People* (fiction). New York: Viking Penguin, 1981.

Mathabane, Mark. *Kaffir Boy: The True Story of a Black Youth's Coming of Age in Apartheid South Africa.* New York: Macmillan, 1986.

*Paton, Alan. *Cry, the Beloved Country.* New York: Scribner's, 1961. Basis of film of same title (directed by Zoltan Korda, 1952). Basis of musical play *Lost in the Stars* (music by Kurt Weill, book and lyrics by Maxwell Anderson, 1949).

———, *Ah, But Your Land Is Beautiful.* New York: Scribner's, 1983.

Sarafina! The Music of Liberation (a musical play performed by black South African high school students who create a play about Nelson Mandela). Book, music, and lyrics by Mbongeni Ngema, with additional songs by Hugh Massekela. *Sarafina!* premiered in South Africa in 1987, opened at Lincoln Center in New York City later that year, and is currently (1989) running on Broadway.

Voices of Sarafina! (film). Directed by Nigel Noble, 1988.

*Woods, Donald. *Biko—Cry Freedom* (biography). New York: Holt, 1987. Basis of film *Cry Freedom* (directed by Richard Attenborough, 1987).

———. *South African Dispatches: Letters to my Countrymen.* New York: Holt, 1987.

Cambodia

Back to Kampuchea (film). Directed by Martin Duckworth, 1982.

Schanberg, Sydney. *The Death and Life of Dith Pran* (nonfiction). New York: Viking Penguin, 1985. Basis of film *The Killing Fields* (directed by Roland Jaffe, 1984).

Eastern Europe and the USSR

The Confession (film). Directed by Constantin Costa-Gavras, 1970.

*Koestler, Arthur. *Darkness at Noon* (fiction). New York: Macmillan, 1941.

*Kundera, Milan. *The Book of Laughter and Forgetting* (fiction). New York: Knopf, 1980. (Czechoslovakia)

Man of Iron (film: fiction and documentary). Directed by Andrzej Wajda, 1981. (Poland)

*Solzhenitsyn, Aleksandr. *The First Circle*. New York: Harper, 1968.

————. *The Gulag Archipelago, 1918–1956: An Experiment in Literary Investigation* (3 volumes). New York: Harper, 1975. (USSR)

————. *One Day in the Life of Ivan Denisovich*. New York: Praeger, 1963. Basis of film of same title (directed by Casper Wrede, 1971).

USA—Civil Rights

Armstrong, William. *Sounder* (fiction). New York: Harper, 1969. Basis of film of same title (directed by Martin Ritt, 1972).

Brown, Claude. *Manchild in the Promised Land*. New York: Macmillan, 1965.

The Color of Honor (documentary film). Directed by Loni Ding, 1987. The incarceration by the U.S. government of Japanese American citizens during World War II.

*Ellison, Ralph. *Invisible Man* (fiction). New York: Random House, 1952.

Eyes on the Prize is both a book (by Juan Williams) and a six-part PBS series. The book is cited in the Bibliography.

*Gaines, Ernest J. *The Autobiography of Miss Jane Pittman* (fiction). New York: Dial, 1971.

Griffin, John Howard. *Black Like Me* (nonfiction). Boston: Houghton Mifflin, 1961.

*Guy, Rosa. *Children of Longing* (interviews). New York: Holt, 1971.

*Hamilton, Virginia. *The Mystery of Drear House* (fiction). New York: Greenwillow, 1987.

————. *Paul Robeson, The Life and Times of a Free Black Man* (biography). New York: Harper, 1974.

Parks, Gordon. *The Learning Tree* (fiction). New York: Harper, 1963.

*Taylor, Mildred. *The Friendship* (grades 2–6). New York: Dial Books for Young Readers, 1987.

*Wright, Richard. *Black Boy: A Record of Childhood and Youth* (autobiography). New York: Harper, 1945.

———. *Native Son* (fiction). New York: Harper, 1940.

Films about Other Countries

Battle of Algiers. Directed by Gillo Pontecorvo, 1966. (Algeria)

The Cause of Ireland. Directed by Chris Reeves, 1983. (Ireland)

Gandhi. Directed by Richard Attenborough, 1982. (India)

Shattered Dreams. Directed by Victor Schonfeld and Jennifer Millstone, 1987. (Israel)

Wedding in Galilee. Directed by Michel Khleifi, 1987. (Palestine)

INDEX

ABOUT THE AUTHORS

MARVIN E. FRANKEL is chairman of the Lawyers Committee for Human Rights, and has investigated and reported on rights abuses in South America, Africa, the Philippines, and the Soviet Union. A former U.S. District Judge for the Southern District of New York, he is now a partner in a New York law firm. He is the author of two books, *Partisan Justice* and *Criminal Sentencing: Law Without Order*, as well as numerous articles on legal matters and human rights.

ELLEN SAIDEMAN is a staff attorney at New York Lawyers for the Public Interest, Inc., and previously worked for the New York City Commission on Human Rights. She has served on the Committee on International Human Rights of the Association of the Bar of the City of New York.